MULTIMEDIA
TECHNOLOGY
FROM A TO Z

MULTIMEDIA TECHNOLOGY FROM A TO Z

by Patrick M. Dillon
and
David C. Leonard

Oryx Press
1995

The rare Arabian Oryx is believed to have inspired the myth of the unicorn. This desert antelope became virtually extinct in the early 1960s. At that time several groups of international conservationists arranged to have 9 animals sent to the Phoenix Zoo to be the nucleus of a captive breeding herd. Today the Oryx population is over 800, and nearly 400 have been returned to reserves in the Middle East.

© 1995 by The Oryx Press
4041 North Central at Indian School Road
Phoenix, Arizona 85012-3397

Published simultaneously in Canada
Printed and Bound in the United States of America

♾ The paper used in this publication meets the minimum requirements of American National Standard for Information Science—Permanence of Paper for Printed Library Materials, ANSI Z39.48, 1984.

Library of Congress Cataloging-in-Publication Data
Dillon, Patrick M.
  Multimedia technology from A to Z / Patrick M. Dillon and David C. Leonard.
  Includes bibliographical references.
  ISBN 0-89774-892-1
  1. Multimedia systems.   I. Leonard, David C.   II. Title.
QA 76.575.D55   1995
006.6—dc20   94-37853
                                                                CIP

DEDICATION

As one gains in wisdom, which is of greater value than knowledge, it becomes clear what is most important in life. This book is dedicated to our children: Nikki and Shane Dillon, and Emily and Christian Leonard. They embody the future and are our most significant work, no matter what else we may accomplish.

CONTENTS

FOREWORD
An Emerging Vocabulary for an Emerging Technology

For those who envision even a fraction of its long-term possibilities, the future of multimedia technology has important implications for several industries. The coming of multimedia technology—the merger between the software, film and TV, publishing, and telephone industries—offers much promise. But, like a gigantic, transglobal, multi-organizational corporate merger, it threatens to bring with it professional tension and possible confusion.

In the first place, this merger calls for the integration of occupations that have previously remained proud and separate nations on the map of professions. For example, in the upcoming age of multimedia technology, film producers must learn to work smoothly with software developers; which means, of course, that both parties, egocentric by nature and with a history to prove it, will need to learn to be sensitive to the intense production demands placed on the other. One highly collaborative medium will become part-in-parcel of another highly collaborative medium. And, in about half the time it takes this synthesis of development processes to take shape, the whole emerging enterprise of multimedia technology may have to take stock of other sets of entrenched and demanding development and production methods from other industries, ad infinitum.

Therefore, delivering on the enormous promise of multimedia technology may result in a transitional period in which applications are created somewhat turbulently and not without conflict. As with any human endeavor that demands large doses of confluence and compromise, one of the first battlefields may certainly be the language itself. Sophisticated technical vocabularies may collide, perhaps as never before. Struggles for lexical hegemony are likely. This conflict may no doubt parallel the inevitable struggles for power and authority that arise as each professional faction jockeys for position in terms of deciding who produces what for whom.

Take the word "frame," for example, innocently useful to so many of the tributary professions that flow into multimedia technology. To the animator, it means a single visual element, one picture in a series of pictures run together to create the illusion of motion. To the filmmaker, the word "frame" means nearly the same thing, though the methods for producing a frame of video are quite different than they are for producing a frame of animation, leading perhaps to misunderstandings, even between these two closely related professions. To the software developer, the word is at least as purposeful, but it means something entirely different—a packet of encoded information punctuated at either or both ends with specific digital patterns that demarcate and identify the contents. Audio producers have, in their own right, a specific use for the word "frame," and it only roughly corresponds to these other uses. We could go on, but the point is a simple one. Terms like "frame," which do such a good job of evoking structural images for the entities they name, abound in all of these professions, and in many cases occupy pivotal positions in the nomenclatures surrounding them. One senses that they may not be abandoned easily for the other profession's meaning of the word.

All of which brings us to the purpose of this book. As the vocabulary of multimedia technology emerges from the fray of converging—some would say colliding—professions, there is an abundant need for professionals to cross-pollinate one another with their most meaningful terms. Clear communication—always at a premium in collaborative ventures—may escalate to a new level of significance as filmmakers try to direct the activities of computer programmers, and software designers labor to explain themselves to TV programmers. We intend for this book to inform as well as to build bridges of communication between these conflicting professions.

In pursuit of this ambassadorial goal, we have selected key principles and terms from each of the converging industries that we believe represent—at least during this formative era—the cornerstones of the multimedia industry. Thus, from the film industry we have included the term EDL (edit decision list), an everyday item in video production, but an utter unknown to professionals in software development or print publishing. From the world of computing, we have included such commonplace terms as CPU (central processing unit), which are probably familiar to most professionals, but, as the machinery of multimedia technology invades virtually every corner of our homes and offices, may certainly become as central to our everyday household language as, say, terms like baseboard to bevel. In selecting these core terms, we have tried to be judicious, delving only as deeply into the semantic interiors of these tributary professions as we feel may be truly useful to multimedia technology initiates.

In addition to providing this cross-pollination of vocabularies, we have attempted to capture, in as comprehensive a fashion as possible, the body of terms coming into existence as a direct result of the emergence of multimedia technology. This new language is spurred primarily by two forces: the host of enabling technologies ushered into place to bring multimedia content and applications into the home, schools, and the workplace, and the significant design activity surrounding the production of that content.

In the area of enabling technologies, for example, there is now a flurry of activity associated with the digitization and compression of video. Video, which has traditionally been an analog medium, is currently being co-opted into the all-digital computer realm. This process is creating an explosion of new technologies and a corresponding volume of new terminology to describe these technologies. In the fledgling realm of multimedia content creation, the discipline of interface design is expanding to occupy a good part of the academic niche serving this embryonic art form. Like all academic niches, it too is creating a steady stream of new terms.

Finally, because the industry is still young, we felt it is of some value to identify key places and events. Like most of our society, the universities are still a bit stunned by the meteoric rise of multimedia technology and have not yet had the requisite half-decade or so to approve new courses, let alone realign their departmental structures to accommodate this new medium. Of course, that may all come in due course. Presently, however, there are a number academic pioneers who have surfaced, some of them privately funded and outside of the university structure. Since these few institutions are now having a relatively large impact on the conceptualization of multimedia, we felt it was worthwhile to include them in the book, so that some of the early doers may know where to find some of the early thinkers.

We are firm believers in the power and importance of language. To the extent that any human enterprise is governed by vague, ambiguous, or even misguided language, it is likely that the enterprise itself may be similarly indisposed. We are also true believers in the future of multimedia technology. We are convinced it stands in the same transformational relationship to the twenty-first century that the sum of its tributary media of film, television, computing, and telephony have with regard to the twentieth century. We are thus motivated to make whatever small contribution we can to setting the language of multimedia on a well-defined initial course. And we welcome your involvement in the activity as the language of multimedia and its corresponding technologies unfold.

PMD/DCL

PREFACE

This book defines for you over 1,000 terms related to multimedia. Generally speaking, these terms were selected around sets of professional functions that relate to multimedia in one of two ways. They either belong to one of the major contributory disciplines that provide the bases for this new industry, or they belong to a set of competencies that owe their origins to the birth of multimedia.

For example, as video becomes "just another data type," the considerable language surrounding the century-old industry of film and video production has become a justifiable concern for those who would talk the language of multimedia. Thus, we have included a large number of film and video terms, though we have not tried to duplicate that industry's entire nomenclature.

Instead, we have made an effort to include those terms that would be of greatest use to developers who are working to incorporate video in their multimedia content, and particularly for those who are producing CD-ROM titles, which is now the most intense locus of video activity in this young industry. Since most of these developers are not blessed with Hollywood-sized budgets, but instead rely heavily on stock footage and other forms of predeveloped video, our most concentrated effort in the video realm is in the area of post-production, where the general move toward all-digital, computer-based tools provides us with a reinforcing motive to include these terms. Thus, you will find a cluster of terms around such areas of video post-production as digital video effects, which has earned itself the status of an acronym, DVE.

We also selected terms centered around areas of professional competency that owe their very origins to the birth of multimedia. For example, certain software tools that owe their newborn existence to this industry are called "authoring systems." These software toolsets have many dimensions and subclasses, and we have made an effort to be as inclusive as possible with regard to the rapidly growing language that describes their emergent richness and diversity.

Hence, as with any professional nomenclature, the semantic network that is the language of multimedia is centered around an overlapping system of conceptual nodes, many of which owe their origins to earlier sources and centers of meaning, and many others of which owe their genesis to the birth and growth of the profession. Because there are so many clusters of interrelated terms, the reader will find a large number of cross-references contained within the entries to this dictionary. We have used *italics* wherever we have included a word within a definition that we have also defined in its own right elsewhere in the dictionary.

In many instances, we introduce a new, and often esoteric, term as part of another term's definition, but have elected not to define it in its own right, typically because that esoteric term lies below what we have determined to be a sort of threshold of interest. Based on our judgment, any terms lying below that threshold do not carry enough weight in the industry, or perhaps lie so far to its fringe that they do not merit their own entry. In such cases, we have enclosed those terms in quotation marks, and made an attempt to define them insofar as they contribute to the definition of the entry in which they appear.

If you were to pursue the cross-references, and all of our embedded definitions, as if riding the associative trails of a hypertext document, you would eventually start to see the multinodal pattern of meanings by which this young and vibrant industry is erecting its own language. It is our hope that you will enjoy and be instructed by our efforts to define the industry.

Acknowledgments

As with any book, there are many individuals to whom we are indebted. In particular, for providing us with professional vision, we are indebted to Nicholas Negroponte of the Media Lab at MIT and to George Gilder, noted author of multimedia and virtual reality works. We also wish to personally thank Mike Vollmer of the Federal Deposit Insurance Corporation, Pam Schaepe of CSS Multimedia, L.W. Leonard and T.P. Rud of IDC Information Design Corporation®, and Dr. Marjorie Davis, School of Engineering, Mercer University, Macon Campus. Thank you.

Trademarks

Every effort has been made to identify any trademarks mentioned in this book in the list below. However, all products listed in this book are trademarks of their respective companies, whether or not they are included in this list. In the text, only defined terms in boldface are given trademarks to distinguish brand names from generic terms.

The following are trademarks of the indicated companies: PostScript and Premiere, of Adobe Systems Inc.; IconAuthor, of AimTech Corporation; America Online, of America Online, Inc.;

HyperCard, Macintosh, Newton, QuickDraw, QuickRing, QuickTime, TrueType, and IIE, of Apple Computer Inc.; AutoCAD, of Autodesk, Inc.; Where in the World is Carmen Sandiego?, of Brøderbund Software Inc.; Amiga, of Commodore Business Machines, Inc.; Compton's Interactive Encyclopedia, of Compton's NewMedia; Compuserve, of Compuserve, Inc.; Kodak Photo CD, of Eastman Kodak Company; 3D0, of Electronic Arts; Neuro-Baby, of Fujitsu; DigiCipher II, of General Instruments Corporation; Hypertalk, of Hypercard; IBM Atlanta Usability Lab, IBM Multiples Marketing Program, OS/2, and Primary Editor Plus, of IBM Corporation; Power PC, of consortium of IBM, Motorola, and Apple; IMAX Theatre, of IMAX Theatre; DVI (Digital Video Interleaved), Indeo, PCI (Peripheral Component Interconnect), and Pentium, of Intel Corporation; Special Delivery, of Interactive Media Corporation; Script-X, of Kaleida Labs (joint IBM and Apple consortium); Kleenex, of Kimberly Clark Corp.; 1-2-3 and Notes, of Lotus Development Corporation; Action, Director, and Authorware Professional, of Macromedia Inc.; SimCity, of Maxis; AVI (Audio Video Interleaved), Encarta, Flight Simulator, Modular Windows, MSCDX (Microsoft CD-ROM extensions), MS-DOS, PC Paintbrush, VFW (Video for Windows), and Windows—Note Pad, Alarm Clock, MCI, and Media Player—of Microsoft Corporation; DAG (Data Acquisition Glove) and TeleTact Glove, of National Advanced Robotics Research Center in conjunction with Airmuscle Ltd; MovieStudio, of OptImage Interactive Services; FMV (Full Motion Video), of Philips Corporation; AIV (Advanced Interactive Video), of Philips UK; Polhemus Tracker, of Polhemus Navigation Sciences; Prodigy, of Prodigy Services Company; Genesis, of Sega; PAS (Performance Automation System), of SimGraphics; SPOX, of Spectrum Microsystems; Cinepak, of SuperMac; VIS (Visual Information System), of Tandy Corp.; RIP (Remote Imaging Protocol), of TeleGrafix; Targa, of TrueVision; VL-Bus, of the Video Electronics Standards Association; The 7th Guest, of Virgin Games Interactive; DataGlove, DataSuit, and EyePhone, of VPL Research; OPL3, of Yamaha.

INTRODUCTION
The Multimedia Industry

After two decades in the great technology incubator, banished to such threadbare regions as corporate training departments, and to such deprived platforms as the first generation of personal computers, the phenomenon we are now calling multimedia has exploded onto the technological landscape with a force that even its most vocal advocates had not imagined possible. But what is it? Most of the authors of the considerable volume of what is being written about the subject are downright bewildered when pressed on this blunt question. It would appear that, in spite of abrupt and blaring pronouncements in the media, the identity of this new medium is very poorly understood.

Could it be that the future of multimedia is now happening so fast that we have totally lost our place in the procession of technological history? Probably. But there are a number of reasonably cogent things that can be said about multimedia and about where this emergent medium is heading. Based upon the reflections of a handful of industry leaders and early conceptual pioneers, it is possible to round up at least a thimbleful of useful ideas. We offer them here as a provisional explanation of what's happening.

Three Industry Segments

The early market for multimedia applications appears to have divided itself into three fairly distinct segments:

1. **The Home Market**: which owes its origins to the likes of Sega, Nintendo, and the other adolescent video games, is now on the verge of blossoming into a much, much more robust enterprise. The games themselves are becoming more sophisticated and intelligent and are now offering some of the first genres capable of attracting and holding an adult audience. Just around the corner looms the promise of interactive television, which threatens to turn the standard American couch potato into the newly rejuvenated couch commando.

2. **The School Market**: which owes its origins to the small-scale, curriculum-based programs that ran on Apple IIe's, has recently played host to the large-scale integrated learning systems that rank among the most sophisticated forms of instructional software yet created. These systems integrate the electronic delivery of course content across broad, multigrade spans of content, and deliver that content via network-based client server systems that monitor learner performance in specific, objectives-level detail. With all of the great debate over the declining quality of the American education system, the pressure to explore various forms of instructional technology will keep this market growing at a rapid pace into at least the near future.

3. **The Business Market**: which is, ironically, the most backward segment of the interactive market, has great growth potential. The tremendous pressure to reengineer business practices and processes in almost every sector of our economy will likely elevate the attractiveness of interactive training solutions. Corporate America will be seeking ways to quickly and efficiently train large and geographically dispersed workforces as never before, and now that the corporate desktop is coming to be occupied by MPCs (multimedia personal computers), rather than just plain old vanilla PCs, the inclination to use interactive multimedia should grow dramatically.

In sum, every segment of the multimedia market will be growing during this last decade of the century. The business market will be driven by the need to constantly train and re-train a diverse workforce. The school market will be fueled by mounting pressures to modify—if not overhaul—an antiquated instructional delivery system. And the home market will likely be the liveliest of all, as the twitch-and-shoot design model of first-generation electronic games matures into several successor genres, including the first interactive forms of fiction and cinema, and various other forms of increasingly immersive media.

The hype is not foundless. The wave of mergers and acquisitions we are now witnessing between previously segregated portions of the information economy are nothing if not early harbingers of an explosively innovative future. The massive and cash-rich telecommunications firms are buying entertainment and computing companies. Print publishing firms are seeking alliances with software companies. In fact, virtually every permutation of linkage between these various stewards of information is being pursued with almost frantic vigor.

All of these enterprises must be positioning themselves for something. But for what?

Multimedia Is about Converging Industries and Technologies

In 1978 Nicholas Negroponte, one of the true savants of multimedia, used a Venn diagram and his intellectual track record as an MIT professor to raise $70 million to launch the Media Lab, an organization dedicated to contemplating the far-flung technological horizons of communications. In the Venn diagram, Negroponte showed that three industries were converging to form a single technological powerhouse, one that would dominate the future of human communications. Those three industries were the printing and publishing industry, the computer industry, and the broadcast and motion picture industry.

He projected that the overlap between these three industries would approach a near union by the end of the century. And while many futurists would just as soon have us forget their projections once the time of their foretold future has arrived, Negroponte's premonitions seem more and more worthy of acknowledgement the closer we get to the year 2000. Clearly, these industries are converging.

If anything, that convergence is ahead of schedule. And the multifarious outcomes of that convergence are a large part of what we are calling multimedia. They involve new products, new services, and new genres of art and entertainment. In fact, the impact that can be attributed to the interindustrial convergence that is multimedia seems to broaden with each passing year and certainly with each new journalistic interpretation.

The span of topics covered in the trade and academic presses by articles that have the term "multimedia" in their titles is truly staggering. Much of what is written focuses on the enabling technologies, such as networking, transmission, and new forms of mass storage, on to the playback environments and the ever-expanding array of authoring tools. Many of the articles claim that in the final analysis content is king, and then proceed to spray the journalistic canvas with widely diverging interpretations of just what exactly constitutes multimedia content.

Many writers think of multimedia as videoconferencing and its various derivatives, such as document conferencing, distance learning, and video mail. Others see multimedia technology as a new form of publishing, and thus see these media as those that are quickly replacing all major forms of paper documents with superior, interactive versions: electronic catalogs and brochures replace their passive and inferior ancestors of the same name (sans the "interactive"); likewise, electronic encyclopedias and computer based training programs replace the static encyclopedia and textbook, respectively; and, not to forget the arts, interactive fiction and fantasy games replace the most venerated form of document in our cultural history, the novel.

Still others see multimedia technology as a natural step in the direction of increasingly sophisticated and immersive media. These writers and thinkers are prone to let their thoughts drift among such topics as 3-D audio and video, motion platforms and force feedback, even on to the exotica associated with cyberspace and virtual reality. Regardless of how one chooses to judge these various attempts to describe and classify the things associated with multimedia, one thing is absolutely clear: multimedia is a serious phenomenon.

It connects to our most salient historical arcs. The merging of computers and media now permits the author—or, as in film, the authoring team—to enlist and engage the audience as never before. Rather than watching the performance of a protagonist from a detached and safe-harbor seat in the theater, the listener-reader-viewer must now become something new and unprecedented in the history of the narrative arts. The audience member must now become an active participant, must now become the very protagonist whose performance is the thing that is judged.

The convergence of publishing with computers and media means that shoppers and learners and explorers will be able to take control of their media in ways that enable them to find just the right advertisement relative to their immediate needs; to individualize their training experiences to match instructional content to personal skill and knowledge deficiencies; and to select entry points on the ladder of challenge that are most likely to lead to the optimal gaming experiences.

As we contemplate the consequences of the converging technologies that are now being called multimedia, it is prudent to take stock of a lesser known, but highly appropriate, quote from Marshall McLuhan:

> The hybrid or meeting of two media is a moment of truth and revelation of which new form is born . . . . The crossings of media release great force.
>
> *Understanding Media*, 1964.

And, as we further devote our thoughts to the proposition of responding to a steady flow of new, hybrid forms of media, it is also prudent to ask . . .

Why Bother?

Imagining—for just a moment—that it might be possible for us to seize control of the fuel line that feeds our capitalist engine with the flow of innovations upon which it now so obviously depends, what type and amount of pressure would we want to place on the nozzle that regulates the pace of new media? Imagining—for just a wildly speculative second—that ours might become the invisible hand of Adam Smith's economy, how would we adjust our grip when it came time to determine the rate at which we permit our traditional media to transform themselves via the synthesizing force of digitization?

To inform the grip in our thusly deified hand, it would be appropriate to ask the larger question: what is the value of these new forms of media? In other words, what are the advantages of multimedia? By way of framing the answer to this question, we must first conjure at least a working definition of the proper scope of the term. In other words, we must first answer the question: Over what span of human interests will this upstart and wildly hybrid medium have a significant impact?

Even at this relatively early juncture, the answer to this question seems obvious: the impact of multimedia will be global, both in a literal and a figurative sense. Like all major forms of communication that have gone before, multimedia will—in the fullness of time—have a significant impact on every industry and population segment.

Using this perspective to frame the question "why bother?" and, thereby, to inform our decision making with regard to our imagined control over the rate of appearance for new media, it would seem appropriate to respond by looking at two very broad divisions of our economy: the arts and entertainment industries, on the one hand, and the remainder of the business world, on the other.

What beneficial impacts will multimedia have on the arts and entertainment industries? More to the point, what benefits will multimedia bestow on the creators of artistic and entertainment product—or, if you will, on what is being broadly referred to today as "content"? Stated with just one more minor twist: why would our most gifted creators of content take leave of the venerable media of our ancestors and contemporaries (novels, film, painting, etc.) to risk their highly valued time and effort on producing the emerging artifacts of multimedia?

To provide at least a provisional answer to these critical questions, we would like to turn to the insights of an individual whose career predated multimedia, but who is of great contemporary moment because he is the man who many would consider to be perhaps the most credible practitioner of the avant garde in the twentieth century. That person is Alain Robbe-Grillet (the last name pronounced "Robe Gree-ay"), the French novelist who visited more experimentation on the narrative form than any other writer in this century with works such as *The Voyeur* and *Last Year at Marienbad*.

During his career, Robbe-Grillet penned several essays on the transformation of the narrative form, a subject on which—as we have stated—he had unparalleled expertise. Robbe-Grillet understood the restless nature of art, particularly in this, our most restless of centuries. Several of these essays were gathered together into the little known 1965 volume *For a New Novel*. In analyzing the motivating forces that are currently driving us in the direction of new, interactive forms of art, it is appropriate that we exhume some the thoughts contained in this mid-sixties collection.

More than anything else, Robbe-Grillet—both in his novels and in his philosophical reflections—believed that the great historical arc of our storytelling tradition is the trend toward increasing levels of realism.

> It has always been the same: out of a concern for realism each new literary school has sought to destroy the one which preceded it; this was the watchword of the romantics against the classicists, then of the naturalists against the romantics; the surrealists themselves declared in their turn that they were concerned only with the real world.

Central to this trend toward greater realism, in Robbe-Grillet's mind, is the ability for the author to gain increasingly direct access to the audience. In a comment that clearly anticipates the dawn of interactive art forms—though it is fairly clear that he was not specifically thinking of anything like interactive multimedia or virtual reality at the time—Robbe-Grillet states: . . . *"far from neglecting him, the author today proclaims his absolute need of the reader's cooperation, an active, conscious, creative assistance."*

Reading a Robbe-Grillet novel, even today, two to three decades later, is still a strange experience. Many people find his works impossible to penetrate. This is not the time or place to explore the specific attributes that make them seem so out-of-the-ordinary; but what is appropriate to mention here is their most stunning attribute. Once one sees what Robbe-Grillet is trying to do—once one breaks his code, so to speak—it is clear that the effect he is most trying to create is the elimination of the usual gulf that separates the reader's psyche from that of the main character; one sees that he is laboring to place the reader as far *into* the action of the novel as is possible via a literary instrument. In a sense, Robbe-Grillet is trying to make the presence of the author disappear, and thus bring the reader into direct and naked contact with the protagonist's experience.

Robbe-Grillet speaks so directly to the issues surrounding the emergence of new media precisely because he did not foresee those media in any specific detail, but rather saw the larger forces and trends of which they are a part, of which they are the natural, late-twentieth century extension. Like its immediate predecessor, film, an interactive multimedia program provides the author with a leap forward in terms of the power to recreate the scenes and dramas of man, and thereby extends our storytelling tradition's venerable drive towards greater realism.

More vividly, though, interactive forms of storytelling and entertainment force the audience into the work of art by making them active participants in their creation. When an audience member plays the role of a protagonist and makes decisions that influence outcome, something fundamental and powerful has happened. As if in a Robbe-Grillet novel, the consumer of an interactive fiction experiences direct contact with the narrative circumstances of the story.

The forces motivating the emergence of interactive and increasingly immersive forms of art and entertainment are powerful. They are deeply rooted in much larger historical trajectories, and therefore must seem inevitable to us, no matter what fits and starts and skepticism may greet them during their initial stages. But what of more practical applications? What of the role of multimedia in the world of commerce and industry?

Here, again, we see powerful trends, but they issue from a different set of motivating forces. Multimedia will play large in the business world, but the forces that write the history of interactive media in this market segment will not be the same as in the arts and entertainment world. Here, the key motivating factor appears to be something that we might refer to as *the velocity of information.*

If we follow the major themes that have appeared in the business literature over the past few decades, we see that there is fairly wide agreement on what the key trends are: the globalization of the world economy, leading to increased levels of competition in almost every industry segment; the need to compress every aspect of the product life cycle, from R&D to manufacturing and especially into sales and marketing; the penetration of microprocessor-based forms of machine intelligence into almost every type of product and service, leading to an amplification of the forces behind technology-driven change; and, most critical of all, the need for organizations to employ a dynamic and flexible workforce, thus enabling them to change course quickly in response to sudden opportunities and/or competitive threats.

All of these themes relate directly to the need for organizations to change quickly; which, of course, is as much as saying they need to increase the rate at which they are able to learn and absorb new processes and technologies. As never before, the pressure to increase the velocity of information beats down on us, both from an individual and an organizational standpoint.

Thus, any technology that can make this acceleration more bearable, that can speed our rates of learning without breaking the bank, will hold great appeal. And while the first generation of interactive training programs has had its fair share of disappointments, there is no doubting that the long-term potential of interactive media in the business world is great.

In fact, a number of studies have appeared over the past few decades that document the power of well-designed interactive training programs. It has been validated that a well-conceived interactive product can be more effective than any other form of instruction, save perhaps the one-on-one mentoring that occurs between learner and expert. But, of course, experts are almost always scarce, and therefore very expensive, resources. They can be leveraged somewhat by using a seminar format, but then this form of instruction abandons the intense levels of interaction that confer so much value on mentoring.

The features of interactive multimedia that make for an effective instructional delivery platform are abundant and are by now fairly well known. They include the ability to offer learners an appropriate level of control over the learning experience; to ask questions of learners, thereby forcing their direct involvement; to track the performance of learners over a range of questions and other interactive challenges, thereby building up profiles of learner knowledge and skill; to prescribe entire learning sequences on the basis of objectively determined levels of knowledge skill; to use multiple and appropriate forms of media to meet the unique needs of particular instructional challenges and student populations; to track learning preferences, as well as performances, thereby enabling programs to match delivery formats to learning styles; and to link a diverse database of training resources to the even more diverse learning needs of large audiences, thus providing the long-awaited power and promise of individualized instruction.

The benefits of an effective piece of interactive multimedia to a business organization are both numerous and potentially profound. It enables an organization to leverage the knowledge and skills of its strongest performers by encoding their expertise in the pedagogical logic of the program. It makes it possible for large and geographically dispersed companies to significantly reduce—if not eliminate—the high travel and lodging costs associated with offering seminars. It offers learners the ability to take the training wherever and whenever they need it, the so-called just-in-time learning phenomenon. It enables organizations to discern knowledge levels in their workforce, and thus be able to address specific strengths and weaknesses. And it offers managers the ability to track the effectiveness of their investments in training, and therewith better allocate their future training expenditures.

Though the business world has been slow to adopt interactive solutions, the mounting evidence that these programs can deliver some powerful benefits will no doubt work to reduce the resistance. More important, though, the pressure on organizations to increase the velocity with which information travels through their ranks will make interactive forms of instruction a near-necessity in the very near future.

But Will It Be Easy?

Increasingly, interactive forms of media appear destined to stand in the same relationship to the twenty-first century as film and TV have to our own. The current floodtide of journalistic interest is almost willing the transition from linear to interactive. But there are many factors which will make that transition difficult, expensive, and painful. In fact, at least two of the most significant problems have already made themselves quite apparent.

In the first place, the most obvious aspect of the interactive revolution is also its most problematic, at least here in the early going. The most fundamental aspect of interactive is the digitization of audiovisual forms of information. This relatively straightforward process holds the potential of unleashing some of the most powerful change agents in the history of the capitalist world. Unfortunately, there is no question about its having unleashed a tremendous set of technological problems.

If we consider the past three decades to be the formative years of computer technology—as most experts do—then it can be said that the formative period in the history of computing was all about the processing of symbolic forms of information, i.e., of text and numbers. As it turns out, digitally encoded forms of symbolic information are very compact, though this was certainly not the prevailing sentiment even just a decade ago, when personal computers were only capable of storing and manipulating a few million characters, or about the equivalent of a few healthy books. With the subsequent advent of hundred-plus megabyte hard drives, and then the 600+ megabyte CD-ROM, we now comfortably hold the view that computers have risen up to swallow our books and accounting records. The lone problem remaining seems to lie in getting this information better organized.

But when we move on to the task of digitally encoding audio, and especially video, sources of information, we re-enter the domain of the humble—the very humble. One second of uncompressed, television-quality video requires over 27 megabytes of storage. Pursuing this equation to some of its more painful conclusions, we find that the mighty CD-ROM player is capable of handling just about 30 seconds of uncompressed video, and that a full-length motion picture would require close to 200 gigabytes, or approximately the amount of storage that one would expect to find handling the entire data processing needs of a medium-sized corporation. Cough.

The digitization of media—of audio, image, and video—has created a crisis in the computer *and* the communications industries. Though a multitude of compression/decompression schemes have entered the marketplace in the past half-decade, the problems associated with displaying and storing and transmitting the volumes of data needed to encode media are still immense. Computers are not fast enough. Storage devices do not have enough capacity. And the networks do not have nearly enough bandwidth. If you look at a multimedia title and wonder at the relatively poor quality of its media assets, consider it a manifestation of this larger problem. Barring some unforeseeable innovation, the challenge of mastering this undercapacitation will be at the center of the multimedia industry for at least the next decade.

But this technical problem is not the only one that threatens our transition into the age of multimedia. Nor is it perhaps even the most difficult. As one contemplates the convergence of media—of print and publishing with computers, and of both of these with film and television—the most tumultuous proposition would appear to be the imminent collision of the cultures that preside over these various media with decisively different styles, values, and knowledge-sets.

Take, for example, the separate cultures that preside over the computer industry, on the one hand, and the film and TV industry, on the other. Both are global leaders. Both require extremely large numbers of finely specialized and highly talented individuals. Both are proud to a fault, even ethnocentric. Neither tribe will take too kindly to the inevitable turf intrusions of the other. And lest we agree to fool ourselves, it is impossible to imagine that there will be many safe passages on the corporate battlefield that will serve to adjudicate the struggle for multimedia booty.

It Will Be All of These Things

The coming decades will see the rise of multimedia, replete with opportunities and pitfalls. The convergence of multiple industries of the most powerful sort will further accelerate the forces of technology-associated change. New forms of media—electronic brochures, interactive fictions, system emulation programs, even virtual reality—will appear with clockwork regularity. Some of them quickly ascend to the role of major social change agent, much as telephony and television, for example, have done in our century.

There is no reason not to feel the same sort of excitement about the prospects of multimedia that one indulges in over such phenomena as major space exploration programs. This enthusiasm, however, should be balanced by some equally legitimate anxieties. As individuals with careers that will be impacted by these new media technologies, how should we govern our career path decisions? As organizations, which of these risky and expensive technologies should we commit to, and when? And, as a society, how should we manage (regulate) these new industries so as to minimize some of their potentially destructive influences?

We have written this present and humble volume in an effort to make our contribution to easing the anxiety and conflict that will no doubt accompany the coming of multimedia. As we stated in the Foreword, one of the most substantial conflicts will appear early—has, in fact, already appeared. It is the clash of professional vocabularies, of nomenclatures. If we can help some of these contributory industries understand and appreciate the language and concepts and potential of the others, then we will have hit our mark.

MULTIMEDIA TECHNOLOGY FROM A TO Z

—

If interactive breaks through the barriers between entertainment and the entertained, the next step may be to break down the wall between the real world and the artificial computer world.

—The Hollywood Reporter

A/B roll editing: This process of splicing and combining two or more videotapes, the most common of editing functions, is now being made far more flexible and easy to do by the advent of digital video production tools.

Accelerator board: This term refers to a class of *expansion board* used in personal computers to speed up their performance, usually in relation to processing the display of visual information. Machines built to process alphanumeric forms of information now need to process *mixed media data types* (e.g., audio, image, video). These accelerator boards, directly connected to the computer's monitor, process the movement of *pixels*, taking the burden off of the computer's *CPU* (central processing unit). High-end, high-performance boards use a special type of memory known as *VRAM* (pronounced *vee-ram*, and stands for video random access memory), which allows the computer to write new information to a memory location while the old information is being read.

Access key: With the advent of the massive storage capabilities made possible by *CD-ROM*, and *optical storage* in general, an increasing number of application developers are making use of this technology, which is a software-encoded key allowing access to a group of files protected by a file protection code. With large *clip media* libraries, for example, the developer can enable users to pay for only those portions of a particular library that they need.

Access time: Refers to the location and recovery time of information requested by a user on the computer.

Accuracy aids: With reference to computer graphics, this term refers to various pre-programmed techniques, such as *snap-to grids*, that enable a designer to achieve positioning accuracy on an interactive display.

Acoustic coupler: A nearly obsolete piece of data communications hardware, an acoustic coupler functions as a *modem* by converting a computer's digital signals into chirps to be sent over the telephone line, and, conversely, by converting the chirps received back into digital signals intelligible to the computer.

Active display: With reference to handling *digital* video in memory, this term refers to that portion of the video memory currently being displayed, as opposed to screen contents being held in memory for later display (if needed).

Active window: With graphical user interfaces (*GUIs*) based on the *desktop metaphor* (such as the Apple Macintosh or the Microsoft *Windows* interface), it is always possible to have several *windows* open on the desktop at any one time. However, for the sake of maintaining order, it is only possible to have one of those windows active at any one time. Thus, the window where the user's actions are directed at a given moment is referred to as the active window.

ADC: Stands for *analog* to *digital* conversion of data.

A/D converter: A device that samples an *analog* signal at regular intervals and *quantizes* each sample. An A/D converter stands as the primary translator between the real world of analog phenomena and the computer world of *digital* phenomena. The most important aspect of the A/D conversion process is the *sampling rate*, which measures the frequency with which the analog phenomena are converted into digitally encoded numbers, and, therefore, expresses the resolution, or quality, of the A/D conversion. The higher the sampling rate, the more accurately the digitally encoded data represent the analog phenomena being measured or captured. Any type of probe or sensor that interfaces to the computer (e.g., a *digital thermometer*) is an example of an A/D converter. As the world becomes increasingly computerized, the presence of A/D converters will be widespread.

Address: With regard to computing, this term refers to a character, a group of characters, or other *bit* pattern that occupies and can be accessed through a particular storage location in computer memory.

ADF: Stands for automatic document feeder, a mechanism that attaches to a *scanner* and allows unattended scanning of multiple images. This relatively simple device is a great labor-saver for the emerging document imaging industry.

ADPCM: Adaptive delta pulse code modulation is a technique for translating *analog* audio into *digital* audio. As the term "delta" implies, this technique belongs to a large family of digitization techniques that rely on correlating patterns of amplitude over time. It is a direct descendent of *pulse code modulation* (PCM).

ADSL: Otherwise known as the asymmetrical digital subscriber line, this technology was developed by Bellcore (the research arm of Bell Labs dedicated to the interests of the so-called baby bells, e.g., Bell Atlantic) to enable the providers of telephone services to supply video services for the residential market over the copper wire transmission lines that have been traditionally used for providing *POTS* (plain old telephone service). This is a strategic technology for the telephone companies. At present, the telephone companies may be at a competitive disadvantage to the cable operators with regard to providing multimedia services like videophone to the home market. Cable operators own the coaxial cable delivering cable TV service to homes, which provides them with a sizable *bandwidth* advantage over the copper lines that telephone companies own for delivering their signals. ADSL may neutralize this comparative disadvantage. It uses specially designed transmitters and receivers that reduce the interference and *noise* normally experienced on a copper line. The technology makes it possible to transmit television-quality, compressed video over ordinary copper wire. Up until the appearance of ADSL, it was thought that the goal of merging the switching capabilities of the *public switched telephone network* (PSTN) with the ability to carry a video signal would require the telephone companies to provide curbside fiber lines to every home, which is an enormously expensive undertaking. This technology may eliminate that need.

Advanced Interactive Video™: Also referred to by its acronym, AIV, this term refers to a *laserdisc* format developed in 1986 by Philips UK and a number of other media and computer interests. The format accommodates *analog* video, *digital* audio, and digital data on the same laserdisc surface. Also referred to as *LV ROM*, this format is suffering from the same fate that has befallen the other laserdisc formats: namely, a diminishing popularity in comparison to the all-digital formats associated with *CD-ROM.*

Advisory Committee on Advanced Television Service: This ad hoc committee was established to recommend from among competing technologies a single set of functional specifications to the FCC for an *HDTV* (high definition television) standard.

Aftertouch: Also referred to as "pressure-sensitive," this is an attribute of more sophisticated *MIDI* (musical instrument digital interface) keyboards with which the amount of pressure placed on a key is encoded as part of the MIDI data stream. In other words, when a player presses a key on the MIDI keyboard, not only is the code for that particular key generated, but so too is an additional code that describes how much pressure was employed in pressing the key. Obviously, this attribute enables the MIDI standard to encode a finer set of distinctions in its digital representation of music.

Agents: This is a relatively new type of software module that implements technologies to understand the user's spoken or written requests and then complies with them. This term is roughly synonymous with *interface agents*, varying from that term only in the sense that it represents the more general and abstract machine intelligence which lies behind, and makes possible, the functioning of an interface agent.

Age of Interactivity: This term is slowly emerging from the trade journals and carries with it some probability that it will replace the currently popular phrase "Information Age" as the label du jour for describing the technology-intensive era in which we live. The term "Age of Interactivity" bears many important connotations: that we will soon see the mass media of broadcast TV and film turn to interactive forms of presentation and entertainment; that ye olde technology of telephony will soon be revitalized by the video dial tone; that the classroom model of education—dominant for the entire history of public education—will begin to give way to interactive forms of instructional delivery, such as we are now calling educational software (a.k.a. *CAI, CBT, IVD,* etc.); and that interactive cinema and a number of the other *cyberarts* will gradually replace linear, one-way forms of narrative, such as fiction and film, as the dominant modes of storytelling and mass entertainment.

Alerts: From the world of graphical user interface *(GUI)* design, these interface elements, also referred to as alert boxes, notify the user when an unusual, or possibly damaging, condition has occurred.

Algorithm: This term refers to a series of instructions or procedural steps for solving a specific problem.

Aliasing: These are unwanted visual effects in *raster images*, especially jagged lines and edges *(jaggies)* caused by improper or low-quality *sampling* techniques.

ALU: Arithmetic logic unit refers to that specialized part of the *CPU* that performs arithmetic and logic operations.

Ames Research Center: Located along Route 101 in Silicon Valley, this NASA research center is responsible for pioneering many of the foundational technologies of *virtual reality* (VR) and *simulation* systems. Home to noted VR inventor Scott Fisher, this center is responsible for developing, among other creations, the *Convolvotron* directional audio system, the Virtual Planetary Exploration (VPE) system, and the Virtual Interactive Environmental Workstation (VIEWS).

Amplitude: With regard to audio and/or video signals, amplitude refers to the strength of a given signal. Amplitude is measured in various units depending on the application. For example, with audio signals, the measurement is in decibels, which is a logarithmic scale based on human hearing sensitivities. For audio, amplitude is a measure of volume; for video, it is a measure of image contrast.

Analog: In electronics, analog is a continuously variable signal. Analog signals are often depicted as waveforms, and in the computer world are always held in contrast to discretely variable *digital* signals, representing separate datapoints in space and time. Analog phenomena in nature include waves, time, temperature, and voltage.

Animated blobs: Created by Carnegie-Mellon University's Joseph Bates, these creations represent the first attempt at automated storytelling using the principles of *object-oriented programming*. The blobs are self-contained, intelligent objects, programmed according to the rules of behavioral theory. The way blobs encounter each other sparks emotional responses that in chain-reaction form cause additional reactions so that they appear to be creating their own spontaneous drama.

Animated map: A series of maps presenting a moving image, typically used to show spatio-temporal patterns such as the distribution of population in the United States over the course of several decades.

Animation: Is the process of displaying artwork over time to simulate motion. Most animation belongs to one of two types: graphic or character. "Graphic animation" is generally composed of a single piece of art whose position changes over time (e.g., a moving logo). To create movement, one piece of art has intermediate positions rather than intermediate drawings. Graphic animation is relatively easy to master, does not require drawing skills, and, in a computer environment, requires only modest storage and processing power. "Character animation," in contrast, entails generating a different piece of art for each *frame*, as is done for TV cartoons. In traditional character animation, an artist works at a light table, creating each frame by transferring a drawing from paper to acetate (called a *cel*) and hand coloring it with paint. Two key drawings—which are the principal points of movement for each frame—punctuate several "inbetweens" which, as the name implies, are the intermediate drawings between *key frames*. With desktop animation tools, many of the more arduous tasks of traditional animation, such as *inbetweening,* are automated, leaving open the potential for an enormous growth in the use of character animation for many purposes, such as *edutainment* products.

ANSI: Stands for the American National Standards Institute, a standards-making body for the computer industry, most famous for its *ASCII* standard format for encoding characters in the PC environment.

Answer analysis: From the realm of *educational software*, this term refers to the simplest, lowest level form of *performance tracking*, where the programmer writes code to analyze a learner's response to a single question. The most common form is the multiple choice question, where the program simply branches on the basis of whether or not the learner answered the question correctly.

Anti-aliasing: *Aliasing* is perhaps the most commonly cited visual *artifact* of computer graphics, whereby boundaries take on a stairstep pattern, often referred to as the *jaggies*. Anti-aliasing refers to techniques designed to sharpen the image by switching *pixels* to intermediate intensities along either side of otherwise jagged diagonal lines. Anti-aliasing techniques are particularly important with displays that feature relatively low *resolution*.

Architectural walkthrough: A sub-type of the *surrogate travel* genre, walkthroughs are also a form of *virtual reality*, wherein the user can control a simulated passage through an architectural structure such as a hallway in a building. The underlying or *enabling technology* of architectural walkthroughs is *CAD* (computer aided design) programs. In the coming age of interactive artforms, the capabilities and techniques made possible by walkthroughs will become a tool within the larger toolkit for those making highly immersive forms of electronic games, *interactive fictions*, and training *simulations*.

ARM: Otherwise known as the Argonne Remote Manipulator, this is a prototypical telerobotic device developed at the Argonne National Laboratories. The ARM is a long, multijoint arm suspended from the ceiling. The device provides basic control and force feedback to the user's hand, wrist, elbow, and shoulder along three axes and three torques. It is designed to give the user control of a remote robotic arm and was developed initially for handling radioactive materials. Many of the techniques and devices used in the construction of the ARM are now finding their way into the design of *virtual reality* systems.

Art director: A key figure throughout much of the history of the collaborative fictional enterprises, such as theater, film, video, and feature animation, the art director is one role that, if anything, will be enlarged by the advent of *interactive multimedia*. The primary responsibility of the art director is to create the total visual look of the product, which requires a highly creative and artistic sensibility. Many art directors from the film and video sector have made excellent contributions to the discipline of *interface design*. Their skills at manipulating color and lighting, translating functions into metaphors and metaphors into *button* designs, and specifying spatial relationships have made their presence welcome on many interactive projects. Art directors are often assumed to be good *illustrators*, which is not necessarily the case, though they are certainly dependent on good illustrators to implement their vision. In the interactive world, art directors design the visual aspects of the interface, while illustrators execute their designs; i.e., they create the artwork for the buttons, graphics, animations, etc.

Artifact: This term is widely used to describe flaws that can be detected in all forms of media, both *analog* and *digital*. More precisely, though, it is used to describe a flaw—a random sound or visual effect—that was not present in the original source signal, but that has been introduced by one of the components in the recording or reproduction chain. For example, *flicker* is a common artifact in the analog video world, while *pixellation* is one of the most common artifacts found in digital video.

Artificial intelligence: This term refers to the part of computer science concerned with designing machines that exhibit human characteristics and do things in a way that would require intelligence if done by people. The classic measure of AI, more relevant today than even perhaps when it was conceived, is called the *Turing Test*. Named after its author, Alan Turing, this test is passed by a machine if its ability to carry on a conversation is indistinguishable from that of a human, as exemplified by "HAL," the fictional computer in Stanley Kubrick's (director) *2001: A Space Odyssey*.

ASCAP: Stands for American Society of Composers, Authors and Publishers, an organization that has become best known for working out a detailed set of licensing specifications for recording artists that helps ensure that royalties and other usage fees get paid to the copyright holders and artists. Many people feel that this set of specifications—or something very much like it—will be in great need in the *Age of Interactivity*, where, for example, the widespread use of *clip media* will make it difficult to track and manage the payment of royalties to all of the contributing artists.

ASCII: Stands for American Standard Code for Information Interchange and represents one of the most important and enduring standards of the personal computer market. ASCII is a standard table of 8-bit digital representations of uppercase and lowercase Roman letters, numbers, special control characters, and various graphic characters. This widely adhered to standard makes it possible for the vast majority of PC software programs to exchange information at a basic text-and-number level.

Aspect ratio: In the most general sense, the aspect ratio is the width-to-height ratio of a rectangular object. With respect to computer displays, this can refer to either the screen shape or the *pixel* shape. Video has a screen aspect ratio of 4:3, and film an image aspect ratio of 3:2. Converting from one presentational medium to another—the classic example being from motion picture to television—can be problematic, often forcing some form of distortion.

Asymmetrical codec: Refers, for the most part, to *interframe* forms of compression-decompression, where the encoding (compressing) side of the process is much more time-consuming and expensive than the decoding (decompressing) side. Both *DVI* (Digital Video Interactive) and *MPEG* (Motion Picture Experts Group) are asymmetrical, *interframe codecs*. The primary reason for the asymmetry rests on the arduous computational task associated with finding the patterns of temporal change and stability in video sequences. Once these patterns have been found and subjected to the *delta encoding* techniques, it is not nearly so difficult to decompress (reconstruct) the original image.

ATM: Stands for asynchronous transfer mode, a term which everyone interested in the networking of *mixed media data types* should commit to memory. This technology possesses several traits that make it the favored networking protocol for the future of high-*bandwidth, multimedia, data communications*. It works by splitting data into small chunks, giving it the key attributes of a *packet switching* protocol. But instead of routing each packet individually, as is characteristic of most packet switching systems, ATM establishes a virtual circuit between origin and destination so that it can accommodate the time-sensitive *streaming data* associated with digital video. Thus, ATM also possesses the essential characteristic of a *circuit switching* system. Because of this combination of attributes, ATM is noted for its ability to allocate bandwidth on demand, a trait often referred to by the popular computer term *scalability*. Because it is scalable, and because it can handle ultra-high capacities, ATM is favorably viewed by media futurists for its ability to scale way up in response to a request for transmitting image or video, thus being responsive to the needs of networked multimedia; but also for its ability to scale back down after the multimedia transmission is complete, thus saving the user from having to pay for such high bandwidth when it is not needed.

Audiographics: This term refers to an early form of *picturephone* that features two-way audio on a voice-grade telephone circuit with computer and/or video still images sent over the same line or a second line. Synchronization of the audio and visual components is not sought with audiographics, since the time required to send the visual components (an image, for example) is often delayed in the range of several seconds to several minutes, whereas the audio is transmitted in typical, real-time fashion.

Authoring system: This term is given to systems that contain software tools designed to empower individual developers and development teams to produce various types of *multimedia applications*. Though there is obviously considerable variation from one system to the next, the categories of tools provided in most of these applications include media integration tools, i.e., tools for digitizing *mixed media data types* and for interfacing to media peripherals such as *CD-ROM* players; media production tools, such as *paint systems* and other routines for building and managing screen objects; *answer analysis* and *performance tracking* routines; a high-level programming interface designed for ease of use, such as the time-line interfaces featured in such programs as Macromedia's Director; and, some form of programming or scripting language, such as HyperCard's HyperTalk. Though virtually every authoring system sells the idea that it can be used by computer-neophyte authors, this is only true in a limited way. Most authoring systems can be used in a restricted fashion by uninitiated authors. In general, though, the development of sophisticated multimedia products is a highly collaborative undertaking that requires numerous specialists, utilizing several tools all working under expert direction.

Auto assembly: In the world of video production, this term refers to the penultimate portion of the editing process whereby a master tape is constructed from the *EDL* (edit decision list) under the control of a computerized editing system.

Autochanger: This term refers to the critical component of an optical juke box (or any other form of juke box), which is responsible for fetching and loading optical discs using some form of robotic device.

Auto iris: From the world of film and TV production, this device is useful when filming a scene during dawn or dusk. It is a camera lens function that automatically adjusts to compensate for changes in light levels.

AVI™: Stands for Audio Video Interleaved, Microsoft's movie file format. The *interleaving* refers to the fact that under this file format, video and audio files that relate to the same captured media event are interleaved with one another so that synchronizing them (*lipsynching*, for example) can be more readily accomplished.

This is not Hollywood on a disk or a computer in Hollywood—it's something new altogether.
—Paul Saffo, Researcher, Institute for the Future

Backchannel: In the emerging world of *interactive television*, this term refers to the channel over which users (home consumers of interactive programming) will communicate back to the entity from which the programming initiates. Because TV has historically been a strictly one-way medium, with programming that originates with the broadcaster and is sent to the home user, there has never been any infrastructure put in place to handle backflows of data from the user to the broadcaster, other than informal channels that lie outside of the cable system (e.g., cable users can pick up the phones and call their local cable operators, but this communication channel is not part of the cable system per se). With the perceived need for *interactivity* at an all-time high, cable operators are now experimenting with various ways of supplying their users with backchannels so that these users can potentially interact with the programming. At present, these backchannels possess relatively low *bandwidths*, but this should change in the near future.

Backdrop: From the realm of *digital* video, this term refers to the background image plane displayed when all other *picture planes* are made transparent.

Backfile conversion: When an organization contemplates the conversion of its various documentation (e.g., paper documents, microfiche, slides, etc.) to a *digital* format, and then to long-term storage on one or more of the many emerging optical mass storage technologies, it must confront the (often massive) chore of converting all of its historical records. With paper document sources of information—by far the most common case—the process usually involves scanning, touch-up, indexing, and then, finally, transfer to disk. This whole process is called backfile conversion, and it represents one of the meat and potatoes applications of the age of multimedia. The primary advantage to organizations that undertake this process is that it brings all of their historical sources of information under the control of some form of information storage and retrieval system. The "converted" sources of information can then be searched and retrieved in an automated fashion, as well as subjected to various statistical analyses. In contrast, with traditional sources of archival storage, such as microfiche, the user must first read an index—which may be computerized—and then must manually fetch target information from the archival vaults, a procedure that backfile conversions seek to eliminate.

Background task: This is a task that a computer performs while the primary or foreground program is not using the *CPU* (central processing unit). In a true multitasking environment, the user is typically unaware that a background task is being processed.

Back-of-the-book index: In the world of traditional book publishing, this term refers to the index that appears at the back of the book, with which we all have great familiarity. It is of importance to the dawning era of multimedia because it is now viewed as part-in-parcel of a thing called document design, which in turn is attached to such emerging media as electronic reference documents (ERD). With many desktop publishing systems, the construction of back-of-the-book indexes can now be automated by simply tagging the terms in the body of the text that one wants to appear in the index. The program then tracks the location of these terms as the document changes in size, and automatically writes their respective page numbers to the index upon command. Going one step further, with many ERD *authoring systems*, these indexes can be made "live," meaning that by clicking on one of the entries in an electronic back-of-the-book index, one is immediately transported to the indexed location (page number) in the body of the text.

Back plane: From the world of *DVE* (digital video effects), this term refers to the lower of two visual planes used in *two-plane effects* to create transitions from one screen to the next.

Bandwidth: This term is of such applicability to our emerging era of multimedia that it now rolls off the tongues of technological babes, "wannabe" business tycoons, and hardcore telecommunication wizards. In its widely used contemporary sense, bandwidth refers to the information-carrying capacity of a transmission link between any two devices. In its more traditional sense, it means the range of frequencies, usually measured in cycles per second, that a piece of audio or video equipment can encode and decode. Video uses higher frequencies than does audio, and so is said to possess a higher bandwidth. In the field of information processing, the stream of digitally encoded alphanumeric characters that dominated computer usage before the era of multimedia represents one of the smallest forms of bandwidth. Thus, from a technical standpoint, one of the great struggles of the era has to do with transforming the computer so that it can gracefully handle the higher bandwidth sources of information—namely, audio, image, and video.

Bandwidth reduction: In the television industry this term is commonly heard, especially among those who are wrestling with the transmission demands and constraints of *HDTV* (high definition television). It is roughly equivalent to the term *compression*, in that it refers to the host of techniques that can be employed to reduce the overall *bandwidth* requirements of a television broadcast. *RLE* (run length encoding), *DCT* (discrete cosine transform), and *motion compensation* are just some of the compression techniques enlisted in the overall effort to reduce bandwidth.

Banff Center for the Arts: This Canadian institution is considered by many to be the leading organization in the world for exploring how *virtual reality* can be used within the arts.

Bar sheet: Used extensively in animation productions, this diagrammatic form is used by the director to make a blueprint of the action, music, dialogue, and sound effects for the entire picture. It illustrates how all of these elements are to be timed, and unfold in parallel, as each scene progresses. Perhaps most importantly, though, the bar sheet deserves a bright historical footnote, as it has served as the basis for the *time-line metaphor* that has informed so many of today's multimedia presentation and *authoring systems*.

Batch processing: From the world of traditional mainframe data processing, this term refers to a form of information processing that is typically held in contrast to *real-time* processing. With a batch process, information is gathered and stored in advance of being processed, or analyzed. Thus, when a bank stores up all of its transactions for the day and then updates all of its customer records at night, this is said to be batch processing. The data is stored up into a "batch" before anything meaningful is done to it. In contrast, with real-time processing the data is analyzed or processed immediately upon receipt. In the era of multimedia, most applications demand real-time, as opposed to batch, processing, because when users are interacting with media—as when they are playing video games—they want their processed data now, not later.

Bed: This term emanates from the world of film and TV, where it is used to describe the instrumental portion of music which serves as an underscore to the visual proceedings.

Benchmark: This is a task used for measuring some aspect of a computer's performance.

Beta-Test: It has long been the practice of software developers to send pre-release versions of their programs to expert users who get some form of consideration (like discounts or free licenses) for testing out those products before they are released to the general public. Given the extremely complex nature of most software programs, it is to be expected that the developers will be unable to catch all of the bugs (technical flaws in the code). The process of beta-testing helps to clean up the code. As entertainment developers begin to produce interactive products—which, after all, possess a strong software component—they will need to avail themselves of the culturally acceptable habit of beta-testing.

Binaural fusion: From the world of perception, this is the process by which the brain compares information received from each ear and then translates the differences into a unified perception of a single sound issuing from a specific region of space. Any manufacturer of *3-D sound* equipment must take this phenomenon into account.

Bit: The smallest unit of data, a bit refers to the on-off signals stored in computer memory.

BITC: Stands for burned in time codes and is pronounced "bit-see." This term refers to a characteristic of video required in video editing and other *post-production* activities whereby the time codes for each video frame have been burned into a set location, or field, on the frame. Time codes are very important in editing, because they represent the logical equivalent of a memory address, enabling users to move quickly to the locations in the video stream they wish to be working with at a particular moment. In the analog world of videotape, these time codes are actually "burned" into the surface of the tape. In the digital world of *nonlinear video*, the time codes are also digital and are embedded in the video datastream. Though fundamentally different, the digital time codes appear to the end user much as their burned-in forebears of the *analog* era.

Bit map: This refers to a software object that represents visual data in a form where each *pixel* location corresponds to a unique memory location accessible by the computer *CPU*.

Bit-mapped displays: Are made up of tiny dots, called *pixels*, and stand in contrast to the older-generation character displays, which are only capable of representing information out of the *ASCII* character set. Bit-mapped displays are capable of much higher resolution than character displays and represent the primary instruments of graphical user interface (*GUI*) design. Bit-mapped displays have manipulation capabilities for both *vector* and *raster* graphics, which allow presentation of information appearing in the final paper form.

Bit resolution: With *digital* forms of media, bit resolution is a measure of the quality of the *digitized* audio, image, or video. Bit resolution represents the number of bits used to represent each sample taken in the *ADC* (analog-to-digital) process to form a data stream of digitized media. Thus, with reference to digital audio, the industry standards are 8-bit, 12-bit, and 16-bit audio, with the higher bit lengths representing a higher quality form of digitized media.

Blind: From the realm of digital video effects (*DVE*), this term refers to a *two-plane effect* in which the image on the *front plane* becomes like a Venetian blind that opens to reveal the image on the *back plane*.

BLOB: Stands for binary large object, a term that belongs to the language of relational databases and is often referred to as a *memo field*. The best way to understand what a BLOB is, is to compare it to standard relational database fields. The standard database fields, because they must fit into a tabular model, have a fixed length. Thus, a relational database always has some intrinsic limit on the amount of information that a single text item, or field, can store. In contrast, a memo field uses the fixed-length part of a table only as a pointer to a large body of information with a virtually unlimited size. Thus, a memo field can be used to store a paragraph, a page, a book, ad infinitum, all using, in the database proper, only the amount of space required to hold the *pointer* (memory address). This data structure is ideal for *hypermedia* forms where an orderly, navigable structure must be maintained (which corresponds to the database), but where numerous large information objects (*digitized* images, animations, film clips) of widely varying size must be made available.

Block: This is an amount of data moved or addressed as a single unit within the computer's memory.

BMP: Stands for bit-mapped file, and refers to the internal picture file format used by Microsoft *Windows*, versions 3.0 and higher. This *raster file* format is also supported by OS/2, the IBM operating system.

Board: This term is synonymous with "circuit board" or "card." The primary function of a computer board is to hold the chips and wiring that control either some essential function of the computer's *CPU* or a peripheral device such as a *CD-ROM* player. Throughout the volatile history of computing, boards have been used as a vehicle for scaling up the capabilities of computers, adding, for example, audio capabilities to a computer that was manufactured before such capabilities were a standard part of the computer's (built-in) motherboard. Thus, boards should be thought of as a major source of *scalability* and *extensibility* in the computer world.

Bookmark: Also referred to as an electronic bookmark, this graphical user interface (*GUI*) design/navigational feature is employed to facilitate multisession uses of electronic documents, interactive *multimedia applications* for training, and *hypermedia applications* for reference. Bookmarks simply record or save the point at which one decides to exit a program, making it possible to re-enter at that exact point when one starts the next session. As the size and use of electronic forms of publishing continue to grow, bookmarking is becoming a standard feature of most forms of electronic documents.

Boundary detection: This is considered one of the key problems associated with *virtual reality* environments, where a user's body may interact with, or actually pass through, a virtual object, such as a chair or wall. It presents a perceptual problem because these objects should have a solid consistency but, in the VR environment, may put up no resistance at all, thereby taking on a ghostly character. The emerging technologies associated with *tactile feedback* are considered to hold the ultimate solution to this problem, enabling the user to move around in a virtual environment and, when the system is appropriately cued by boundary detection logic (or devices), to feel the appropriate sensations when bumping into things. Virtual reality research is a long way off from perfecting such systems. In the meantime, designers are experimenting with a number of ersatz solutions, such as sound systems that correlate varying sound effects with the detection of different types of boundary collisions.

Boundary representation: From the realm of computer graphics, this term refers to one of the main methods of "solid modeling," in which the object is described by its geometry and topology.

BPS: This term stands for *bits* per second and is a standard measure of transmission speed or *transfer rate* in the computer world.

Branchpoint: The basis of machine intelligence relies on the computer's ability to change its preset sequence of instructions, a most common phenomenon in programming known as branching—the code branches from one location in the program to another. A branchpoint is, quite simply, a location within a program where a branch occurs. With regard to interactive forms of entertainment—video games, *edutainment* programs, and the like—most of the branchpoints are dedicated to giving the user (learner, gamer, etc.) some element of control over what happens next in the program.

Brightness: Along with hue and saturation, this is one of the three fundamental dimensions of color. Brightness refers to the differences in the intensity of light reflected from or transmitted through an image.

Broadband: This term is used frequently in communications to refer to *transmission media* and *channels* that possess relatively larger carrying capacities or *bandwidth*.

Browsing: In the current *hypertext* and *hypermedia* environment, this term describes the oft-practiced user behavior of meandering through the available electronic information, looking simply for interesting associations. The metaphor corresponds with paying a desultory visit to your favorite bookstore to peruse the stacks.

Browsing path: Based on the *browsing* behavior of users, this term refers to the specific sequence of *hyperlinks* that a particular user selects while moving through a large *hypertext* or *hypermedia application*. This information can be very useful, especially if the designer of the hypermedia application wants to establish usage patterns relative to the content and preference patterns relative to specific user profiles.

Brush: With reference to computer *paint systems*, a brush is a marker that draws a line or pattern on the display surface, thereby emulating the action of a real paintbrush.

Buffer: Is a small part of a computer's memory that temporarily stores data. Buffers can compensate for a difference in data flow rates when transmitting data between two devices or can hold data likely to be used in the near future.

BUFR: This term stands for binary universal form for representation, a standard *digital* imaging file format used by meteorologists to represent the visualizable aspects of weather data.

Burst: This term has become a popular one for describing flows of data, otherwise known as data transmission. It acknowledges the almost universal aspect of reality that phenomena are not evenly distributed in time, but rather tend to occur in bursts, separated by periods of relative quiet.

Bursty traffic: From the world of network management, this term refers to the types of data flow experienced with respect to traditional, alphanumeric (i.e., character) forms of data. On the traditional network, traffic is said to be bursty because, for the most part, the network is clear of traffic and so single data conversations are able to be quickly established and released without degrading the overall performance of the network. From time to time, though, the volume of requests for access to the network surges, which in turn leads to the need for invoking some sort of contention scheme to determine who has access, and in what order. Owing to this variable traffic pattern, the traditional PC network is said to experience bursty traffic.

Bus: This commonly used computer term refers to the circuit or pathway through which data is transmitted. It most often is used to refer to the **main** such pathway that serves to connect the major components of a computer system to the *CPU*.

Bus interface: From the realm of computer design, this term relates to the fact that everything in a computer is attached to the *CPU*—that is, every device that is a part of the computer must communicate with the CPU in some way. To do this, these devices (e.g., disk drives, monitors, printers, etc.) must be connected to the computer's *bus* so that they can exchange data. This point of connection is called the bus interface.

Button: An important term in graphical user interface (*GUI*) design, a button is a relatively small screen object, usually labeled with text or an *icon* or both, and typically used to initiate instantaneous actions, such as completing operations defined by a *dialog box* or acknowledging error messages. Buttons represent *hot spots* on the screen—by clicking or touching them, one initiates some computer-mediated action. In designing buttons, the traditional wisdom has it that the label of the button should describe the **result** of using (clicking, touching) the button, rather than some abstract term about the function that is being performed.

Byte: In the world of computers, the ubiquitous byte is a unit of measure of 8 binary digits (i.e., 8 *bits*) representing either two numbers or one character.

Bytes per second: Again, in the world of computers, this is a unit of measure for the speed of digital transmission of information.

The problem ... is that most of the people who have the trades of screenwriting, cinematography or whatever are utterly ill-equipped to build nonsequential, highly interactive programs.
—Nicholas Negroponte, Director, The Media Lab at MIT

Cable headend: This term belongs with the emerging language of the *information superhighway*, as it represents one of the key distribution nodes on the network. Within that segment of the highway dedicated to cable TV, the cable headend is the central point at which TV signals are downlinked from satellites and are modulated onto the cable by local stations. In other words, it is a key port of entry for the distribution of video content.

Cabling: Any discussion of the technical aspects of communications—*telephony*, data communications, *LAN,* and *WAN*—usually makes reference to one of its most fundamental features: the type of cabling, or *transmission media*, being used. There are three major forms of cabling in use today. In order of lesser-to-greater capacity, they are the following: **Twisted-pair:** the copper wire medium that connects the household telephone to the *Public Switched Telephone Network* (PSTN*)*. It is the oldest cabling technology and can be either shielded, or not. Reliance on this largely outdated medium is what is considered to be the largest disadvantage for the telephone companies in the heated competition to control *home interactive media.* **Coaxial cable:** long been used for cable television connections because of its ability to handle a relatively large number of signals or, in other words, different channels, simultaneously. "Coax," as aficionados like to call it, has four basic parts: a solid metal wire forms the core of the cable, surrounded by insulation; a tubular piece of metal screen surrounds the insulation, and an outer plastic coating completes the cable. Coax is capable of high *bandwidths* and is therefore a popular choice for LANs that must carry a large amount of network traffic. **Fiber optic cable:** considered the transmission medium of the future, fiber carries light pulses rather than electrical signals. There are several advantages to fiber: immunity from electromagnetic interference, enormous bandwidths, and the ability to carry signals for a very long distance. Fiber cable consists of a core fiber enclosed in glass cadding, with a protective outer coating that surrounds the cadding. *LEDs* (light-emitting diodes) are used to send the signal down the optical fiber. At the receiving end, a photodetector is used to receive the signals and convert them into a *digital* computer format. Owing to its very large bandwidths, fiber is the core transmission technology of the integrated services digital network *(ISDN)*, and is considered by many experts to be a necessary ingredient in the future extension of *multimedia applications*.

Cache: In its traditional usage, cache is a temporary storage area for data requiring very quick access. Most contemporary *CPUs* (e.g., Intel's 80486, Motorola's 68040) carry a specification for their cache size, which denotes the size of the memory held on the CPU itself. This CPU cache is the location where frequently accessed code and data from the current application are stored. But the CPU is not the only "place" in a computer system where the strategy of supplying a cache is commonly employed. As a process, caching is now a commonly employed strategy for building bridges between every form of memory and its next-slowest, but higher capacity companion. Thus, caching is done between optical and hard disk storage, between hard disk and *RAM*, and between CPU cache and RAM. In the coming era of multimedia, where extremely large amounts of *digital* data will need to be moved on a constant basis, the importance of using caches will grow dramatically. In this usage of the term, a cache is roughly synonymous with the term *"buffer,"* and caching is synonymous with "buffering."

CAD: Otherwise known as computer aided design, it is a widely used term most typically associated with engineering and architectural applications for computer graphics. With the advent of *virtual reality* systems, especially those that render visual scenes in *real time*, CAD is taking on a new role as an integral support component in these complex programs. In a very real sense, CAD is becoming an *enabling technology* for the *virtual reality* industry.

CAI: Stands for computer assisted instruction; along with *CBT* (computer based training), this is one of the early acronyms for describing programs that use the computer as an instructional tool, rather than as an automation machine. As the computer becomes the *teleputer*, historians may view CAI as a truly seminal use of the first generations of computing machines.

Camera field: In film and video, this is the area being photographed by the camera. The camera field constitutes what is visible to the audience at any given moment.

CATV: Stands for community-antenna-television, which is the separate transmission infrastructure that was created to meet the needs of the cable television industry. This infrastructure was needed to serve cable TV, because the copper wire transmission system that serves the ubiquitous residential and business needs of *telephony* is not capable of handling the *bandwidth* (carrying capacity) demands of television broadcasting. Thus, during the decade of the eighties, the cable industry was forced to create its own ubiquitous transmission infrastructure by laying the higher bandwidth coaxial cable into millions of homes and businesses around the country. This higher-capacity infrastructure now gives the cable operators a somewhat serendipitous advantage over the telephone companies with respect to offering interactive services, especially to the home market.

CAV: Stands for constant angular velocity, one of two distinct *videodisc* formats (*CLV* [constant linear velocity] being the other). With CAV, the frames are laid down in concentric circles. Each frame has its own 360-degree track on the videodisc, thereby making it possible for the laser reader to jump from one track to the next. This format is the strongest option for providing rapid random access to *frames* and is thus the preferred format for interactive videodisc applications.

CAVE: A *virtual reality* project under development at the *EVL* (Electronic Visualization Lab) in Chicago, the CAVE is a room in which a viewer stands and becomes totally immersed in a 3-D audiovisual experience. The visual components of the CAVE are produced by multiple projectors, with each projector being responsible for flooding one of the wall sides. The images are projected in an *interlaced* video fashion, and the viewer wears *stereoscopic glasses*. Fallout applications of the CAVE include biomedical imaging, architectural rendering, interior design, and mechanical design of heavy equipment.

CBR: Stands for content based retrieval and represents an emerging class of programs that seek to automate the process of searching large information bases. Operating on the grounds of user-defined content characteristics, these programs automatically perform search and retrieval functions against large information bases in an effort to unearth gems of information from the mountains of data. An example of a CBR program would be one that scans the massive flow of stock data that emanates from Wall Street each day and culls from that dataflow just the information that relates to the user's individual portfolio of stocks. Negroponte's concept of *personal television* may be implemented through what we are today calling CBR.

CBT: Stands for computer based training and represents one of the oldest acronyms in the interactive business. The term was dominant during the early PC era and was used to describe interactive training programs that—owing to the constrained presentational capabilities of early PCs—was limited primarily to text and *ASCII* graphics. By far, the most common application for CBT was the software *tutorial*, where the computer was used to teach end users how to use common computer software applications such as word processing, database, and spreadsheet. The term is still alive, and there are those advocates who are trying to migrate it to the more updated, multimedia-based forms of interactive training. For the most part, however, the term is now used to describe older generation interactive courseware.

CCD: Stands for charge coupled device and represents the dominant technology used in *scanners* and other devices for converting light to electronic impulses, the first step in *digitizing* lightsources of information. CCDs consist of a silicon semiconductor and a series of electrodes. When light passes into the silicon, that light frees electrons within the silicon atoms. The brighter the light at a given point on the image, the more electrons are freed.

CCITT: Stands for Consultative Committee on International Telephone and Telegraph, a telephone industry standards-making body.

CCITT H.261: Also known as *Px64*, this is the video *compression* standard for *video teleconferencing.*

CD-DA: Stands for *compact disc*-digital audio, and represents the earliest standard in the CD industry. Also referred to as the *Red Book* standard, CD-DA is an audio-only standard, specifying how audio CDs should be formatted.

CD-I: Stands for *compact disc*-interactive, a self-contained multimedia platform developed by Philips Corp. One of the early platforms for home multimedia, CD-I possesses its own proprietary operating system, known as CD-RTOS. As a standard for multimedia, CD-I is also known as the *Green Book* Standard. Currently, there are about 100,000 CD-I players in commercial use.

CDMA: Stands for code division multiple access, one of two emerging standards for *digital wireless* communications. CDMA works by splitting a single radio channel into a large number of voices, using a unique identifier code for each voice. The receiver uses a code book of sorts to detect and capture the desired signal from the substantial background *noise*. The accepted analogy for CDMA is that everyone in a room filled by many people can hear just the message intended for him or her because each person is concentrating on (is decoding) a single conversation. Along with its sister technology, *TDMA* (time division multiple access), this standard represents a new form of transmission capacity and is therefore being heralded as being able to address the emerging *bandwidth* crisis that threatens to thwart the vitality of *multimedia*. In a sense, because digital wireless does not use cabling, as do all other forms of data communications, CDMA and its near cousin TDMA represent "found" bandwidth in a contemporary world that is increasingly bandwidth-scarce.

CD-R: Stands for *compact disc*-recordable, which represents a recent family of CD players that make it possible for end users to record their own data, albeit only once. CD-R is part of the emerging *Orange Book* standard, which includes most of the CD technologies that enable end users to record, including the emergent magneto-optical technologies.

CD-ROM: Stands for *compact disc*-read only memory and refers to the dominant form of direct access, mass storage for the early years of multimedia technology. Refer to "compact disc" for a more complete discussion.

CD-ROM-XA: This is an extended architecture for *CD-ROM* that permits the *interleaving* of sound and data for purposes of synchronization when these two data types are merged in motion picture and animation segments.

CD-RTOS: Stands for *compact disc*-real time operating system, which is the proprietary operating system developed by Philips for its *CD-I* platform.

Cel: Short for celluloid, this term actually refers to the sheets of acetate laid down on top of one another to produce a single *frame*, or *exposure*, of an animated feature.

Cel Animation: Refers to a moving picture produced by displaying a series of complete screen images in rapid succession.

CELP: This acronym stands for code excited linear prediction, and it represents one of the more innovative forms of digital audio communication. As *MIDI* (musical instrument digital interface) works with respect to music, CELP works by transmitting an encoded representation of the voice, rather than a waveform signal of the voice itself. The technology is based upon a "codebook" that stores the basic sound elements of the human voice. The transmitting end of the communication decomposes the sounds of the "sending" human voice into their codebook values, and then transmits a set of pointers, plus any modifying parameters needed to capture the unique characteristics of the speaker, to the receiving station. In turn, the receiver uses the pointers to look up the codebook elements, which it then incorporates into a decoded version of the speaker's voice. The primary advantage of this technology—like its MIDI cousin—is that it greatly reduces the *bandwidth* needed to transmit the human voice. In a sense, it is a form of *compression*. Its primary disadvantage is that it is extremely *CPU-intensive*, and typically requires the use of a special purpose *DSP* (digital signal processor).

Center for Creative Imaging: Opened in May of 1991 by Eastman Kodak Company, this training center is designed to help videographers, photographers, and graphics artists make the transition to the new media artforms made possible by the many new and sophisticated electronic imaging products entering the market. Located in Camden, Maine, and founded by longtime Kodak executive Raymond DeMoulin, the Center provides hands-on experience with a broad range of *scanners*, cameras, printers, storage media, and software applications.

CGA: Stands for color graphics adapter, a vestigial remnant of the early days of *desktop* computing, a time when any form of graphics was considered a luxury. As some will recall, the original IBM PC came with a monochrome monitor that could display text only. As the forces that would ultimately lead to *multimedia* began to take shape, IBM responded with the first of its graphics adapters, namely CGA. Equipped with a color monitor and a CGA card, the user could display up to 16 colors in *RGB* format, with a *resolution* of 640 x 200 *pixels*. However, if you want to remember how bad a standard this was, recall that if you wanted to display graphics, you had to first go into a thing called "graphics mode." And, if you wanted to display text while in graphics mode, you had to switch out of 80-column and into 40-column mode. This technical compromise produced some of the least attractive type fonts in the history of communications. Early forms of *CBT* (computer based training) were particularly haunted by this standard, because if you wanted to incorporate graphics and text on the same screen—which is a pretty compelling combination when you're trying to teach something to somebody—you had to use the extremely blocky and *pixellated* type fonts of 40-column mode. In the lineage of PC graphics standards, CGA comes just after "MDA" (monochrome display adapter) and just before *EGA*, which then gave way to *VGA* and *SVGA*.

Channel: In the computer world, this term refers to a path or circuit along which information flows. Most channels are measured in terms of how much information they can carry, which is also referred to as their *bandwidth*.

Channel explosion: This term is now in popular use by observers of the rise of the home media market. It describes the rapid expansion in the number of TV channels that, in the first phase, was made possible by the creation of the *CATV* (cable TV) infrastructure. This first phase resulted in the laying of coaxial cable into cable-connected homes, which provided a form of transmission media that has much more effective *bandwidth* than the copper wire of *POTS* (plain old telephone service). With the application of *compression* technologies to the signals being transmitted over CATV, it is expected that home cable will soon offer upwards of 500 channels, making possible a whole new generation of home media services. In the near future, a second phase is expected to appear in which TV will move to an all-*digital* format and, more importantly, make use of *fiber optic*, rather than coaxial, cables. This move to a digital, fiber optic transmission infrastructure will cause yet another "explosion" in bandwidth, which, in turn, will likely serve to keep this term in vogue well into the next century.

Chapter-level entry points: In an effort to join the *Age of Interactivity*, many film producers are manufacturing interactive versions of their feature films. However, as the process is currently being managed, the interactivity is "put into" these movies as an afterthought—as a sort of high-tech adornment—rather than being designed into the artworks from the outset. In order to put the interactivity into these pictures without disrupting their narrative flow, many producers have found a safe bet is to create entry points at obvious locations, such as at *edit points* between scenes. Using the obvious analogy of text-based narratives, these entry points are often referred to as chapter-level entry points.

Character-based applications: This historical term is used to describe PC software applications before the current era of graphical user interfaces (*GUIs*). These applications were said to be "character-based" because they did not make use of *bit-mapped* graphics, the *desktop metaphor*, *mouse* input, or any of the GUI elements that are part of contemporary computing. Rather, they were constructed entirely out of *ASCII* characters. For example, many PC-users will remember the old, character-based version of Lotus 1-2-3, which was an industry standard for spreadsheets until the late eighties. Most applications have either migrated up to a GUI format or simply migrated into the blissful sunset of extinction.

Character generator: From the realm of traditional video post-production, this term refers to a device dedicated to creating and superimposing text on top of video. Hence, when a person's name appears below their talking head in a televised interview, you can be sure that you are witnessing the work of a character generator. In the coming age of *desktop video production*, the function of placing text over video will become almost trivial.

Check box: With graphical user interfaces (*GUIs*) that are based on the *desktop metaphor* (such as the Apple Macintosh interface or the Microsoft *Windows* interface), this is a standard *interface design* element. Used most commonly in *dialog boxes*, the check box is a square structure that operates like a toggle switch to turn particular functions on or off. To activate or de-activate a function, the user simply positions the cursor within the confines, or *hot spot*, of the corresponding check box, and then clicks the *mouse* button.

Check disc: Manufacturing a long run (large number) of any form of optical disc (e.g., *CD-ROM* or *laserdisc*) has traditionally been a relatively expensive and, because of their read-only nature, permanent venture. Because of this, it is customary to proceed with an abundance of caution by first printing one, or a few, test discs that can be thoroughly checked for accuracy before launching the full quantity run. These preliminary discs are usually referred to as "check discs."

Chroma keyer: A commonly used device in video production, a chroma keyer is used to process two video sources where one source— referred to as the "foreground"—is to be laid down on top of the other source, referred to as the "background." The device works by first specifying a particular color that plays the role of the "key." Once this key is specified—the most common key being blue—any object in the background that is the same color will drop out and let the background show through. Perhaps the most commonly known use of chroma keyers occurs where they are used to show TV meteorologists, apparently standing in front of a weather map, but in fact standing in front of a blue wall. (Is nothing sacred?)

Chrominance: This term refers to one-half of the information that typically goes into making a video signal. Chrominance is the color portion of the information contained in a full color electronic image. The other half is *luminance*, or light intensity, which an image requires to make it visible. Of the two, chrominance is the component with regard to which the human eye is less sensitive. For this reason, many of the *compression* techniques employed to handle the transmission of *digital* images do more to reduce the presence of chrominance information than they do to reduce the presence of luminance data.

Cinepak™: Considered one of the most popular motion video *codec* (*compression-decompression*) standards, Cinepak was developed by SuperMac. It is capable of playback at 320 x 240 *pixels*, the same resolution as the first generation of the *MPEG* (Motion Picture Experts Group) standard, but can only do so at 15 *fps* (frames per second). Also, Cinepak is a severely *asymmetrical codec*, with the compression process taking 300 times longer than decompression.

CIRC: This term stands for cross interleaved reed-solomon code, an error detection and correction method for audio CDs.

Circuit switching: A less flexible form of *data communications* than its leading rival, *packet switching*, this term refers to a method of handling data transmissions in which a circuit is established for the entire duration of a particular transmission, no matter how large the associated files or the amount of time required to complete the transmission. For long, data-intensive transmissions, this method is considered quite rigid because it makes no provision for re-routing the data flow even though the availability of bandwidth may shift around on the network during the time of the transmission. However, in the case of digital video, where it is critical that the flow of the *streaming data* not be interrupted in any way, the establishment of a circuit is almost mandatory.

Clipboard: This term refers to an *interface design* component that is used to supply temporary storage for elements that are being *cut and paste*d from one application or place in a document to another.

Clip consciousness: The growing awareness that original media content—image, audio, and especially video—is laced with value in the form of clipable pieces of image, audio, and video. For example, the well-known animation firm Hanna-Barbera has turned over some its best known sound effects to Microsoft for inclusion in digitized clip audio CDs.

Clip media: This is an overarching term used to describe the increasing propensity to cut, index, store, retrieve, and revise media elements, much as we have done with alphanumeric data during the early decades of the computer age. Common subtypes are clip art, for small pieces of artwork; clip audio, for small pieces of music and speech; and clip video, for small, categorizable segments of video. The move to clip media is one that possesses profound implications for society. The primary purpose of "clipping, indexing, and storing" these various media elements is so that they can be recombined with other elements for various commercial, artistic, or other purposes. It is just like the boilerplating behavior that occurs with respect to documents, especially with legal documents. One of the most profound consequences is that, as our *cut and paste* technologies gain sophistication—which they already have a good bit of—it will become virtually impossible to tell real from constructed media. Thus, audio recordings, printed images, and recorded video—all traditionally thought of as accurate and unimpeachable sources of information—will now become subject to all sorts of distortion and forgery. Also, legal issues will require resolution regarding re-usability with authorship, copyright, and licensing of clip media elements.

Clock: In computers, this is a device that marks the time and generates periodic signals that control the timing of all computer operations. One of the primary functional specifications for a computer is its clock speed, which is a measure of how fast its clock pulses and, therefore, is also a measure of how quickly it turns over its instructions and other processes.

Close-up: From the world of film and video, this term refers to a camera shot used to establish a desirable intimacy between the subject and the viewer. The close-in shot of the romantic interlude represents the exemplar of close-ups. This term is often held in contrast to the long shot, which is a camera *POV* (point-of-view) that is distant from its subject and is typically used to establish the general setting of a scene.

Closure: This term refers to a psychological habit of the human mind exploited by every manner of artist—but especially filmmakers—wherein a partial view of a subject is provided with the intent that the audience will use its imagination to construct individual versions of a completed subject. In film, for example, a close-up of a tapping foot is often used to signify impatience, instead of showing the entirety of the impatient subject. In the *Age of Interactivity*, *branchpoints* may be used as a way of getting audience members to externalize their sense of closure.

CLUT: This term stands for color lookup table, which is an image encoding method. Under this method, the numeric value of each *pixel* is used to look up an *RGB* (red, green, blue) value in a table of color registers. This reduces the amount of data required to store an image by limiting the number of colors available. CLUT is a method that is usually employed for "computer-style" or "cartoon-style" graphics and animation.

CLV: This term stands for constant linear velocity, one of two distinct formats for *videodisc* (the other being *CAV* [constant angular velocity]). With CLV, the information is laid down on the disk in one continuous spiral, as opposed to the separate, concentric tracks of CAV. For this reason, CLV is the preferred format for videodisc applications with long, continuous video plays, such as would be characteristic of a feature-length film.

Codec: A contraction for "compression-decompression," this term describes one of the key technologies of the information age. One of the first applications of codec technology was facsimile transmission, where it was realized early-on that the massive amounts of information generated by faxing documents all over the globe dictated a need to compress the documents for transmission and then decompress them back to their original form when they arrived at their destinations. Using this transmission strategy made it possible to increase the effective transmission *bandwidth* by a factor that was directly proportional to the amount of *compression* that could be achieved. For example, a 10:1 *compression ratio*—not at all uncommon—made it possible to increase the transmission carrying capacity of one's communication lines by 10 times without changing any aspect of the transmission medium. With the advent of *multimedia*, codec technology has become an even more important area of research and development, underscoring the need to facilitate the dramatically increased bandwidth required by digital forms of the various media—audio, image, and video. Reflecting the magnitude of this pursuit, there are now a large number of codec techniques (e.g., delta techniques), and an even larger number of commercial codecs (e.g., Apple's *QuickTime*, Intel's *DVI* [digital video interactive]) which are streaming into the market. Much of the debate over today's computer standards has to do with the search for an agreed-upon codec standard.

Codes of resemblance: This very useful term is one of many invented by the famous French film theorist Andre Bazin. Writing in the first half of the century, Bazin felt as though the primary secret to the power of film was its ability to encode reality in ways that resembled reality. Put in simple terms, film is successful because it represents the world in a very familiar form. As we enter an era of increasingly immersive media, i.e., an era dominated by the new forms of *virtual reality*, it would appear that Bazin's term should wear well with time. The new forms of *tactile feedback, motion platforms*, and the like are nothing if not new codes of resemblance.

Collaboration technology: This term seeks to embrace a group of technologies and behavioral science concepts and approaches that may be defined by their collective goal of facilitating and enhancing the daily work and interactions of people and machines bound together under the umbrella of a common goal, project, or job.

Color space: This term refers to all wavelengths in the electromagnetic spectrum that produce a visible color effect—that is, color perceptible to the human eye.

Combination view: From the realm of graphical user interface (*GUI*) design, this term refers to any screen in a windows-style interface that has two or more windows open at one time. The purpose of seeking such a view is that it permits comparative perspectives on, and/or interchanges of data and information between, the contents presented in the combination of views.

Combinatorial explosion: Perhaps the most troublesome aspect of our early days of *interactive fiction*, this term refers to the phenomenon that occurs when an author of interactive content permits each decision point in a *decision tree* to spawn several outcomes. When every decision point spawns several outcomes, and every one of those outcomes, in turn, leads to its own multi-outcome decision point, the tree-like structure of the program spins out of control, exploding into an insupportable number of branches, or combinations of outcomes. This problem was first encountered in the computer world by scientists who were attempting to build problem-solving programs that they thought would lead to *artificial intelligence*. As they attempted to define the ways in which even a simple problem might be solved, these early pioneers discovered that there might be literally trillions of ways in which the computer program could pursue the solution—many, of course, leading to incomplete solutions or down blind alleys. This intractable problem is now revisiting the industry by vexing the efforts of those who would attempt to build convincing interactive stories.

Command-line interface: This is a term used to describe an *interface design* that preceded the now popular graphical user interfaces (*GUI*s) like Microsoft's *Windows*. With the older interfaces, the user interacted with the computer's operating system by typing in commands on a rather spartan interface that featured only a drive designation followed by a colon. Often referred to as the "DOS-prompt," this approach to obtaining input from the user has been replaced, for the most part, by a *mouse*-driven world of *desktop metaphors* and the like. Still, there are a few propeller-heads left who prefer the command-line interface to the graphical user interface.

Compact disc: Is an injection-molded aluminum disc that stores high-density *digital* data in the form of microscopic *pits and lans* that a laser beam can read. Conceived by Philips and Sony, it was originally designed to store high-fidelity music, for which *CD-DA* is the standard now accepted worldwide. Because of its large capacity when compared against magnetic disks, the CD was seized upon by the computer industry when it became evident that computers were processing the higher *bandwidth* sources of information—audio, image, and video. Thus, *CD-ROM* (compact disc-read only memory) has become the first viable direct-access storage standard for the *MPC* (multimedia personal computer). However, its origin as primarily an audio storage device has created some early problems for multimedia computing, most of which have to do with the standard transfer rate of 150 Kbytes between the CD player and the computer. This transfer rate is ideally suited for audio, but does not completely serve the needs of high density graphics, digital images, or video. Consequently, while optical storage may be the storage medium of the near future for multimedia computing, it is likely that storage manufacturers will soon be called upon to make fundamental changes to the original compact disc technology so as to make much higher transfer rates possible.

Compiler: This is a computer program that converts the source code of a high level language program into the machine code of a computer for processing.

Component video: One of two major types of video, the component video stream is transmitted as separate *luminance* and *chrominance* signals to provide a higher quality image. Often compared against *composite video*, which combines all of the video elements into a single signal, component pays a price for its higher quality in that it requires more than one connector and takes up a greater amount of *bandwidth*.

Composite signal: Most signals received by the human sensory system are of a composite nature. Reflecting the multisource nature of sensory reality, composite signals consist of many separate components that propagate at different frequencies and amplitudes. A simple example of a composite signal is that generated by a pipe organ. Each note produces a single tone, but when several notes are combined—as they typically are when playing an organ—the several notes that emanate from the instrument merge to form a complex waveform, which is another way of describing a composite signal. In the era of modern media, the scientific analysis and understanding of composite signals has made it possible to electronically decompose and recompose those signals. In the coming era of digital media, this process will reach a new level of abstraction and flexibility through the exploding media manipulation capabilities made possible by *DSP* (digital signal processing) and other media-processing technologies.

Composite video: One of two major types of video, the composite video signal economizes on *bandwidth* and connectors by combining the *RGB* (red, green, blue) and synchronization signals into one. This is the type of video used by television and VCRs. It is often compared against component video, which transmits the video stream as separate *luminance* and *chrominance* signals to achieve a higher quality image, but at a higher cost.

Compositing: Typically thought of as a part of video *post-production*, this term more generally refers to the practice of layering one media image (sound or picture) on top of another. The practice of building a complex image with multiple layers usually proceeds in phases, with intermediate stages called "pre-composites" and the last stage, where the finishing element is laid down, called the "final composite." In the coming era of *desktop video production*, this practice will become fairly simple, and with the more sophisticated tools, raises the much feared specter of digital forgery, whereby a skilled user creates a fraudulent visual or audio recording that, for example, incriminates an innocent party by placing him or her at the scene of an illegal deed.

Compound document: This early term covers the business communications usage of multimedia and refers to electronic documents composed not only of text and graphics, but of audio and video segments as well. As an example, tomorrow's business letter as a compound document may contain a textual introduction, followed by video clips taken from a corporate *hypermedia* process knowledge database, accompanied by an executive's *voice annotations*.

Compound document architectures: An extension of the *tagging languages* that govern the structural characteristics of highly formatted (published) documents, these architectures seek ways to encode, and therefore make manipulable within the context of a single document, all of the *mixed media data types* that go into making up *compound documents*. A relatively recent phenomenon in the industry, the *ISO* Open Document Architecture (ODA) and DEC's CDA (Compound Document Architecture) are the two early leaders in the effort to create these standards.

Compression: Any effort to understand the technical problems of the emerging *multimedia* industry must start with a simple fact of life: computers were originally designed to handle alphanumeric forms of information, not high *bandwidth* forms such as audio, image, or video. That audio, image, and video should have enormous value added to them once they become *digitized*, and therefore be susceptible to the program control of the computers, is an absolute revelation, and one that is fairly governing the entire computer industry at present. But it has introduced one enormous problem. Consider this: one second of video digitized at a *resolution* (image quality) comparable to today's broadcast television takes up no less than 22 megabytes of storage. One second! That means that a feature length film of, say, two hours would take on the order of 158 *gigabytes* of storage. Hence, there is now a huge research and development effort around the world to find new and better ways to compress digital forms of image and video. The goal of these efforts is to achieve compression—that is, smaller file size—while only throwing away information that will not be visually significant. As an indicator of the magnitude of the effort to find new and innovative compression techniques, consider that a substantial portion of this glossary is given over to terms which name and describe the techniques thus far concocted by the industry (e.g., *JPEG, MPEG, QuickTime, DVI, Fractal Transform*).

Compression ratio: A term of great significance in the *multimedia* industry, compression ratio refers to how good a job a particular *compression* technique does at reducing the size of a file made up of some form of *digitized* media. At the low end, compression ratios for fax machines—which work with *bit-mapped* images of black-and-white documents—average in the range of 10:1. Thus, if an uncompressed bit map of a document takes 100 K of storage, its compressed counterpart at this ratio will take only 10 K. The current *JPEG* (Joint Photography Experts Group) standard for compressing color still images ranges up into the neighborhood of 40:1. *Fractal transform* techniques, the most ambitious compression technology to date, can range comfortably up into the 200:1 range.

Console cowboy: This term refers to *cyberpunks* who prove their valor by donning *virtual reality* headgear and performing heroic feats in the imaginary world of *cyberspace*. Not to be confused with real cowboys as depicted in John Wayne and Clint Eastwood movies, though many console cowboys must certainly view themselves as such. In both worlds, various mythic behaviors are embodied whose sources, among others, are Greek drama and mythic initiation rituals.

Construction visualizer: From the world of scientific visualization, this is an exemplar of the industry, a program that helps contractors plan site layouts by visualizing the movement of materials, machines, and trucks for real estate development projects.

Consumer software: This is the popular term used in the business media that includes *home interactive media* programs. Of the titles that today would fall squarely into the category of interactive multimedia technology, Broderbund's *Where in the World is Carmen Sandiego?* is commonly thought of as the first major success among consumer interactive software programs.

Contention protocols: From the world of computer networking, this term describes the dominant and traditional form of managing dataflow over networks. Under contention schemes, only one data conversation can have control of the network at any given time. However, because most traditional data files are based on alphanumeric (character-based) sources of data, and are therefore of relatively small size, most data conversations are of relatively short duration. Thus, the strategy of limiting flow on the network to one data conversation at a time is eminently tenable and only leads to degradation during atypical bursts of dataflow. This contention protocol, however, is not well suited to handling the high *bandwidth* sources of data that make up *mixed media data types*. With the audiovisual data types, networks must be able to handle large, continuously flowing, time-critical streams of data. Consequently, as we enter the era of multimedia, this network management protocol is likely to be on the decline.

Context-sensitive help: Considered one of the seminal ideas behind *performance support systems*, this term refers to an intelligent extension of the help screen whereby the help is specific to the situation that the users find themselves in at the moment they invoke the help function. It implies a help system that is intelligent enough to interpret what the user is trying to accomplish at any given moment and has given rise to such related concepts as *embedded training* and *job aids*.

Continuity: In the film and video industry, this term is used to refer to the importance of maintaining the logical order and consistency of what is seen on-screen. With the advent of *interactive cinema*, where the audience may travel a multitude of possible paths through the film experience, maintaining continuity—what Aristotle called "unity"—will be among the most difficult challenges of the enterprise.

Contrast ratio: A measure of image quality in video playback equipment (e.g., *CRTs* and *LCDs*), this ratio describes the ability of a device to capture the differences between bright and dark areas. Generally, CRTs have a much better contrast ratio than LCD screens, meaning, for example, that they have better shading and smoother lines. This concept is somewhat analogous to the audio notion of *dynamic range*, which measures the ability of an audio playback device to capture the differences between loud and soft tones.

Convolvotron: Based on technology developed at the NASA *Ames Research Center* in collaboration with Crystal River Engineering of Groveland, California, this is an extremely powerful audio *DSP* (digital signal processor) that changes, or convolves, an *analog* sound source using *HRTF* (head related transfer functions) to create a 3-D digital sound effect. Sound that is computer-synthesized, or that is drawn from an external source like a *compact disc,* can be filtered through the Convolvotron and placed in a space around the listener. The sound-space *resolution* of the Convolvotron is virtually infinite, meaning that it can take analog sounds and distribute them to as many sound source positions within the 3-D sound space as is desired.

Couch commando: This is a term held in contrast to the "couch potato," signifying an individual in the next generation of the viewing audience, who will interact with, and participate in, the content.

Courseware: This is a general term used to describe programs that embody the convergence of software and instruction. The term *educational software* is a near-synonym, though many purists in the field of instructional technology would insist that the term "courseware" applies to any form of instructional media, including paper-based products, instructional videos, etc. However, in general, courseware has become synonymous with educational software.

CPU: One of the most common terms in the computer industry, this acronym refers to the central processing unit. Also referred to as just the processor, the CPU is the brains of the computer, the engine that drives all other aspects of the system that is a computer. The entire personal computer industry is subdivided on the basis of which CPUs are employed by the manufacturers. The DOS/Windows portion of the industry is based on processors manufactured by Intel Corporation (the popular 80x86 family), while Commodore's Amiga and Apple's Macintosh systems are based on processors manufactured by Motorola (the famous 680x0 family).

CPU-intensive: As we enter the age of multimedia, this term is becoming a veritable catch phrase because so many applications—from *3-D animation* to *compression-decompression*—are pushing the limits of the current families of processor technology. An application is said to be "CPU-intensive" when it demands a large number of CPU cycles in order to be performed. The *rendering* of a 3-D animation is a good example of a CPU-intensive application. The terms "compute-intensive" and "processor-intensive" are widely used synonyms.

CRT: This term stands for cathode ray tube and refers to the most common type of video display technology, both with regard to computing and television. With this technology, a vacuum tube with an electron gun at one end and a *phosphor*-coated screen at the other is used to convert voltages into patterns of images on the screen for viewing.

Cropping: A process common to the manipulation of *digital* images, this term refers specifically to the discarding of unwanted portions of an image. Cropping is most commonly done with freshly scanned images where the *scanner* has picked up unintentional debris around the edges of the target image.

Cross fader: From the realm of audio engineering, this term refers to a knob or slider that enables the engineer to balance the level of two audio inputs, performing a smooth transition between the two. At one end of the continuum, it passes only one source, and at the opposite end, it passes only the other. In between, it blends the two sources proportionately.

Cue sheet: From the world of video production, this is a form that shows the mixer where various sounds on a track stop and start. It is used during post-production when combining the tracks (components) of a picture onto one master track. Much of the production "logic" communicated by cue sheets is now embodied in the timeline interfaces used by several popular authoring systems.

CUI: This term stands for character user interface, and it refers to the computer precursor to the graphical user interface (*GUI*), in which the entire interface was constructed from alphanumeric characters. Users of earlier generations of personal computers will recall that the CUI phase in the history of desktop computing was characterized by the DOS-prompt, a total reliance on the *ASCII* character set, and the need to use typed commands in order to get anything done on the computer.

Curator file: This term refers to a use of *hypermedia applications* that is becoming increasingly common. A curator file is an encyclopedic, hypermedia collection of items that represent a museum's stock of artifacts. Typically, these hypermedia programs will include *digitized* images of the artifacts, text, and audio overlays that explain their origins, meaning, and/or significance. Many producers of these programs are now adding video sequences that add depth to the meaning of selected artifacts. More and more, museums are building such hypermedia creations as a way of capitalizing on their unique *media assets*. In so doing, they are also—perhaps unwittingly—adding to the growing canon of *surrogate travel* products, which, of course, are designed to eliminate the need to travel to the places where the artifacts originated.

Cursor: This refers to a position indicator that can be a symbol on the screen (a screen cursor) or a handheld device for entering coordinate points (a hand cursor).

Cursor plane: In the world of digital video, this plane is the uppermost *picture plane* used to render the computer screen. It is a small area, typically no larger than 16 x 16 *pixels*, and is used to display the current position of the *cursor*.

Curtain: From the realm of *DVE* (digital video effects), this is a *two-plane effect* in which the image on the *front plane* parts or closes like a pair of curtains to reveal the image on the *back plane*.

Cut: From the world of filmmaking, this term refers to the end of one scene, to be followed by the beginning of the next scene.

Cut and paste: This is an interactive technique for moving items from one location to another within an electronic document. Originally, this term referred exclusively to the movement—the cutting and pasting—of text segments within word processors. However, as *mixed media data types* have found their way into the computing environment, this term has gained much wider application, and it can just as easily refer to moving audio, image, graphic, or video segments from one place in a *compound document* to another.

Cuts-only editing software: Among the slew of new video post-production software tools, this is one of the simplest, specializing in the automation of some of the tedious tasks associated with *A/B roll editing*. Basically, these products offer many of the same controls found on *analog* editing decks, such as enabling the video editor to view, catalog, and tag video segments, as well as create *EDLs* (edit decision lists).

Cutting room: This is the editor's work area, and in traditional filmmaking, the central place of post-production activity.

Cyberarts: This is a general term for describing the various emergent forms of interactive entertainment and art. Included in these forms would be *interactive cinema* and *interactive fiction*, the various immersive gaming devices associated with *virtual reality*, and a number of entertainment genres that rely on high *bandwidth* communications to bring geographically dispersed parties together in order to benefit from some type of shared experience (a.k.a. *cyberspace*).

Cybernetics: This term, which now stands for an entire discipline, was coined by Norbert Weiner of MIT during World War II. At the time, Weiner was designing a system for anti-aircraft guns. During this project, he realized that the key element in a control system of any making—natural or artificial—is a feedback loop that gives a controller information on the results of its actions. He called such systemic considerations *cybernetics*, a term that has been expanded to refer to the science of communication and control theory. Obviously, with the prospects of such technologies as voice and optical recognition in the offing, the future of this discipline is very bright.

Cyberpunk: A term originally used to describe a specific type of individual—a modern-day beatnik of sorts—it has recently expanded to refer to an entire subculture. It is a subculture that combines an infatuation with high-tech tools and a disdain for conventional ways of using them—a sort of counterculture taken with such postmodern phenomena as psychedelics, smart drugs, and cutting edge technology (especially *virtual reality*). Cyberpunk seems to be part-in-parcel of the shift from a reverence for the wisdom of the past to the veneration of a technology-driven future.

Cyberspace: This now-famous term originated in the cult classic *The Neuromancer*, written by William Gibson in 1984. A basic definition of cyberspace is a 3-D domain in which *cybernetic* feedback and control occur. As currently defined, a cyberspace system is one that provides users with a 3-D, interactive experience that includes the illusion they are inside a world rather than observing an image. It will seem obvious that one of the reasons why this term has gathered so much popularity is that in its multiple meanings, it tracks very closely with the concept of *virtual reality*.

Digital technology challenges the traditional relationship between the artist and the viewer/ listener. The director will have to give up some of his autonomy . . .

—Paul Schrader, Film Director

DAC: Stands for digital-to-analog conversion. It is the reverse process of *ADC* (analog-to-digital conversion) that occurs on the playback side of the digital equation for producing computer-mediated media. For example, with digital audio, the ADC converts analog, or waveform, audio into a digital stream of data, and the DAC converts it back to an analog form that drives loudspeakers or headphones.

DAG™: Stands for Data Acquisition Glove, a device developed at the National Advanced Robotics Research Center in the United Kingdom in conjunction with Airmuscle, Ltd. This device is used in tandem with the *TeleTact Glove*, developed by the same principals. The DAG, as the name implies, is a glove used to capture the *force pattern* data associated with grasping various real world objects (e.g., the gearshift of a racecar). When you put this glove on and grasp a real object, the force-sensitive resistors register distinct force patterns. These patterns are in turn converted to proportional electrical values (i.e., they are *digitized*) and are stored in computer memory. Engineers then use this data to create templates of how various objects feel, and, over time, build up a library of force pattern templates in much the same fashion that makers of *MIDI* (musical instrument digital interface) *wave tables* build up *patch* sets of musical instrument sounds. These digitized force feedback patterns are then used with the TeleTact Glove, which is the output device used to recreate the tactile sensations associated with a particular *virtual reality* application.

DARPA: Stands for Defense Advanced Research Projects Agency, a military organization that has been responsible for funding innumerable research and development projects that have led to new media prototypes. A recent example is *SIMNET* (simulated network).

Data capture: This commonly used term in the computer industry is nearly synonymous with the term "digitizing." It refers to the point in the information processing sequence where noncomputer sources of information (like pictures of the real world, and the real world itself) become digitally encoded so that they may be subsequently submitted to some form of manipulation by the computer.

Data communications: This is the general term used to describe the very general phenomenon of exchanging digital forms of information between two or more locations.

Data conferencing: An enhanced derivative of *document conferencing*, this term refers to a form of all-digital communications in which there is simultaneous voice and data transmission on the same communications line. With data conferencing, the voice is digitized and treated—in *multimedia* fashion—as just one more element in the data stream.

DataGlove™: A prototypical *virtual reality* (VR) product from VPL Research, this "input" device permits users to reach into the 3-D environment of a virtual world and, while viewing a virtual hand corresponding to their own real one, grasp and move virtual objects, as well as perform various gestural commands. It works through the performance of *fiber-optic* bundles located along the glove's finger, thumb, and palm surfaces. These bundles work by responding to degrees of flexibility and positioning of the various hand feature, and then by sending encoded signal pulses to the processor. In just the short time in which this product has been on the market, it has taken on generic status, such that VR aficionados now refer to data gloves as a type of virtual reality device, much as the general public uses a term like Kleenex in lieu of "facial tissues."

Data rate: This term refers to the maximum sustainable throughput for an input/output device. In the era of multimedia, this rate often determines the fitness-for-duty of a given peripheral device.

DataSuit™: Produced by VPL Research, this *VR* concoction makes total immersion possible through the electronic performance of inertial and positioning sensors. The wearer of this suit can move (either freely around a room or on a treadmill) and interact through the full range of the body's movements.

Data tablet: Also referred to as a "digitizing tablet," this term describes a flat working surface drawn upon by a stylus or hand *cursor* to produce an input stream of coordinate data.

DATV: Stands for digital advanced television, which is a term recently invented by FCC-sponsored efforts to establish a set of transmission standards for the soon-to-emerge all-digital television. This standard may eventually replace *NTSC* (National Television Standards Committee), which has reigned as the standard for television in the United States for several decades.

DCT: Stands for discrete cosine transform, an increasingly common *compression* technique used, for example, with the *JPEG* (Joint Photography Experts Group) standard. Essentially, DCT algorithms throw out redundant *pixel* data and analyze the frequency of the color data, *chrominance*, contained in a video *frame* so as to discard the least important visual data.

Decision-based scripting: This is another term for interactive scriptwriting, or the writing of scripts for interactive programs. It reflects the fact that scriptwriting in the interactive domain must take account of the user's ability and desire to participate in the decision-making process. In this regard, scriptwriters must think in terms of decision trees, alternate scenarios, multiple outcomes, and the like.

Decision tree: For those who would attempt to build *interactive fiction*, or any form of *multimedia* like it, the decision tree is a key concept. Drafted into the world of multimedia development from such business and scientific disciplines as management science and *artificial intelligence,* this term captures the notion that a single decision point will have multiple outcomes, each of which will spawn additional decision points, each of which will, in turn, spawn several more outcomes, ad infinitum, leading to a program that bears a logical, flowchart-like structure that imitates the visual form of a tree—especially a Christmas tree—that has been turned on its side. Thus, without any type of reconvergent or other constraining strategy, the natural progression of an interactive fiction or business case study will likely lead to a *combinatorial explosion* of decision points and outcomes—one of the early, crucial development problems faced by authors of interactive multimedia.

Declustering: Another term for *file striping,* declustering is a high performance strategy allowing for distribution of a single file over several storage devices. This strategy is important in the age of multimedia technology because it permits rapid movement of the enormous amount of files associated with *mixed media data types*.

Decompression: The flip side of *compression*, this term refers to the process by which compressed forms of *digitized* media are reconstructed for presentation or further processing. With many of the simpler *codec* (*compression-decompression*) technologies, the decompression process is roughly comparable in effort to its compression counterpart. However, for the more sophisticated techniques that achieve higher *compression ratios*, the decompression process takes much less effort. For this reason, these more sophisticated techniques are called *asymmetrical codecs*—that is, they take more time and computing resources to compress the media than they do to decompress it. Whatever the codec, however, because decompression typically occurs in *real time*, just before the media is presented to the end user, it is the extremely time-sensitive half of the codec process.

De facto standard: This refers to any standard that arises outside of the formal, standard-setting activities of industry-sanctioned committees. Most commonly, de facto standards come into being because an innovative, often entrepreneurial solution appears in the marketplace. Because this previously unheard of solution is so far superior to the current standard being offered up by the industry majors, the invisible hand of consumer selection chooses it to be the standard for its particular industry niche. It is the result of capitalism, and it occurs with almost maddening frequency in the fast world of computer technology and the ultra-fast world of multimedia technology. It leads to that most wonderful, yet dreaded, economic phenomenon known as functional obsolescence.

Degrees of freedom: This term is commonly used as a gauge of sophistication with regard to the forms of *virtual reality* (*VR*) that seek to immerse the user in a virtual world. The most sophisticated VR systems accommodate up to six degrees of freedom: three in the Cartesian coordinate space of left/right (x), up/down (y), and forward/backward (z); and, three having to do with the changes in orientation known as pitch (motion around the x-axis), roll (motion around the z-axis), and yaw (motion around the y-axis).

Delivery system: This general term refers to the combination of hardware and software components needed to deliver a particular *multimedia* or *courseware* program. For most of the industry's history, multimedia solutions have been brought to their audiences via *stand-alone systems*, i.e., delivery systems not connected to any network. Typical of these traditional standalone systems is the interactive video workstation, which usually includes a *laserdisc*, a personal computer, and a television, all interconnected and controlled by a program developed using an *authoring system*. Rarely have these workstations ever been connected with one another over a network. However, as we sail into a future occupied by such technologies as *interactive television* and the *information superhighway*, multimedia delivery systems will increasingly involve the same sorts of networking features that now characterize advanced data processing systems in the corporate world.

Delta encoding: This term refers to one of the more common strategies for *compression* of image data. With this technique, the actual value of each *pixel* is **not** what gets stored and/or transmitted. Instead, what gets stored is the amount that must be added to the current pixel value to produce the value of the next pixel in a *scan line*. For each scan line, the true value of the first (leftmost) pixel is stored, but thereafter a series of differences, or deltas, is stored for each subsequent pixel. The assumption underlying this technique for compression of visual data is that the range of deltas will be small relative to the range of the true pixel values.

Desktop: As with the use of the term "environment" in public discourse, the use of the term "desktop" in the computer industry is gathering so many references that it runs the risk of losing any of the semantic specificity required of useful terms. However, there are two major areas of meaning to which this term may be confined in its contemporary usage: 1) as the central metaphor of the Apple Macintosh and Microsoft *Windows* graphical user interfaces (*GUIs*), and 2) as an adjective for describing various computing devices and functions that have been so thoroughly down-scaled in size and price that they are capable of being employed on the individual desktop, as in *video* production.

Desktop accessories: With regard to the Apple Macintosh *desktop* graphical user interface (*GUI*) and the Microsoft *Windows* GUI, these are programs of relatively limited scope that can be opened while other applications are running. Examples are the Note Pad, Alarm Clock, and Calculator.

Desktop entertainment systems: This term relates to the emerging assembly of media production features that enable personal computers to 1) interface with the various audio and video instruments normally associated with traditional media production, and 2) offer software-driven post-production capabilities covering most of the *mixing*, editing, and refining functions traditionally associated with the large post houses. Taken together, these board and software combinations now make it more affordable and possible for individuals to create their own film productions without incurring the great expenses typically associated with such undertakings. It is projected that these emerging capabilities will become standard components in the *MPC* (multimedia personal computer), and will give rise to whole new class of amateur film authors.

Desktop metaphor: One of the early centralizing concepts of graphical user interface (*GUI*) design, the desktop metaphor was first utilized in the marketplace by Apple Computer to serve as the key organizing principle of its Macintosh GUI, and was taken up later by Microsoft *Windows*. This *interface design* has become ubiquitous and has virtually replaced and outdated the *character-based application* interfaces of DOS and the older mainframe, text-heavy, graphically sparse environments predominant in the '70s and part of the '80s. Some of the standard components of the GUI desktop interface include the use of *windows* as a visual model for accessing and viewing documents, the use of the click-and-drag method for moving objects about on the desktop, and the use of the trash can as a receptacle for files that the user wishes to delete. As an *interface paradigm*, the desktop metaphor may be falling out of favor, as many feel that a more robust user interface is required to handle the rich data types of multimedia.

Desktop video production: This term arises out of the fact that at some point in the near future desktop computers will be equipped with all of the electronic tools necessary to perform the essential functions of today's video production studio. In other words, the everyday user will be able to do all of the editing, *mixing, titling,* and special effects needed to produce a professional video. This mix of tools will help launch the age of the *compound document,* where professionals communicate with one another by composing documents that have image, audio, and video components.

Desktop virtual reality: The low end of *virtual reality (VR)*, it is also commonly referred to as "Window VR." Using the broadest definition, it includes early products like Microsoft's "Flight Simulator" but typically refers to programs that enable one to navigate through 3-D rendered worlds. *Architectural walkthroughs* and other *surrogate travel* programs represent common, early examples of this form of VR.

Device driver: Refers to the systems-level code, usually written in assembly language or C, responsible for translating high-level instructions from the computer into codes that a particular hardware device can understand. Thus, we often speak of a display driver or a printer driver, these being the codes that make it possible for the computer to work in harmony with specific models of display and printer, respectively.

D1 digital video: This high-end form of *component video* has become a popular input source among the service bureaus that perform *MPEG* (Motion Picture Experts Group) *compression*. Owing to its digital format, D1 can be copied any number of times without suffering *generation loss*.

Dialog box: From graphical user interface (*GUI*) design, this is an interface element where a windowed portion of the screen is set up to enable the user to more completely specify the details of a particular function before launching it. Selecting the number of copies that one wants before launching a print process provides a good example of how a dialog box might be used.

DIB: Stands for Device Independent Bitmap, an *interoperability* strategy for interactive video. In a market that is constantly introducing new multimedia devices and platforms, a DIB enables the developer to move programs from one platform or device to another without having to re-digitize or reformat the images.

DICOM: Stands for Digital Imaging and Communications in Medicine, a standard file format used by the medical industry to represent digital images and other forms of medical information.

DigiCipher II™: This is a *codec* that intends to compete with *MPEG* (Motion Picture Experts Group) *2* for the right to become the standard among cable operators for all-digital TV transmission. DigiCipher II has a *compression* quality that is on par with that of MPEG 2, plus it has the additional ability to scramble, or encrypt signals to prevent piracy. This codec is a product of Chicago-based General Instrument Corp., a leading supplier of cable TV decoder boxes.

Digital: This is a term of such wide applicability and appeal that one suspects it gets involved in the naming of things that aren't even digital. To be digital, something must be encoded in binary format, where all information is ultimately stored in the on-off signals that computers can process.

Digital audio production systems: The aural counterpart to *desktop digital video* systems, these hardware-software creations are now rivaling their analog, tape-oriented, studio forebears in terms of being able to produce sophisticated, broadcast-quality sound tracks.

Digital audio special effects: Like their video (*DVE*) counterparts, these *digital* tools now make it possible for audio editors to produce entirely synthesized forms of audio special effects, such as reverb, flanging, and chorusing.

Digital imaging: Is an emerging, technology-based artform made possible by the digitization of visual elements, especially the photographically captured image. Perhaps the most powerful form of artistic manipulation made possible by this technology is that of electronic compositing, which enables the artist to integrate disparate visual elements into a single imagistic metaphor. Thus, for example, an artist can create a sense of irony by placing a device like a traffic light in the middle of an otherwise all-natural scene like a meadow.

Digital puppetry: This is a new form of puppetry in which the movements of on-screen animated actors are controlled by real-life humans wearing tracking booms and special facial sensors. The most well-known digital puppet to date is the commercially available *PAS* (Performance Animation System) by SimGraphics, which allows actors to control the movements of computer generated 3-D characters in *real time*.

Digital thermometer: An example of an A/D converter, which is a probe or sensor that performs *sampling* of temperature data to convert it from *analog* to *digital* form.

Digitize: This widely used term refers to the process by which some form of analog media source (picture, slide, audiotape, etc.) is input to computer by converting it into encoded signals that can be stored digitally and processed electronically.

Dimmed: In the world of pull-down menus and *interface design*, this term refers to the gray tone applied to menu items that, for whatever reason, are not available to the user for selection at a given moment. As we move into the era of *interactive cinema*, it is easy to imagine an analogous artistic instrument whereby certain on-screen objects possess dull tones when they cannot be interacted upon by the user (participant).

Direct manipulation: A graphical user interface (*GUI*) design term, direct manipulation refers to the simplification of the interface that occurs when the user can manipulate objects directly without having to memorize and use abstract commands. The classic example occurs in the Apple Macintosh or Microsoft *Windows* GUI, where one *drags icons* of files from one place to another to execute the same copy function that, in the old *command-line interface* of the DOS world, required the strict syntactical construction of a "copy" command.

Direct neural input: This is one of the most feared and even hated visions being contemplated today for new media. The idea is obvious: bypass the body's sense organs and send information directly to appropriate areas of the brain.

Discovery learning: A term made popular in the educational world by Jerome Bruner, it refers to an approach to learning that emphasizes the intrinsic motivation and self-sponsored curiosity of the learner. This term has now become popular among *instructional designers* because it matches well with the inherent design characteristics of *hypertext* and *hypermedia* in that both rely upon the associative thinking patterns of a naturally curious learner.

Disk, Disc: These two terms are often used interchangeably, though the tendency now is to use disk, spelled with a "k," to refer to magnetic storage media, and disc, spelled with a "c," to refer to optical storage media. In either case, the term refers to a circular platter used to store *digital* information in a format that makes that information randomly accessible, rather than sequentially accessible (as is the case with sequential media like magnetic tape).

Display list: With reference to computer graphics, this term describes a list of display instructions for specifying how an object is to be drawn on the display surface. *Vector* graphics, for example, make use of display lists.

Display mismatch: One of the principal types of bug found in *virtual reality* systems, it occurs when the visual, auditory, or tactile systems get completely out of sync or are otherwise mismatched. For example, if you stepped on a virtual gas pedal and got the toot of a car horn as a response, you would be safe in saying that your virtual car had a display mismatch.

Display surface: That part of a computer graphics display device (such as a *CRT* or *pen plotter*) that actually displays the graphical data, i.e., the screen itself or the plotting surface.

Dissolve: This term refers to a transitional effect between scenes that makes it seem as though one scene has dissolved into the next. With the explosion of PC *paint systems*, there are now virtually hundreds of dissolve routines available for *desktop video production*.

Distance learning: A popular term in educational circles, distance learning simply refers to the use of broadcast media to extend the geographic span of (presumably) high-quality teaching. The most commonly cited application of distance learning has to do with transmitting instruction into rural and otherwise remote geographic areas.

Distractor: This term comes from the world of education, where it is used to name an option in a multiple-choice question that is incorrect, i.e., that is put in place to distract the learner. With all forms of computer based learning, the distractor has become a potentially powerful design tool, often put in place to induce learners to exhibit that most dreaded of learning blocks, the intuitively appealing misassumption. Good *instructional designers* will use distractors to lead learners into alternative pathways that *remediate* these common misassumptions, thereby accelerating the path to enhanced learning. This term even has utility in the field of video game design, where it can be used to describe lures placed in the game to challenge the player's ability to exercise sound judgment.

Dithering: An *anti-aliasing* effect common to most graphics packages, dithering is used to give objects the appearance of higher *resolution* by blending their edges (boundaries) into the background so as to help remove the unappealing affect also known as the *jaggies*.

DLL: Stands for dynamic link library and represents one of the more prominent elements in software design today. With so many aspects of our lives being automated, and therefore encoded in software routines, there is an increasing concern about duplication of effort and the needless decrease in productivity it causes for all of us. The dynamic link library is a generic software design concept intended to combat duplication of coding effort, and therefore, to make a significant contribution to productivity in the software industry. More specifically, the DLL concept is based on the notion that most applications call on a standard set of routines which are so commonly used that they need to be duplicated in nearly every application. To avoid this duplication, DLLs are created as a way of sharing these routines among their constituent applications. The routines are stored on disk in only one place—the dynamic link library—thereby saving space on a computer's hard disk and the effort involved to incorporate them into the compiled versions of the various applications that need to use them. This idea of making a public resource out of widely used elements is as old as the ages, but in computing, and especially in software engineering—where localized sources of complexity and uniqueness seem always to foil the best-laid intentions—the concept of the DLL is welcome.

DMA: Stands for direct memory access, which is a technique used to transfer large amounts of data into or out of computer RAM off of or onto peripheral storage devices without involving the *CPU* to carry out the operation. This frees the CPU to take on other tasks. In the age of multimedia, where vast amounts of *digital* data for representing the various forms of media will be involved, the use of DMA as an architectural strategy will grow increasingly important.

Docugraphic system: Is a network that contains and links scanners and printers.

Document conferencing: A hybrid form of *interactivity*, this term refers to a type of activity that combines the benefits and features of *videoconferencing* and *groupware*. As two or more geographically separated parties work on a shared document, a *window* embedded in the document is supplied that enables the current speaker to be viewed by others on the team while—one assumes—the communication is directed toward some aspect of the document-as-shared-work product.

Document exchange format: This term refers to text formatting and styling standards intended to support cross-platform *portability* of highly formatted documents. *SGML* (standard generalized markup language) is perhaps the best known example. The present challenge is to create such formats for files that contain audio, graphics, and full motion video, the *mixed media data types*.

Document mapping: This term refers to a process by which the contents of a traditional text document are made more accessible, i.e., where those contents are more readily matched to specific user interests and needs. There are now special purpose *authoring systems* that help automate the process of document mapping. These tools help create, among other things, tables of contents with live links to the content sections named in the table, *back-of-the-book indexes*, chapter outlines, and maps of *hypertext* links (*hyperlinks*).

Dolly: From the world of film production, this term refers to a tracking structure that allows a scene to be shot by a moving camera. Thus, this cinematographic device is used to create a moving *POV* (point-of-view). Increasingly, *digital* video software, especially those programs associated with *virtual reality*, are able to create this effect entirely within the software, where it is referred to as *flying* (i.e., the user, in essence, takes control of the POV and flies through the computerized setting).

Download: In the most general sense, the copying of information from one computer to another. Traditionally, this term has been viewed as the transfer of documents, database files, or other text-oriented data from a larger system to a smaller one. For example, a user would download a desired news item from one of the online information services. Increasingly, though, the process of downloading will involve *mixed media data types*, and, in the near future, it may become common parlance to say that one wants to download a movie, for instance.

DPI: Stands for dots per inch, a common measure of *resolution* for devices, such as *scanners*, associated with image processing. It represents, for example, the number of *pixels* that a scanner can physically distinguish in each vertical and horizontal inch of an original image.

Dragging: This interactive technique, made very common through its use in the *desktop metaphor*, is used to reposition an object on the screen. The most common form of dragging is effected by positioning the *cursor* over the target object, holding down the *mouse* button, and then dragging the object through the movement of the mouse until one has moved the object to its destination, at which point the mouse button is released.

Draw systems: Used as a term that contrasts with *paint systems*, draw systems are programs that create *structured* or *vectorized* graphics images. Paint systems are programs that create *bit-mapped* graphics images. Draw systems can be simple or very complex: they can range from tools for creating simple two-dimensional images, all the way up to *CAD* (computer aided design) programs that support 3-D modeling of solid objects with surface shading. With these systems, the artist manipulates objects rather than *pixels*. Most programs include, at a minimum, commands for creating various geometric objects (such as circles, rectangles, or boxes), assigning them attributes (such as color), and manipulating their spatial properties (such as location on the screen).

Drill and practice: From the world of *instructional design*, this term refers to a commonly used design strategy for programming *CBT* (computer based instruction). Drill and practice programs, as their name implies, are typified by long strings of multiple-choice, fill-in-the-blank-type questions that strive to sharpen the learner's skills with respect to a fairly narrow range of academic concerns. Math programs, in particular, have exploited the drill and practice paradigm. For example, a student might be asked to answer a series of short answer questions regarding the addition of two two-digit numbers. Easy to program, but facetiously referred to by many as "drill and kill," this mode of instructional design has (thankfully) fallen out of favor with educators over the past few years.

Driver software: This is a nearly ubiquitous type of software that provides communications at the machine level between computers and their peripheral devices. For example, one could not use an external *CD-ROM* player with a computer without first installing that player's driver software in memory. With regard to peripherals that are permanently attached to the computer (e.g., a printer), the driver software becomes a part of that computer's boot (i.e., startup) program and is automatically loaded into memory when the machine is turned on without requiring any user intervention.

Drum: This term generally refers to *scanning* equipment at the high end of the publishing application spectrum. Film or paper is inserted on a drum which is rotated past a focused light source. Drum devices are generally very high *resolution* machines.

Drum plotter: A type of *pen plotter* device in which the paper is rotated on a drum while the pen moves along the opposite axis.

DSP: Stands for digital signal processing, a chip-based technology responsible for converting analog signals (such as sound) to a computer-readable digital format and vice-versa. DSP chips promise to find their way into PCs in a massive way in the near future. In fact, most industry analysts agree that without DSPs, multimedia technology would remain a pipe dream, because general purpose *CPUs* simply do not have the horsepower to handle multimedia data efficiently. Thus, DSPs will fast become one of the central components in the emergence of the *multiprocessing* architectures to make the concept of a true *MPC* (multimedia personal computer) possible. A DSP-equipped PC can function as a digital answering machine, a fax modem, a CD-quality audio recorder or player, and a file *codec* (compression-decompression), without requiring additional *expansion boards*.

DTD: Stands for document type definitions, utilized by *tagging languages* such as *SGML* (standard generalized markup language) to define specific processing rules for encoding and decoding a document's structure and the *markup tags* that determine the document's structure.

DTM: Stands for digital terrain models, a texture mapping technology for building 3-D, photorealistic landscapes. With high-end systems, scenes may be computed on the fly, enabling the user to freely explore the terrain. DTM could become a powerful tool, or *enabling technology*, for creating the referential context of *interactive fictions* as well as for training simulations.

DTVC: Stands for desktop videoconferencing, an emergent use for the PC which relies upon levels of connectivity and network *bandwidth* that are not quite in place as yet.

Dual-resolution displays: This technology is used by *virtual reality* engineers to manufacture wide *field of view* systems that restrict the high resolution portions of their screens to *windows* that approximate the area of human foveal attention (which is the high resolution portion of human sight). All other portions of the screen have a much reduced resolution (smaller number of *pixels*), but, in theory, should not be noticed because they are only visible to the low resolution portion of the human eye known as peripheral vision. This type of display is used in close conjunction with *eye tracking* technology to keep the high resolution window in front of the user's *fovea* and the low resolution portions of the screen affixed to the user's peripheral vision. The advantage of this technology is that it dramatically reduces the total number of pixels to be used, thereby reducing the computational load and increasing the *frame refresh rate*.

Ducking: From the world of audio production, this term is used to describe the technique by which the volume (loudness) of a music track is reduced to accommodate narration. This process, designed to eliminate sources of competition in a production's sound track, is readily handled using numerical methods with *digital audio production systems*.

DVE: Stands for digital video effects, the growing library of digitally constructed visual effects that are being made available to desktop computers through a growing number of *desktop video* products. The most common form of DVE is the transition, or digital wipe.

DVI™: Stands for Digital Video Interactive and represents one of the earliest technologies to attempt to *digitize* video and then compress the resulting datastream. Originally developed by RCA at their laboratories in Princeton, New Jersey, during the mid-eighties, DVI eventually ended up in the hands of chipmaker Intel, who purchased it from interim owner GE in 1988. A multifaceted product that revolves around its own proprietary *codec* (compression-decompression) technology, DVI has built a fair degree of support for itself in the marketplace. IBM has endorsed the technology, several third-party software houses have developed authoring systems around it, and the technology now has a Microsoft *Windows* version known as *Indeo*. However, DVI suffers from the fact that it does not conform to any of the widely accepted standards for digitizing visual information: namely, *JPEG* (Joint Photography Experts Group), *MPEG* (Motion Picture Experts Group) and *H.261*. The differences between DVI and, in particular, MPEG and H.261, go to their respective product cores, namely, their respective *codecs*. Where both MPEG and H.261 are based on the mathematics of *DCT* (discrete cosine transfer), DVI is based on a kind of math called "region coding." (Because JPEG is concerned with still image, it is not appropriate to make direct comparisons.) Many technologists believe that DCT is the superior form of math for doing compression-decompression. The bottom line is that, in spite of the considerable progress that DVI has made, its future in the digital video market may be uncertain.

DXF: A file format that somehow stands for drawing interchange format, this acronym refers to a platform-independent format for *CAD* (computer aided design) files developed by Autodesk. As *virtual reality* brings such phenomena as the *architectural walkthrough* into the mainstream of desktop computing, expect standards like DXF, and its near-cousin *IGES* (initial graphics exchange specification), to become increasingly common.

Dynamic range: In the world of digital audio, this term describes the difference between the loudest and softest sounds that can be expressed by a system. It represents a measure of audio *resolution* and is often expressed in decibels.

DYUV: Also known as delta luminance color difference, this image *compression* technique takes advantage of the fact that data for neighboring *pixels* are often similar. Thus, instead of recording each pixel separately, it records only the difference between pixels, line by line. Like its *YUV* image encoding parent, it also exploits the fact that the human eye is more sensitive to differences in brightness (*luminance*) than in color (*chrominance*), and thus saves data space by storing less information about color changes than about changes having to do with brightness.

If you want a song in interactive, sing it.
—John Barlow, Songwriter, the Grateful Dead

EDI: Stands for electronic data interchange, which is a general term that refers to the data communications technology needed for trading partners to transmit various forms of business document correspondence—such as purchase orders, bills of lading, and shipping orders—electronically across a network instead of sending them physically through the mail. It is expected that this form of electronic communication, like most others, may increasingly be enhanced by the inclusion of various forms of *mixed media data types* such as *digital images* and *voice annotations*.

Editor: Is one who deletes or adds scenes to a picture by following the instructions of the director, and who also keeps the sound tracks in *sync*. It has often been said that it is the editor who actually makes the movie, because it is the editor who controls the overall pacing of the film and thereby determines much of its emotional impact.

Edit point: From the world of film and video, this term refers to any place in a video where the editor has intervened with respect to the visual flow. An edit point is typically associated with some form of cut from one shot to another. Producers who wish to make aesthetically appealing interactive programs will need to remember the fact that virtually all points of interaction (*branchpoints*) will also be edit points of one type or another.

EDL: Stands for edit decision list, which in the world of film production is a list of instructions for creating a final, single videotape out of multiple source tapes. This particular film production technique is now a popular one among producers of *desktop video production* tools because, from a systems analysis standpoint, it represents little more than a straightforward database function.

Educational software: Nearly synonymous with the terms *courseware* and *CBT* (computer based training), this growing type of application represents the use of software to educate, rather than automate. Rarely heard of in the corporate world, this term is much more commonly spoken of in the school market, where it is used to describe what many educators feel to be the next major form of instructional publishing.

Edutainment: This contracted term is given to software that merges the functions associated with educational **and** entertainment software. This new breed of software exploits the media capabilities of the *MPC* (multimedia personal computer) and seeks to expand the home market for software by blending the youth appeal of electronic games with the parent appeal of educational software. More than just a marketing whim, the concept of edutainment is based on the well-researched overlap between sophisticated, multidimensional games and the higher-order thinking skills associated with problem-solving.

EGA: This stands for enhanced graphics adapter, which is a vestigial remnant of the graphical ascent of DOS-compatible personal computers. Falling in the lineal path just after *CGA* and just before *VGA*, the EGA standard permitted 64 colors with a *resolution* of 640 x 350 *pixels*.

EISA: This term stands for extended industry standard architecture, a now somewhat dated update to the original (and even more dated) *ISA* architecture of the personal computer. The EISA standard provides for a broader data path than its ISA forebear, which became a necessity in the late 1980s (1988, to be specific), when computer manufacturers began to accelerate their attempts to enrich the computing experience with *multimedia* data types. Because this effort has continued to grow in the '90s, the EISA standard has fallen behind, and is now being patched by various *local bus* strategies, such as Intel's *PCI* (Peripheral Component Interconnect).

E-journal: Short for electronic journal, this phenomenon issues from the "Net," or, to be more precise, the *Internet*. Considered to be the latest, best manifestation of democracy, the E-journal embodies the concept that anyone with access to a computer equipped with a modem can produce and distribute an electronic magazine through a computer network. E-journals are exploding in number and are—predictably—oriented around special topics such as computer law and AIDS prevention. The beauty of E-journals is that they enable many to publish who simply do not have the finances or other resources to bring their ideas to fruition in the print publishing arena.

Electronic content: This term was created in the world of document processing to refer to documents stored in the form of electronically encoded characters such that each character of the document has its own encoded representation. Documents that have been converted to their constituent *ASCII* codes for storage on the personal computer system are an example of electronic content. This form of representing document content is often distinguished from electronic image, wherein the document is represented as a *bit map* of *pixels.* Electronic, or ASCII-encoded, content is more useful because it can be searched on a character-by-character basis (i.e., it can be *parsed*).

Electronic likeness rights: Related to intellectual property rights, this term refers to an emerging trend for multimedia content vendors to create animated, or *quasi-video*, representations of famous people, clearly making use of the publicity value that those people possess. These rights help protect the publicity value owned by those people, and, in most cases, translate into some form of royalty arrangement.

Embedded PC: This term captures the notion that all of the technical components associated with the personal computer can now be embedded in other, traditionally low-tech, devices. Actually, the process of embedding PC-like intelligence in other technologies has been going on for some time: witness the microwave oven, the logical functions of which are based entirely on microprocessor technology. The significance of this term in today's market is that as the PC becomes the *MPC* (multimedia personal computer), media-based applications, such as navigational systems for automobiles, will become common.

Embedded training: From the world of *instructional design*, this term refers to use of *CBT* (computer based training) in small, granular units that are brought as close as possible to, and therefore become "embedded" in, the tasks for which they provide training. This concept is held up as being superior to the traditional form of delivering instruction, where all of the training is packed into a single session or period of time, and is thereby separated from the time in which the learner will actually make use of it. Embedded training is used extensively in *performance support systems*, where the embedded training pieces are also often referred to as *job aids.*

Emulation: The widespread use of this term in the computer industry in many respects serves as an indicator of the volatility of the computer marketplace in general, and the multimedia market in particular. Emulation occurs when the hardware-software combination that constitutes one delivery *platform* is made to operate like (emulate) the hardware-software combination of another platform. In the computer industry, one of the earliest widespread uses of emulation occurred when intelligent personal computers were made to operate like dumb terminals so that PC users could make use of the programs and data stored on large mainframe systems. In the current era of multimedia computing, with hardware-software combinations proliferating from every direction, developers of *multimedia applications* are faced with an unprecedented need to emulate all sorts of delivery platforms so as to make their programs as widely usable, and therefore as marketable, as possible.

Enabling technologies: Refers to the growing mass of data storage and transmission products, computing/media platforms, system software, authoring tools, etc., that taken altogether make it possible to deliver *multimedia applications* to the end user. Put in a bit more general sense, the term refers to any technology that makes another, more humanly accessible, technology possible. Thus, a *fiber optic* transmission line is an enabling technology for *picturephone*, and picturephone is, in turn, an enabling technology for *videoconferencing*.

Endpoints: In vector graphics, these are the points that specify each end of a line segment.

Environmental systems: This refers to a form of *virtual reality* consisting mostly of externally generated 3-D objects, but with little or no body paraphernalia. Users move within a real physical space that reacts to cues triggered by their motions and actions.

Equitagonist: This term refers to an audience member who participates in a game that is so multivariate in nature as to have the feel of a real life narrative. Thus, it refers to a human player in an *interactive fiction*. It is derived from the traditional literary terms of protagonist and antagonist; it implies that the participants will have their performances assessed (scored) on the basis of criteria that are equally applied to other (both electronic and human) players in the interactive fiction.

ERDAS: Stands for earth resource data analysis, a standard file format for representing remote sensing images.

Ethernet: This venerable standard for *LANs* (local area networks) is now getting a bit long in the tooth. Capable of only handling 10 Mbps (megabits per second), Ethernet is overwhelmed by any substantive effort to network *mixed media data types*. A recent upgrade to this standard called "Fast Ethernet" is capable of 100 Mbps, but represents only a stopgap measure in the face of the multi-*gigabyte* demands of true *multimedia* networking.

Event loop: One of the key design elements in constructing an interactive program, the event loop is the central routine that at any given time determines the range of acceptable user actions. All other things being equal, the broader this range of acceptable actions, the more flexible and interactive the program will appear to be.

EVL: Stands for Electronic Visualization Lab, a branch of the University of Illinois at Chicago dedicated to leading-edge 3-D audiovisual systems for use in *virtual reality* applications. The *CAVE*, a virtual reality environment that features a room whose walls and floor flood the viewer's senses with projected images, is the EVL's leading project.

Expansion board: This term refers to the many plug-in boards that expand the capabilities of standard personal computers. With the rapid onset of market demand for *multimedia* capabilities, video and audio expansion boards have proliferated in recent years because single-processor PCs simply cannot handle the demanding computational requirements of image, audio, and video.

Experiential prototyping: From the world of practical *virtual reality* (an oxymoron?) applications, this term is a near-synonym for *architectural walkthrough*. It refers to entire environments—such as buildings—that are created by the virtual reality media so that they may be experienced by the user as if they were real.

Expert system: From the world of *artificial intelligence*, an expert system is a genre of AI designed to solve problems at the expert level in some scientific, mathematical, or medical domain. To date, expert systems have only been successfully used with regard to relatively restricted problem domains. The key step in constructing expert systems is known as *knowledge engineering*, wherein a knowledge engineer works closely with a subject matter expert to untangle the decision rules and sources of knowledge that make the expertise work. As expert systems become joined to *multimedia applications*, taking advantage of such newborn software design techniques as the *interface agent*, their usefulness will likely become dramatically extended.

Exposure: In film and video, this term refers to one frame of film that has been exposed.

Extensibility: A term used frequently in software engineering, it refers to a desirable system characteristic wherewith new features can be added easily, i.e., they can be added without having to undertake major redesigns. Extensible systems help avoid rapid functional obsolescence. Very extensible systems are said to be *future-proofed*.

Extrusion: This is an interactive modeling technique in which a further dimension can be added to an existing definition, e.g., a line can be extruded from a point, a plane from a line, or a solid from a plane.

Eye candy: This insider term refers to the richness and texture of the computerized image generated on a *multimedia* screen.

EyePhone™: Manufactured by VPL Research, this was the first commercially available stereoscopic *HMD* (head-mounted display) for *virtual reality* applications. This apparatus uses color *LCD* displays with a resolution of 360 x 240 *pixels* to provide a horizontal *field of view* measuring 100 degrees.

Eye tracking: This emergent technology, first developed for military applications and now being annexed by makers of *virtual reality* gear, tracks the movement of the human eye for purposes of machine interaction. The primary methods of eye tracking in use today involve bathing the eye in low-intensity infrared light. This light creates a bright image of the pupil and a bright spot reflecting off the cornea, both of which can be captured by a video camera focused on the user's eyes. Image processing software then analyzes the video image, finds the pupil and cornea, and calculates where the eye is looking. Once the system knows where you are looking, the computer can be controlled through measuring *gaze duration*. Thus, for example, the user could press a button or select a key by staring at it for a specific length of time. Or, in a virtual reality environment, the user could navigate, or *fly*, through a landscape by simply staring in the desired direction.

. . . you're building a process . . . not a composition.
—Randall Packer, Founder, New Music Theatre

Face armature: Consisting of sensors to track the user's head, face, and lip movements, this *virtual reality* equipment attaches to the head and permits real-life actors to animate corresponding features of animated on-screen agents.

Fade in/out: A transitional effect whereby a scene starts as black and is gradually brought, *frame* by frame, to full exposure, or vice versa. The process of creating "fades" has been automated by the powerful *pixel* processing routines available in many PC *paint systems* programs.

Fade margin: From the technical side of communications, this useful term refers to the level of signal decay tolerated before communications cease. One of the problems with the emerging forms of all-digital communications is that with digital, the distance between a completely valid signal and one that is utterly useless is both small and abrupt.

Fantasy role player: From the world of video games, this term refers to the role that the game player (user) takes while involved in some of the more sophisticated electronic games. This term clearly points toward the future of electronic games, where these interactive programs will seem less like games and more like the next generation of storytelling products where the audience member will play a participatory role in an *interactive fiction.*

FAQ: Stands for frequently asked questions, a module that has become so common in online help, software *tutorial,* and *CBT* (computer based training) programs that it has earned the status of an acronym. It derives from the widely recognized tendency that, for most products or systems, anywhere from 5 to 20 questions end up representing about 90 percent of all questions asked about that product or system.

FAT: Stands for file allocation table and refers to a common data structure used with erasable storage media, such as hard disks. FATs are based on the notion that data sectors are erasable and, therefore, reusable. Generally located on the outermost sectors of the disk, the FAT keeps track of files with regard to the addressable disk sectors they occupy. FATs are generally considered to bring with them a considerable amount of overhead.

FDDI: Stands for fiber distributed data interface and represents the industry standard for *LANs* (local area networks) based on *fiber optic* transmission. FDDI is a token-based standard, which means that a station must have possession of the system's lone token in order to place an object on the LAN for transmission. The advantages of FDDI over the more common copper- and coaxial cable-based LANs are several: fiber is high capacity, capable of transmitting up to gigabits of data per second; FDDI LANs possess electromagnetic isolation properties, which means that they are not affected by external electromagnetic fields that might cause interference, impulse noise, and crosstalk on nonfiber networks; and, these fiber networks do not, themselves, emit radiation that can cause interference with other equipment. The FDDI standard is in its second generation, termed FDDI II, which expands the capabilities of FDDI I by supporting *circuit switching* for users who need LAN support for voice, video (*picturephone*), or other constant-data-rate applications.

FDX: Stands for full duplex, which is simply communication in two directions simultaneously on a communications channel.

Feature extraction: From the realm of optical character recognition (*OCR*), this term refers to one of the more common techniques for recognizing characters on source documents. This techniques studies the structure of the character: the angles, slopes, inflection points, holes, etc. The shape of the character is compared with sets of rules (called "operators") about character shapes. For example, a shape with two vertical lines that meet at the top with a horizontal line in the middle fits the rules for the letter "A." This technique is often compared with *template matching*, a less expensive, but less powerful, alternative.

Feelies: What is today being referred to by *virtual reality* aficionados as *tactile feedback* was (perhaps originally) foreseen by the famous twentieth-century author Aldous Huxley. Huxley wrote about 3-D movies that he called "feelies."

Fiber optics: This term refers to the use of an *optical fiber transmission* of data by means of a light beam.

Field of view: This term of visual anatomy is gaining popularity in the world of *virtual reality* because it helps define the parameters of visual immersion. Large screen technologies like *IMAX Theatre*, which seek to immerse the audience from a visual standpoint, are quite concerned with field of view. Research has shown that to be totally immersive, a screen must cover a 270-degree arc in front of the audience member. This number is arrived at in the following way: When a user is looking straight ahead, each eye is capable of providing visual information as much as 90 degrees of its central axis. Combining the images from both eyes provides a lateral field of view of approximately 180 degrees. Because you can pivot your eyes to the left and right about 45 degrees, it is possible (even easy) to perceive an additional 90 degrees, making for a total lateral field of view of approximately 270 degrees. Current research suggests that a sense of immersion in an image requires a field of vision of at least 90 degrees.

FIF: Stands for fractal image format, the emerging standard for image data that has been *compressed* using techniques derived from *fractal geometry*. The standard was created by Michael Barnsley of Iterated Systems, Inc.

File striping: Also called *declustering*, this term refers to a high-performance algorithm based on the principle of distributing a single file over several storage devices. Each device, then, holds a stripe of the same file. Because these drives can then work in parallel, each one storing and retrieving data in near-simultaneity, striping offers a much higher *transfer rate*. Reads, for example, are performed in a fashion whereby a single read request is broken into multiple requests, each serviced by a different storage device. This strategy holds great currency in the age of multimedia, where moving enormous files rapidly poses one of the industry's greatest challenges.

Fill: From the world of computer *paint systems*, this term refers to a widely available feature in commercial packages in which enclosed areas in a picture can be given a gray shade, color, or pattern with a single click of the *mouse*.

Film scanner: This type of *scanning* device specializes in *digitizing* slides and transparencies.

Firmware: This term refers to computer programs stored in programmable read-only memories (PROMs) that can be replaced but not reprogrammed by the user. Firmware is common in the various *board* products that are used to increase the media processing capabilities of multimedia personal computers (*MPC*s).

Flanging: From the realm of audio engineering, this term refers to an audio effect created by placing two copies of the same sound in and out of temporal phase with one another.

Flatbed plotter: Is a *pen plotter* in which the paper (or film-based material) is held on a flat drawing table where it is traversed by one or more pens in a pen carriage.

Flatbed scanner: One of the most commonly used types of *scanner*, it is distinctive for having a flat surface onto which users place their artwork or documents one at a time for scanning as the light source moves under the item-to-be-scanned. Many flatbed scanners have optional document feeders for scanning multiple pages automatically.

Flat panel displays: These are an emerging family of *VDU* (video display unit) that most often uses technologies other than the *CRT* in order to reduce the bulk and power requirements of the VDU. Good examples include the *LCD*s (liquid crystal displays) and plasma panels that are often used with small portable computers.

Flicker: One of the most common artifacts of analog video, flicker can be seen as a vibration of the entire screen, the horizontal lines, or the colors.

Flying: This term has been abducted by the *virtual reality* community to refer to movement through a virtual world that is enacted by hand gestures (such as pointing one's data-gloved finger in the direction of movement). Thus, with reference to an *architectural walkthrough*, one can say that they are flying through a particular structure.

Flying mouse: Is a *virtual reality* version of the *mouse* input device that tracks motion in three, rather than just two, dimensions.

FM synthesis: One of two primary forms of *MIDI* (musical instrument digital interface) synthesis (FM stands for frequency modulation, in case you didn't know). The other primary form is *wave table synthesis*, which is generally considered to be the superior of the two. FM synthesis is the elder of the two, and it is by far the most common amongst the first generation of add-in sound boards. With FM synthesis, at least two digitally generated sine waves are required. One of these waves is called the "modulator" because it modulates or changes the frequency of the second waveform, which is called the "carrier." While FM synthesis requires only two sine waves, FM synthesizers typically use multiple carriers and modulators. Each of these sine waves is called an "operator." FM synthesis was invented in the 1970s by Stanford's John Chowning. Yamaha holds an exclusive right to the patent for his invention. Yamaha's first-generation chips used only two operators and produced sounds that were adequate to the early game market. Yamaha's latest chip, the OPL3, uses four operators and, predictably, is capable of generating more sophisticated sounds.

FMV™: Stands for Full Motion Video, Philips' *MPEG* (Motion Picture Experts Group)-compressed full motion video option. OptImage incorporates FMV in MovieStudio, an authoring tool designed specifically for use with *CD-I* (compact disc-interactive) technology.

Foley effects: From the world of film production, this term refers to sound effects that are manufactured, usually in a studio, for use in a specific film scene. These effects can be as mundane as someone walking across a linoleum floor, as spectacular as a volcanic eruption. In traditional film production, foley effects are created in a post-production setting where the appropriately equipped individuals (e.g., foley walkers on sand, wood, or linoleum surfaces) make the sounds while viewing the actual film events with which those sounds will be later *mixed*. This process is similar to looping, which refers to the studio creation of voiceovers to replace dialogue recorded at the live shoot. As *MIDI* (musical instrument digital interface) equipment becomes more common, thus enabling the *digital* creation of sound effects and the construction of *clip media* audio libraries, much of the creation of foley effects will become an automated process in which the effects are selected from a database.

Footage: In film and video, this term is generally used to refer to film that has been exposed by the camera operator.

Force feedback: Part-in-parcel of the effort to master the human-machine elements of *tactile feedback*, this subdiscipline of *virtual reality* is involved with the re-creation of *force patterns* that give users the sense that they are coming into tangible contact with some object from the real world, such as the gearshift of a racecar. The most sophisticated force feedback systems to date make use of tables of digitized force patterns, with each pattern representing a particular object and/or sensation.

Force patterns: Analogous to the sound *patches* stored in a *MIDI* (musical instrument digital interface) *wave table*, force patterns are digitized patterns of *force feedback* that emulate the human experience of interacting with various objects in the real world. Thus, the feel of moving a gearshift from first to second speed might be recorded and stored in a *tactile feedback* database of force patterns.

Format longevity: A feature of any media-related technology that describes its duration or length of stay as a useful standard. The *NTSC* (National Television Standards Committee) standard for television is now into its fifth decade of format longevity. By way of contrast, the *CGA* standard (the what?) for computer monitors was a mere flicker in the technological night, lasting for about two years before it gave way to *EGA*, and then its successor, *VGA* (video graphics array).

Form factor: This term refers to the physical size and shape of devices such as computers and interactive televisions. With an increasing move toward special purpose equipment—the portable PC, for example—there is a growing move away from a standardized form factor and toward increasingly customized form factors to meet the needs of specific applications.

Fovea: From the realm of human visual anatomy, this term refers to a region on the rear wall of the retina responsible for one's center of visual attention. This region is both the thinnest part of the retina and the part with the highest concentration of cones. Figuratively speaking, it is the high *resolution* portion of the field of vision. All other portions are, in a sense, low resolution, and are often referred to collectively as peripheral vision. Some *virtual reality* engineers involved in building wide *field of view* devices are now taking advantage of this foveal concentration of high resolution vision by building *dual-resolution displays*. These displays reduce the high resolution portions of their screens to *windows* that roughly approximate the foveal portion of human sight. They keep this portion of the display, or this high resolution window, in front of the user's foveal line of sight by using *eye tracking* technology that keeps up with the location of the user's pupils. The value of this approach to VR engineering is that it dramatically reduces the overall number of *pixels* that must be projected onto the display, thereby reducing the computational demands placed on the system, and making higher *refresh rates* possible.

FPS: Stands for frames per second and represents a primary measure of film quality. The higher the FPS, the smoother the flow of motion, and, all other things being equal, the higher the quality of the motion video.

Fractal geometry: The brainchild of IBM researcher Benoit Mandelbrot, this recent intellectual creation thrives on the notion that nature seems to recapitulate itself at different scales. Thus, large branches scale down into smaller branches, which scale down into twigs, virtually ad infinitum. For the *multimedia* industry, fractal geometry has given rise to a number of promising software technologies: for, among other things, simulating portions of the natural world and *compressing* and *decompressing* images.

Fractal transform image compression: This is perhaps the most innovative, and certainly the most promising, form of *codec* technology yet to appear. Pioneered by Michael Bransley and Iterated Systems, Inc., of Norcross, Georgia, this technology can achieve very high image *compression ratios*, with 100:1 being fairly standard. Based on the mathematics of *fractal geometry*, this codec possesses the desirable feature of creating *scalable* images (i.e., images that are *resolution independent*) and can therefore output (*decompress*) images at any resolution.

Frame: An area of film equal to one *exposure*, this is the principal term used to describe the fundamental unit of both *analog* and *digital* forms of video.

Frame accuracy: This term refers to a device's ability to consistently locate any single frame on a tape. The *SMPTE* (Society for Motion Picture and Television Engineers) time code is, for example, frame accurate. This means that SMPTE is extremely accurate because it can locate any one of 30 frames per second.

Frame dropping: A process that often accompanies the give-and-take of scaling up the size of a *digital* video *window*, this term refers to the lowering of the *frame rate* (*fps*) of a digital video stream in order to maintain a constant data rate. The process of frame dropping often leads to a herky-jerky video image, an artifact that results because key segments of motion are missing after a certain number of frames have been eliminated. The process is required only because of the present *bandwidth* limitations that surround the use of video on the single-*CPU* personal computer and will, in due course, be eliminated by the increasing media-handling capabilities of personal computers.

Frame grabber: This is a system component, usually implemented as an *expansion board* with companion software, used to capture, or *digitize*, the video signal from a motion picture source (e.g., from a TV, video camera, or VCR). Often, the term is taken to be synonymous with a *video digitizer*.

Frame rate: This term refers to the rate at which single frames in a motion picture sequence are displayed on a screen. With TV in North America, broadcast video is displayed at 30 frames per second (fps); the 35mm motion pictures seen in the theater play at 24 frames per second.

Frame refresh rate: Nearly synonymous with *frame rate*, this term has taken on a unique importance in the world of *virtual reality*, where each frame the user sees is dynamically constructed in *real time* from visual data stored in the computer's memory. Obviously, it is far, far easier to create high frame rates when frames are represented by pre-recorded images stored on videotape, than it is to generate photorealistic images on the fly from visual data. For this reason, it is widely accepted that it will be some time into the future before we have virtual reality equipment that can render photorealistic (film quality) images at anything approaching the frame rates of television or movies.

Freeze frame: This feature, common to both analog and digital devices, is used to hold a single frame of video motionless on the screen.

Frequency: With regard to the physical characteristics of a signal, the term frequency is used most often to describe the number of times that a signal varies per second. In this context, frequency is usually measured in *hertz*, or cycles per second.

Front plane: From the world of *DVE* (digital video effects), this term refers to the uppermost of two visual planes used in *two-plane effects* to create transitions between one screen and the next.

Full-body recognition: One of the *enabling technologies* of *full immersion VR*, this is a dreamed-about capability of *virtual reality* that will make it possible for cybernauts to enter a virtual world and have the tracking intelligence of that world recognize what the entire body is doing, e.g., what the arms are doing, what the facial expressions are like, how the body is moving through space, etc. Though this technology is a long way off in any practical sense, early prototypes, such as VPL Research's *DataSuit*, are already on the market.

Full immersion VR: This is the fullest form of *virtual reality*, wherein one dons head gear, *DataGlove,* and bodysuit, and becomes completely immersed in the virtual world (such as it is).

Full text retrieval: This term refers to the most exhaustive form of search and retrieval applied to a large database comprised of text-based documents. With this type of retrieval, users supply target words or phrases (representing the information they are looking for) to the search engine, and the search engine scans, or *parses*, the entirety of the documents contained in the database. Under this search strategy, the user can be confident that no incidences of their target words will be missed. However, owing to the massive nature of many document databases (imagine searching through every article of every issue of the *Wall Street Journal*), many designers back off of this computationally intensive approach and perform only *keyword* searches, in which the only text data parsed is a relatively small number of keywords to summarize the content.

Future-proofed: This is a characteristic of any technology that is **not** subject to the rapid functional obsolescence that has typified the computer and electronics industries from their inception. The only way that a manufacturer of *multimedia* hardware or software can possibly achieve this characteristic is by creating a product that is either highly *scalable* (can be upgraded through several generations without a major re-design) or very far ahead of the innovation curve.

Perhaps the central fact and assumption of the information society is that the world of concrete objects is being controlled more and more by a parallel, but separate, world of abstract objects and concepts.
—Kamran Parsaye, Chairman, IntelligenceWare

Gaffer: From the world of filmmaking, this term refers to the chief electrician, responsible for the safe and efficient setup of lights, cables, and accessories—an important role in film production.

Gas plasma: This is the technology of the future for large, color flat-panel displays (such as those featured in the movie *Total Recall*).

Gaze duration: Simply put, this is the amount of time a human spends looking in a particular direction. This phenomenon is now used as an computer input parameter with *virtual reality* systems that make use of *eye tracking*.

Generation loss: Is a characteristic of *analog* forms of media, such as cassette tape audio or VHS video, where, with each successive copying of the program, some of the original quality is lost. Thus a copy of a copy will possess less quality—more generation loss— than a mere first-generation copy of an original. Generation loss is often cited as one of the most distinct disadvantages that analog forms of media have relative to their *digital* counterparts. With digital media, where the original is stored in the form of a data representation— a binary stream of data, to be exact—there is no generational loss of quality no matter how many times the information is copied.

Genlocking: From the world of video production, this term refers to a device's ability to synchronize video signals from two tape sources so that they can be recorded together onto a third tape. The term has also been used to describe a signal synchronization technique essential to the process of creating a stable signal when overlaying computer graphics with video.

Ghosting: An artifact common on *LCD* screens, ghosting refers to the faint continuation of solid lines—also termed "shadowing"—beyond the actual ends of those lines. This effect is caused by the uncontrolled spread of electricity along the electrodes that turn screen *pixels* on and off.

Gibb's effect: The most common artifact for images that have been compressed using the *DCT* (discrete cosine transfer) technique (which is the base technique for the *JPEG* [Joint Photography Experts Group] standard), this effect appears as ripples running out from sharp edges such as street signs or tree trunks, giving an overall impression of blockiness. As one would expect, this artifact becomes increasingly pronounced the higher the *compression ratio.*

GIF: Stands for graphics interchange file, a file format created by CompuServe to facilitate the exchange of picture files between computer platforms.

Gigabyte: Is one billion bytes; it is also the next level of common storage capacity, now that multimedia technology is making megabytes of storage passé. A gigabyte is typically represented by the initials GB.

Gigahertz: Is one billion cycles per second.

Glass distortion: This refers to a form of *DVE* (digital video effect) in which the image is altered so that it appears as it would when viewed through a piece of unfinished glass.

Glyphs: From the world of *scientific visualization*, these are visual objects whose attributes (e.g., shape, position, color, size, and orientation) are bound to independent variables and serve to provide a symbolic representation of some aspect of nature. Spheres in a molecular structure and color patterns in an anatomical graphic to depict tumors represent just two examples of glyph usage.

Gopher: This term originates from the realm of the *Internet*, and it refers to a navigational aid for searching out specific content from across the vast wastelands of information made accessible on the Internet.

Gourad shading: This is one of the high-end forms of *polygon shading* associated with computer generated graphics.

Gradient fill: This is a feature common to commercial *paint systems* in which the user is able to *fill* a specified area of an image with a pattern, gray shade, or color that displays a gradual transition from the foreground of the fill area to the background.

Granularity: This term refers to the size of the units by which something is structured. The smaller the units, the more granular the structure. Placed in a commonplace example, a foot-long ruler that provides tick marks for every tenth of an inch is more granular in its markings than one that only provides tick marks for every inch. Generally speaking, granularity is considered a desirable design feature for *multimedia applications* because it implies an ability for the program to take greater advantage of the random access capabilities of the computer.

Graphics subroutine packages: The so-called toolbox systems, these packages help programmers build their own graphically oriented application software using pre-written graphics utilities.

Graphics tablet: An input device used by graphics artists, this is a touch sensitive board over which the illustrator passes some form of hand-held input device, typically a pen. Under its most common form of usage, the pressure from the pen as it moves across the surface causes the tablet to generate a stream of x and y coordinates, which a graphics program will then accept and translate into a line drawing that appears on the computer display.

Grayscale: The spectrum, or range, of shades of black an image has. Scanners' and terminals' grayscales are determined by the number of gray shades, or steps, they can recognize and reproduce. A *scanner* that can only see a grayscale of 16 will not produce as accurate an image as one that distinguishes a grayscale of 256.

Great electronic machine: This is futurist Joseph Pelton's term for the world's biggest existing machine: the massive interlinked system of cables, telephones, computers, and broadcasting equipment that constitute the world's communications network.

Green Book: Related to the *Red Book, Yellow Book*, and *Orange Book* standards, this standard for compact disc refers specifically to the *CD-I* (compact disc—interactive) technology of Philips. This standard specifies a specific operating system called *CD-RTOS* and the disc layout. Like XA of the Yellow Book standard, the Green Book allows *interleaving* of computer data and compressed audio on the same track.

Grid: This is an invisible layout that divides a screen into separate visual areas. Grids are quite common in digital video production tools, such as *paint systems*, where they are used as a tool for enabling artists to blend more than one graphic object on a single frame.

Grip: From the world of filmmaking, this term refers to the people who assist the camera and the sound crews by helping to move equipment, props, costumes, and the like.

Grooming: Also referred to as file grooming, this relatively new concept is associated with network file storage systems and describes an automated (defined by algorithm) process whereby files are migrated from *online* to *near-line storage* devices without any operator intervention. As the name implies, the algorithmic intelligence associated with grooming will usually involve some deletion of files (a process traditionally referred to as *purging*). In large scale multimedia systems, where *gigabytes* and possibly even *terabytes* of permanent storage are involved, grooming is a powerful labor-saving technology.

Groupware: This term refers to software designed to enhance the sharing of an information work product (for example, a large document such as a corporate annual report) between and among members of a work group. This emergent technology typically relies upon some form of networking technology to interconnect members of the work team and to provide mutual access to the shared work product. A good example of this is Lotus Notes. *Document conferencing* is a slightly more advanced application of groupware in which members of the work team communicate via video windows embedded in a document work product.

GUI: Stands for graphical user interface, and is pronounced goo-ee. This standard buzz phrase of the late eighties and early nineties refers to the *interface design* goals that became predominant in the industry as PCs began to accrue significant graphics capabilities. In essence, a GUI is supposed to make the computer easier to use by creating graphical objects such as *icons, buttons,* and *windows* for the user to interact with, rather than the sterile systems of text commands that preceded GUIs in the historical evolution of computer software. The *desktop metaphor* of the Apple Macintosh and Microsoft *Windows* interfaces are the classic examples today of a GUI.

If imagining beyond the immediate spatial moment is one of the primal traits that makes us human, then virtual reality can be considered the most natural progression we can imagine.
—Tony Reveaux, Editor, **Computer Publicity News**

Hachures: In the world of computer graphics, this term refers to a series of lines representing the general direction and steepness of slope. Gentle slopes are represented by longer, lighter, or more widely spaced lines, whereas steep slopes are symbolized by shorter, heavier, or more closely spaced lines, just like a topographic map.

Hackers: Are persons who attempt to penetrate the security of a computer system, usually from a remote location, for nefarious purposes.

Hand-off function: This term is used to describe the ability found with the wireless technologies—such as cellular phone or *RDS* (radio data systems)—to automatically switch from one broadcast source to another as a moving destination (e.g., a car) travels from one geographic zone to another. The latest, and perhaps most innovative, use of the hand-off function can be found with RDS, where it will soon be possible in the U.S. for a cross-country driver to have the radio automatically retune itself to another station for nationally broadcast shows as the driver travels from one geographic zone into another.

Haptic system: From the realm of human anatomy, this system has taken on sudden importance with the emerging effort to provide *tactile feedback* in association with *virtual reality* products. The haptic system has two major subsystems. The first is called mechanoreceptors. They are extremely sensitive mechanisms that measure pressure or deformation of the skin. They are critical in providing information about the texture of an object. The second subsystem is associated with the term proprioception, which has to do with the way in which our muscles and tendons work to discover the size, weight, and shape of an object based on how much effort they must exert when encountering that object. Together, the mechanoreceptors and proprioception make up the haptic system and provide haptic cues that convey information to our minds about the tangible environment.

HDF: Stands for hierarchical data format, a file format developed by the National Center for Supercomputer Applications and intended to serve as a standard for the scientific visualization community. HDF is ideal for this role because it is extensible, available in the public domain, and capable of handling data and images as well as scaling information.

HDTV: Stands for high definition television, an emerging standard for higher quality television broadcasts. Actually, the term HDTV has been with us for some time, and, in general, may represent the next generation of television. More recently, though, the term has become increasingly specific, as the *Advisory Committee on Advanced Television Service* in the United States has begun serious deliberations with the goal in mind of recommending a single HDTV standard to the FCC. It is intended that HDTV broadcasting begin by 1996 and air concurrently with traditional *NTSC* (National Television Standards Committee) broadcasts until the year 2008, at which time all NTSC transmissions are to be phased out. There are two primary elements of the HDTV standard: First, and foremost, the new standard offers higher resolution, somewhere in the vicinity of 1,000 *scan lines*, which is roughly twice the NTSC number of 525 scan lines. This resolution delivers broadcast quality that is roughly equivalent to 35mm film (the quality one sees in today's movie theaters). Second, the new standard will include a wider screen *aspect ratio*, another feature that will bring television broadcasts into closer physical harmony with the motion picture industry. The dominant problem facing the various corporate/academic alliances who are in competition for establishing the new HDTV standard revolves around the *bandwidth* reduction that must be achieved to deliver these new capabilities within the bandwidth constraints that have been put in place by the FCC.

Headend: This is becoming a general purpose term for describing source nodes in the architecture of the *information superhighway* that are responsible for storing and serving up the various elements of content that users of the highway want. As the superhighway takes greater shape, headends will provide mass storage of multimedia content, projected to be in the terabyte range within the near future.

Heads-up display: This type of display is soon to become common with respect to *RDS* (radio data systems) that are used in automobiles, wherewith any digitally displayed information is projected onto a small viewing area on the windshield, so that drivers do not have to redirect their line of sight away from the road to see the digitally transmitted information.

Heat mapping: From the realm of *scientific visualization*, this visual procedure produces a surface plot in which height and color are used to represent different variables such as stress intensity or age of data. Obviously, the higher the height and the warmer the color, the greater the intensity one adduces to the variables being represented.

Hertz: This is a measure of frequency in cycles per second.

Heuristics: This term is important to *artificial intelligence*, for it refers to rules of thumb that suggest rules to be used in given situations.

Hidden-line removal: This technique is used in sophisticated graphics programs whereby lines are removed from view that would normally be hidden on a real object by virtue of being obstructed by the front surfaces of the object.

High fidelity simulation: This term represents the convergence of high-end business training applications, such as the flight simulators sponsored by the airline industry, and the use of the immersive technologies of *virtual reality*, such as full field-of-vision video.

High-intensity amusement attractions: One of the leading edges of new media design and production, these attractions form the backbone of the late-twentieth century theme park (e.g., Disney World and Universal Studios in Orlando, Florida). These attractions use a combination of *3-D sound* and video, environmental props, and live actors to create hyper-real experiences for their audiences.

High level language: From the archives of software history, this term refers to a family of software tools that came into existence early on (circa the 1960s) to make it easier for humans to write programs that computers can understand. In the initial years of computing, all programs were written using the binary code of 1s and 0s, a phenomenon called "machine language." This was very difficult, and was mastered by only a few (nerds). Thus, a thing called "assembly language" was invented. It enables programmers to use more human-like commands to build their programs. When they (think they) are finished, they simply submit their code to a thing called an "assembler," which translates the assembly language stuff into machine language. This is still very difficult, and still attracts mostly nerds. Then along came the invention of high level languages, which enable pro-grammers to use almost-human language to write their programs. Again, when finished, they submit their programs to a piece of soft-ware that translates their code into machine language. In the case of high level languages there are actually two such families of translat-ing programs, one called an "interpreter," the other a "compiler." Early examples of high level languages include COBOL and Fortran, both of which are still in fairly wide use. More recent, and currently more popular examples of high level languages include Visual Basic and C++, both of which are commonly used to author multimedia cre-ations. In spite of their name, however, high level languages still re-quire considerable technical training to be able to use them with any proficiency, and, as a consequence, are not the end of the road when it comes to pursuing the dream of inventing software tools that en-able the layperson to program the computer. There are now software tools called "Fourth Generation Languages," or, more popularly, "4GLs." These programs are also called "code generators," because they enable users to interact with a graphical user interface (*GUI*), which then generates useable code on the bases of those interactions. In many respects, most of the programs that pass for *authoring sys-tems* are 4GLs. However, it must be reported that when you use a 4GL, you give up a considerable amount of control and flexibility, and often cannot create what it is possible to produce using a high level language—which is why many multimedia developers still rely heavily upon programmers working with high level languages.

High Sierra format: The first widely accepted standard for positioning files and directories on *CD-ROM*, this terms owes its ori-gins to the fact that it was initially conjured in the mid-eighties at a meeting of industry representatives held at the High Sierra Hotel in Lake Tahoe, Nevada.

HMD: Stands for head mounted display, one of the more noteworthy contraptions of the dawning *virtual reality* medium. This device typi-cally houses *stereoscopic glasses* and headphones and is somehow connected to power and processing sources.

Hologram: Refers to a 3-D optical image formed by storing 3-D information about an image or pattern of light. Where two beams of laser light cross, they produce an interference pattern of microscopic light and dark fringes. If this pattern is recorded, the result is a holo-gram that contains full information about the two beams that formed it.

Home interactive media: This term represents the youngest, but most rapidly growing, segment of the *multimedia* market. The home market, traditionally characterized almost solely by the video games that are computer applications disguised as entertainment, is now starting to expand into a host of other applications, such as home shopping.

Home page: An updated version of the main menu that characterized first generation software programs, this *interface design* term refers to the main point of entry into a *multimedia* program. The home page typically possesses *icons* or *buttons* representing the largest categories into which the program's content has been divided. This screen also usually serves the role of being the first and last screen the user sees when entering and exiting the program, respectively.

Home shopping: Considered one of the true prototypes of *interactive television*, this genre is already being exploited in a very successful fashion by mixing the technologies of television and telephony. With contemporary home shopping, viewers watch a visual procession of products on TV, any one of which they can order by calling the listed phone number. For future interactive versions of home shopping, it is envisioned that this shotgun type of approach will be replaced by systems that enable viewers to navigate through a *hypermedia* collection of products to view content more specifically related to their current purchasing needs.

Horizontal correlation: Also referred to as "horizontal redundancy," this term relates to the fact that with most video images there is a great deal of similarity in the *chrominance* and *luminance* qualities of horizontally adjacent *pixels*. This tendency makes it possible for broadcasters to use various forms of *compression*—for example, *RLE* (run length encoding)—to reduce the *bandwidth* requirements of their broadcasts and recordings. Simply put, horizontal correlation occurs when adjacent pixels on the same *scan line* have the same (or similar) color and brightness qualities. When this occurs, the broadcast signal can be *digitized* in such a way that only one of the values needs to be transmitted or recorded, thus reducing the effective bandwidth requirements in half for that portion of the image.

Horizontal scrolling: Occurs when the developer loads an image into memory wider than the display screen, and therefore supplies the opportunity and motivation for the user to move sideways across the image—to *pan* the image—to see what is there. A common application of horizontal scrolling occurs where the developer loads an image of a town larger than the display, and then makes it possible for the user to scroll back and forth to see the entire town, a screenful at a time.

Hot spot: From the realm of graphical user interface (*GUI*) design, a hot spot is an area of the screen that can be manipulated by the user to launch some activity, such as an on-screen action by a graphic character or by a branch to another screen. To date, most hot spots have been activated by either clicking on them with a *mouse*-driven *cursor*, or by simply touching them if the system has *touch screen* capabilities.

Household buy rates: This term, commandeered from home shopping by *interactive television* savants, describes the rate at which residential consumers make use of such pay per view cable services as *movies-on-demand*. These rates are very important to the cable operators because they determine the capacity, and therefore the investment in hardware such as *video PBXs*, required by these new services.

HRTF: Stands for head-related transfer functions, a term associated with the mathematical modeling of the various sound transformations performed by the human audio perception system. These functions are used to create 3-D acoustic pictures of sound. They are being developed by *virtual reality* engineers so that they can be used as interpretive filters that take incoming sound sources and modify them for output to headphones or speakers, such that the user hears an immersive, 3-D form of sound.

HTML: Stands for hypertext markup language. Written in *SGML* (standard generalized markup language), HTML is a specification for marking *hypertext* documents.

H.261: Also referred to as *Px64* by the *CCITT* (Consultative Committee on International Telephone and Telegraph), this is the *videoconferencing* standard for *compressing* moving video images for transmission over telephone trunk lines. Capable of very high *compression ratios*—on the order of 100:1, all the way up to 2,000:1— this is also a very *lossy compression* technique, reflecting the still primitive state of video telephony.

Hue: This refers to that dimension of color related to wavelength and the classification of the color as, say, a blue, a green, or a red.

Human-centered computing: This phrase was coined by IBM in conjunction with the development of *PowerPC* technology. The idea it conveys is a simple one: computers should be made easier to use by forcing them to conform to how humans communicate, rather than vice versa. Thus, for example, one image of future computing that has been proposed under this conception is an advanced form of graphical user interface (*GUI*) governed by an *interface agent* that possesses speech recognition and works in slave-like fashion to carry out the voice-generated wishes of its user (master?). I dream of computer genie?

Human-factors engineering: This design discipline is focused on creating optimal designs for major technologies such as automobiles, airplanes, etc. It is one of the key applications for *virtual reality* systems, wherein designers are allowed to become immersed (*CAD* [computer aided design] visualizations) in the physical environments they are creating. The primary benefit of such virtual worlds is that they reduce the need for costly prototypes and identify human-factor design flaws that might otherwise go undetected. Examples of the issues that can be addressed by such visual models include foot traffic problems, element positioning, and aesthetic concerns.

HyperCard™: Introduced in 1987 by Apple Computer, this software program is designed to facilitate the creation of hypertext and hypermedia applications. Much of the language used by Apple to describe the functionality of this program has become part of the general nomenclature of graphical user interface (*GUI*) design. Terms such as *button*, card, and stack are nearly universal among those who design and build GUI and *multimedia applications*.

Hyperfiction: This term refers to what is perhaps the most common form of work to be found in the emergent medium of *interactive fiction*. Based on the *hypertext* model of structuring information, readers cut their own paths through the narrative work. Thus, consuming a work of hyperfiction is more like browsing through an interconnected body of information than it is like starting at the beginning and moving in linear fashion to the end, as is the case with traditional fiction. It is a nonlinear, discovery experience. In searching for models to understand this new form of fiction, one is drawn to the 1978 work *Story and Discourse* by literary critic Seymour Chatman. In that book, Chatman made a distinction between two types of fiction: the first, and by far the most common, is what he terms "the resolved plot," by which he means the traditional narrative that uses rising action and climax to hold the reader's interest; the second, and much more avant-garde, form is what he termed "the revealed plot," by which he means the novel that seeks more to reveal the nature of human experience by bringing the reader close to anectdotal events that do not necessarily have to occur in any particular order. With stories told in the tradition of "the resolved plot," the order in which the events are told has everything to do with the impact of the work— one cannot tamper with its authored sequence. For stories told in the form of "the revealed plot," however, sequence is not nearly so critical. Thus, it would appear that this second type of narrative, "the revealed plot," may be the predecessor to hyperfiction and supply us with some form of design model for how these works should be constructed.

Hyperfootage: Currently, most *stock footage* houses organize their libraries with systems that combine electronic and manual elements. The indexes that point to particular clips, or film segments, are electronically encoded—are, in most cases, databases that rely upon *keyword* indexes to enable their users to find the desired footage. However, the film clips themselves are still located on tape, and the huge volume of tapes that make up the stock footage libraries are stored in vaults. Thus, the electronic indexes point not just to particular titles, but also (and perhaps more importantly) to the locations of the particular tapes within the tape vault. Fetching the tape is still a manual procedure. Though systems of this sort are today considered state-of-the-art, the day will soon come when the film footage itself will be digitized and stored on disk, thereby obviating the need for tape altogether and making access to desired film clips as easy as accessing a record in one of today's many electronic databases. When this occurs, stock footage houses will become hyperfootage houses.

Hyperlink: This term refers to the branching logic that connects pieces of related information within a *hypertext* or *hypermedia* program. Hyperlinks are typically implemented through some type of *button* or *hot spot*, both of which enable the user to click on a designated object on the screen to move instantly to the related piece of information.

Hypermedia: This term refers to a form of *information design* that is an extension of *hypertext*, incorporating other media in addition to text. One of the favored design models for multimedia titles, hypermedia permits an author to create a linked corpus of material that includes text, static graphics, animations, video, sound effects, music, voiceover annotations, etc.

Hypermedia applications: As the number of *CD-ROM* titles has exploded during the first part of this decade, hypermedia must be considered one the of the dominant design models for the wave of new media titles. Hypermedia applications are actually quite simple in design and purpose: they provide a visually coherent form of navigation through a thematically interconnected body of material, and they are predominantly exploratory in nature. Three examples of hypermedia applications are: **1) The Electronic Encyclopedia:** with much the same purpose as our voluminous, book-bound encyclopedias, the electronic version has become the early exemplar of hypermedia. Examples of these are Compton's Interactive Encyclopedia by Compton's New Media and Encarta by Microsoft. These programs provide visually oriented navigational interfaces to content that is presented using all of the mixed media data types: image, audio, video, and, of course, good ol' text. **2) The Online Museum (also called a Curator's File):** if you change your normal perceptions a bit, and think of a museum as a physically-embodied database of human artwork, then you will see in an instant why hypermedia is such an ideal design model for bringing the hard-to-reach museum into your home. Many such products use the physical structure of the museum as the interface, permitting the user to view its contents by walking the halls, so to speak. In this regard, the online museum illustrates the overlap between the *surrogate travel* and hypermedia models of *multimedia application*. **3) The Electronic Marketing Brochure:** increasingly, corporations are moving in the direction of building hypermedia programs to serve as powerful marketing information aids. These programs will typically array the company's products, people, and/or services in a thematically oriented fashion, thereby enabling a salesperson or a potential customer to move through the content to find whatever is of interest at the moment. A real estate firm, for example, might have two dominant paths, one that takes the user to visual treatments of their prime properties, and a second that introduces key executives and salespeople. Many such brochures can be given the auto-run logic to flow automatically through selected portions of their content so that they can be used at trade shows and the like. When they follow this approach, with little or no interaction by the user, they become what is referred to as a *rolling demo*.

Hypertext: In the early 1960s, Theodor Nelson coined this word to describe the idea of nonsequential writing. A hypertext system is one that allows authors or groups of authors to link information together, create paths through a corpus of related material, annotate existing texts, and create notes that point readers to either bibliographic data or the body of the referenced text. In essence, a hypertext system is a tool for creating or following associative trains of thought through a document or body of documents. Hypertext is a powerful tool for exploring large bodies of interrelated documents in areas of expertise or of interest to the user. Hypertext has played an instrumental role in the emergent discipline of *interface design*, because many of the principles of this discipline have been created by individuals and teams constructing various hypertext authoring and viewing systems.

And, as imagination bodies forth
The forms of things unknown, the poets pen
Turns them to shapes, and gives to airy nothing
A local habitation and a name.
—William Shakespeare, Midsummer Night's Dream

ICAI: Stands for intelligent computer assisted instruction and refers to forms of interactive computer based training that possess elements of *artificial intelligence.*

Icon: Is a stylized image that graphically conveys purpose or function in graphical user interface (*GUI*) design.

Iconic authoring: This term refers to the category of authoring conducted on the type of *authoring systems* that rely primarily on the manipulation of icons to produce *multimedia* creations. The most popular icons in the world of multimedia authoring are those associated with the flowcharting conventions of software programming. Thus, when individuals perform iconic authoring, they do so by manipulating the sequences and interrelationships between flowchart symbols, typically enacted by dragging the symbols to appropriate positions on the screen. Two popular commercial authoring systems that rely upon an iconic interface are Authorware Professional by Macromedia and IconAuthor by AimTech.

Idea map: From the world of *multimedia application* design, this term refers to a type of document that some design methodologies insist should be created near the front end of a development cycle. It provides an overview of a project's proposed content by displaying links between the major conceptual components.

IFF: Stands for interchange file format, which is a file format standard first developed by Electronic Arts for the Commodore Amiga. It was designed to allow different programs to share a common file format. It works by propounding header information to the file, which describes the amount and layout of the data.

IGES: Stands for initial graphics exchange specification, a standard file format used to represent data in the *CAD* (computer aided design) industry.

IICS: Stands for International Interactive Communication Society, a professional organization charged with promoting the exchange of ideas and opportunities between individuals involved in the *interactive multimedia* marketplace. As an example of the types of activities sponsored by IICS, the San Francisco chapter recently worked to get the city of San Francisco to pass legislation that would ensure future investments in the infrastructure needed to support multimedia development, e.g., local sources of high *bandwidth* transmission facilities.

IID: Stands for interaural intensity differences, a highly technical term that visits us from the land of *3-D sound*. IID is one of the key *HRTF*s (head-related transfer functions) and is based on the fact that sound which originates to one side of the head (as opposed to coming from directly in front or behind) will be received as louder by the ear that faces the sound source. Also referred to as the "head shadowing effect," this phenomenon has become a key element in *virtual reality* systems that seek to create a consistent sense of sound sources, even while the participant is moving around in the virtual environment.

Illustrator: Often compared with the role of *art director*, the illustrator on a multimedia development project is the person responsible for creating the artwork. An illustrator would, for example, be responsible for drawing the icons that go on *buttons* or that serve as *hyperlinks*. Some illustrators are good art directors, but more often the two roles are performed by separate people. The art director develops the visual design of a multimedia product, while the illustrator is responsible for executing the art director's vision.

IMA: Stands for the Interactive Multimedia Association, an international trade association based in Washington, DC. "The purpose of IMA is to promote the benefits of multimedia technology; advance the growth of the industry through public education; develop specifications for hardware, software tools, and applications; develop industry-wide services; and provide government and media relations." Founded in 1987, the IMA's most interesting project to date is its "Cross-Platform Compatibility Project," which seeks to establish industry-wide standards that enable *multimedia applications'* portability across different hardware platforms.

Image-enabled database: As we enter the era of multimedia, one of the first things to do is to enhance our existing database records with all sorts of *mixed media data types*, especially those that are in the form of *digital images*. This term labels that process. Many organizations today are, for example, adding document images of actual invoices to their accounts payable records, *digitized* images of resumes and pictures to their personnel records, and images of correspondence to their customer files. These visual sources add valuable information to the traditional database record, which historically has been based solely on alphanumeric forms of data.

Image extraction: From the realm of *virtual reality*, this term refers to the high end of *position tracking* systems, whereby video cameras are teamed with visual recognition systems to keep track of the location of virtual reality participants in their virtual environments.

Image processing: This term most generally refers to the science of interpreting *digital* images by using computers and computer graphics techniques. The discipline originated in the relatively specialized area that deals with processing data acquired by remote sensing devices placed aboard satellites or other spacecraft. With the onset of multimedia technology, the fruits of this discipline are finding wider usage throughout the computer industry.

Imaging systems: One of the meat-and-potatoes activities of early *multimedia applications* will be that of converting our mass document storage standard from microfiche and microfilm to the eminently more useful—because it is more accessible—medium of *optical storage*. The manufacturing process for achieving this new standard goes by the name "imaging system." With such a system, paper documents are passed through a scanner, which *digitizes* the document, to create a *bit-mapped* image of it. Sometime during the process, the bit-mapped image is assigned keywords. The purpose of the *keywords* is to index the document, making it electronically retrievable. The primary problem with this approach to mass document storage is that the contents of the documents are in a bit-mapped form, and therefore are not themselves searchable. Only the keywords assigned to each image are in *ASCII* (text) format. Thus, the process of assigning keywords must anticipate all of the ways in which future users might wish to search the document base. In other words, all content of a given document **not** represented by the keywords become the textual equivalent of a lost treasure.

IMAX Theatre™: These theme park establishments use large-format motion-picture film and huge parabolic, metallic projection screens. They seek to achieve a vivid 3-D, almost holographic, panoramic realism for audiences. IMAX has become synonymous with the concept of creating a wrap-around or surround environment for entertainment purposes.

Inbetweener: With traditional animation, this term refers to a job role wherein a person is given the responsibility of producing in-between drawings, thereby creating, for example, the sense of a character's motion between a beginning and ending posture. Many of the *paint systems* now provide functions for automating this activity.

Indeo™: A software version of Intel's *DVI compression-decompression* standard, it is delivered in conjunction with *VFW* (Video for Windows). It is *scalable*, compatible across platforms, and compressible in *real time*.

Infomercials: You know 'em when you flip past 'em on the dial: this relatively recent form of television advertising is characterized by a relatively long duration—commonly running up to a half-hour in length—and by a relatively high proportion of in-depth information, often purporting to be scientific in nature. Many media futurists believe that this form of advertising is a prototype of what will be available en masse on the *information superhighway*.

Information design: This field of communications design exploits the online reference and presentation power of the computer to access and show information to the user in discrete, defined units visually segmented and organized so that information is easy to understand and use.

Information designer: An information designer is a professional technical communicator skilled in the methods, techniques, and tools of information design. It is worthy to note that an information designer is capable of working with various forms of *hypermedia applications* and platforms.

Information superhighway: This is a phrase coined by the Clinton administration to refer to the emerging national communications network—the *NII* (National Information Infrastructure)—which will enable an ever increasing level of communications of every sort: data communications, personal communications, and, of course, *multimedia* communications. Most industry analysts believe that the *Internet* is the prototype and origin of the information superhighway.

Information visualizers: A relatively new advance in user *interface design* under development at *Xerox PARC*, this technology strives to take traditional alphanumeric forms of data and convert them into 3-D objects that the user can interact with in ways that are perceptually familiar. With visualizers, it is hoped that users can see their information, touch it, and rearrange it, thereby achieving a deeper, almost tactile, understanding of its structure.

Instruction cache: From the realm of processor design, this term refers to a specialized type of *cache* featured on some microprocessors that enables faster execution by storing frequently used instructions in a form of memory that is physically adjacent to the *CPU*.

Instructional design: This field of communications design exploits the instructional power of the computer. The emergence of instructional design can be directly attributed to the convergence of media and computing.

Instructional designer: An instructional designer is responsible for designing interactive forms of *CBT* (computer based training) and *multimedia applications*. An instructional designer, for example, works with end users to decompose knowledge and tasks into their constituent concepts, skills, and procedural steps, and then use that information to design appropriate forms of programmed instruction. It is worthy to note that an instructional designer are capable of working with various forms of multimedia applications and platforms, including first generation CBT.

Instructional technology: In many respects, this term now has the same expansive meaning to the world of education that the term *multimedia* has taken on with regard to the world of commerce. Instructional technology is an umbrella term that refers to any technology used for training and education. In the literal sense, then, a chalkboard represents an instructional technology. However, when used in the school market, this term generally refers to the burgeoning supply of hardware and software solutions now crowding their way into our schools.

Intellectual property: One of the most explosive topics of the information age, this is an umbrella term for the ownership rights that individuals have when they can demonstrate that they have added value to an information product. Actors in a film, composers of music, programmers of software, and *art directors* of *multimedia* interfaces are all examples of individuals who thusly add value. Their recourse for recording and protecting their rights in this respect are embodied in the laws of copyright, trademark, or patents, or some combination of these. With most multimedia products, because many of the markets are still small and/or poorly defined, the entity that pays for building the product will usually be forced to induce the development talent to sign nondisclosure agreements, most of which contain work-for-hire provisions which transfer all of the ownership rights to that sponsoring entity. Where royalty payments are contemplated, a potential thicket of problems awaits, because *digital* media assets are so fungible, so readily subjected to electronic forms of *cut and paste*, that downstream use of those assets will be nearly impossible to track. *Stock footage* houses and purveyors of *clip media* have a partial solution to this problem, in that they handle all of the royalty arrangements for the various artists, and relieve users of any worry about usage fees beyond those that are embedded in the purchase price—unless, of course, they willingly give those media assets to others, who use them for economic purposes without paying any purchase price. Expect intellectual property to be a bonanza for the legal profession in the age of multimedia.

Intelligence augmentation: One of the goals of all communications media, but especially appropriate in the age of multimedia, this term refers to the general objective of using computer media to increase the capability of people to conceptualize, approach, and gain solutions to complex problems.

Intelligent job aid: Often thought of as an ingredient in *performance support systems*, intelligent job aids are *granular multimedia applications* designed to lead a learner through an interactive training session to solve a specific type of job-related, procedural problem.

Intelligent tutoring system: This is an *expert system* whose domain of expertise is instruction. Such systems usually contain an expert system relevant to the subject domain the tutoring system is teaching about. The objective of an intelligent tutor is to enable a machine to process both the concept to be taught and how best to present that concept to the student.

Interactive cinema: This term refers to an interactive form of entertainment that is most closely related to film. While both *interactive fiction* and *interactive television* have abundant prototypes on the market, interactive cinema is very, very early in its evolution. However, it is worthwhile to note that the New York Film Festival has been offering awards in an interactive category for several years now.

Interactive document: This is a document whose content or sequence of presentation can be altered through direct intervention by the reader at the time of reading.

Interactive fiction: Considered by many to be the next major transformation of our storytelling tradition, interactive fiction refers to the convergence of *interactivity* and narration. Interactive fictions are stories with branchpoints, contingent subplots, alternate outcomes, and the like. As the various genres of interactive entertainment take shape, interactive fiction will be seen primarily as text-based content, whereas *interactive cinema* and *interactive television* will be viewed as the interactive forms that make use of high-end media such as full motion video. In many respects, then, interactive fiction stands in the same relationship to interactive cinema that *hypertext* stands with regard to *hypermedia*. Still in its embryonic stages, interactive fiction has explosive potential as a new medium, perhaps on par with modern film.

Interactive multimedia: *Multimedia applications* are not necessarily interactive. For example, a *rolling demo* has all the characteristics that we are coming to associate with multimedia—audio, image, and possibly video, all running on a computer—but, by design, possesses little or no *interactivity*. Thus, because there are some forms of multimedia that are **not** interactive, it is considered by some to be a worthwhile exercise in language to designate those forms that are.

Interactive television: Most media industry futurists agree that this is the inevitable near-term destiny of home entertainment: a single device that merges the capabilities of the computer and the television. Also referred to as the *smart TV*, this device will make it possible for users to do such things as temporarily store films that they have downloaded from libraries supplied by public media services; play interactive games on their televisions, without the special attachments required by today's games such as Sega Genesis; and create, edit, and store one's own personal video productions.

Interactivity: The defining characteristic of the emerging forms of education and entertainment associated with *multimedia applications* and *hypermedia applications*, this term refers to the ability of users to communicate directly with the computer and have consequential impact on whatever message is being created.

Interface: Taken in its most general sense, this term refers to a shared boundary. In computing, the term refers to the boundary between two subsystems or two devices. In this more specialized context, the term refers to the device (called the interface) that matches these parts of the system.

Interface agent: Can be defined as a character, enacted by the computer, who acts on behalf of the user in a virtual (computer based) environment. The use of interface agents implies an authorial effort to create computer based personae and, through their use, to heighten the naturalness of the interface, both in terms of cognitive accessibility and communication style. Obviously, the fuller implementation of this *interface design* strategy waits on further advances in the field of *artificial intelligence* known as *natural language processing*, which seeks to imbue computers with the ability to speak on a human, conversational level. This term is roughly synonymous with "interactive agent."

Interface design: Also referred to as human interface design or human-computer interface design, this intellectual pursuit is rapidly ascending to the status of an academic discipline. As the term implies, it has to do with designing computer interfaces that make computers easier to use. Originally focused on issues having to do with screen design—e.g., the desktop metaphor that drives the Apple Macintosh and Microsoft *Windows* interfaces—the discipline is rapidly extending itself to include all issues having to do with the input and output of information to and from the computer. In essence, interface design has to do with human-computer communications. With the advent of *mixed media data types*, that is to say, with the coming of *multimedia* and its progression into the marketplace, the potential for extending the purview of this nascent discipline would appear to be virtually without limit. Expect colleges and universities to be acknowledging the legitimacy of this academic pursuit over the next decade by creating subdisciplines or even entirely new departments.

Interface paradigm: One of the truly **big** terms in the industry, it refers to the dominant metaphor that people encounter when interacting with the operating environment of their computer. With both the Apple Macintosh and the Microsoft *Windows* environments, the dominant metaphor has long been the desktop. The designers of these highly similar interfaces have tried to represent all of the objects with appropriate metaphors from the common office environment. For example, files are represented as file folders, and, in the Apple Macintosh environment, there is the well-known image of the trash can, which is used to delete files. Many industry analysts believe that we will soon be ready for a new dominant metaphor, a new interface paradigm. Some of the early candidates are the *personal newspaper*, which would deliver information tailored to the individual's needs in a prioritized format similar to the headline-and-column structure of the newspaper; the geographic information system (GIS), which would give all information items a geographic location—as they actually have in the real world—and permit the user to *pan* and *zoom* to get about to the desired locations in geographic space; and, the 3-D building, which is actually an enlargement of the desktop metaphor that would provide a more variegated set of sub-metaphors with which to access much larger knowledge bases.

Interframe codec: A form of video *compression-decompression* that works on the basis of eliminating the redundant components that occur between (as opposed to within) *frames*. To date, these are the most powerful forms of *codec*, achieving *compression ratios* on the order of 50:1 on up to 200:1. The *MPEG* (Motion Picture Experts Group) standard codec is an interframe technology, and works by, basically, looking forwards and backwards in a video stream and then recording only the information that changes during a given segment. Interframe codecs are said to be *asymmetrical*, because it is much more time-consuming and expensive to encode (*compress*) the video stream than it is to decode (*decompress*) it. This owes to the enormous computational resources that must be expended to define the various visual patterns in a video sequence in terms of their degree of change. Interframe technologies are often compared with the less powerful, but also less expensive, *intraframe* techniques, which lie at the core of today's most popular codec standards, such as *JPEG* (Joint Photography Experts Group).

Interlaced video: The way a standard television picture is created, interlaced video is a technique that can be described as follows: a television picture is drawn onto the picture tube by one or more electron guns, which fire a stream of electrons at the face of the tube one horizontal line at a time. The horizontal lines that make up the arrays of *pixels* that comprise the TV screen are referred to as *scan lines*. The electron gun draws all the even lines first, then goes back to the top of the screen and draws the odd lines. This alternating process is what is known as interlaced video.

Interleaving: This term refers to a technical strategy for laying down *mixed media data types* on storage media, particularly on *CD-*

ROM. With interleaving, as the term implies, one type of information is "interleaved" with another, so that the two types can be physically close to one another on the storage device. The most common example occurs with *digital* video and audio data types, each of which has its own unique format and therefore must be stored as separate files. They are often interleaved when they are laid down on CD-ROM because this storage strategy makes it easier to synchronize the picture and sound—as, for example, when *lipsynching*. This strategy is made necessary by the fact that *transfer rates* on most digital storage devices (especially CD-ROM) are still relatively slow when compared against the demand to load both types into computer memory so that they may be played in synchronization.

Internet: The successor of an experimental network built by the U.S. Department of Defense in the 1960s, this communications system links at least three million computers. A good portion of the connections belong to universities and research and development organizations. Today, many users connect to the Internet by phone (*modem*) to share information or tap into many rich data banks. Also known affectionately by Internet users as "The Net."

Interoperability: This polysyllabic tongue-twister simply refers to the system design feature wherewith a system can operate on several different computer hardware *platforms*.

Interpolation: Used in its most general sense, this term refers to the process of introducing or inserting additional values between the existing values in a series. The process is used frequently in computer graphics, especially in color shading and various *codec* techniques. In a more specific sense, this term is now used to describe any form of *motion compensation* (i.e., temporal codec) in which a *frame* is constructed during *decompression* based upon the difference in information between the original frame (which is determined during the *compression* process) and both its previous and subsequent *key frames*. This process is also known as forward and backward *prediction*, and tends to be a very expensive, *CPU*-intensive process that requires *off-line compression* using mainframe computers.

Interprocessor communications: This term refers to data communications that occur between two processors within the same computing system. The integration of *DSP*s (digital signal processors) into the personal computer to handle the onerous processing requirements of the various media types has made the issue of interprocessor communications of particular importance to *multimedia* computing. The future of media-oriented, interprocessor communications seems to be headed toward the use of specialized operating systems (such as Spectrum Microsystems' SPOX) designed to handle the personal computer-DSP connection. Over time, these programming efforts—and the interprocessor communications they make possible—will make it increasingly easy to add new media capabilities (e.g., *voice recognition*) to the personal computer.

Interrupt: From the world of software engineering, an interrupt is a procedure whereby a program that is currently running on a computer is temporarily suspended so that the *CPU* can devote its time to process another program that has been determined to be of higher priority. It is sort of like relaxing in a colleague's office and then being summoned by a superior—the process of relaxing becomes interrupted by the higher priority task of making a living.

Interrupt-driven: This is a software structure that uses *interrupts* to determine what tasks can run and/or be given control of the *CPU*.

Intraframe codec: This is a form of video *compression-decompression* technology that works by eliminating redundant information within the frames that make up a video sequence. The very popular *Motion-JPEG* standard is based on intraframe and achieves *compression ratios* in the range of 20:1 up to 50:1. Intraframe technologies are often compared to the more powerful *interframe codecs*, such as *MPEG* (Motion Picture Experts Group). The interframe techniques are much more expensive because they are asymmetrical, requiring powerful computers (mainframes) to perform the encoding process. In contrast, most of the intraframe codecs can be done in *real time*, i.e., on the fly.

I/O: One of the earliest, and still most standard, of computer acronyms, I/O stands for input/output. It represents a most fundamental truth about computers, which is that they cannot survive as closed systems, but rather must somehow receive input from the world, and, through the magic of digital processing and the programmer's intervention, provide useful output. Traditional I/O devices include the keyboard and mouse for input and the monitor for output. As we sail into the age of multimedia, I/O devices will become increasingly oriented toward the *mixed media data types* of image, graphics, animation, audio, and video.

Iridium Project: One of the major new telecommunication developments of the 1990s, this project is being carried forward by Motorola and involves the development of a system of small satellites that operate in low Earth orbit, providing worldwide personal communications services. It also complements existing systems by providing telephone service where it does not exist today.

IRIS: Stands for Institute for Research on Information Systems, an organization located at Brown University in Providence, Rhode Island, that has been responsible for much of the groundbreaking research of *hypertext* systems and graphical user interface (*GUI*) design.

Iris out: Is a special video effect in which a series of masks containing circles of diminishing size obliterates the action.

ISA Bus: The ISA stands for industry standard architecture, and the term represents one of the foremost bottlenecks in the computer industry today. The ISA bus problem is particularly acute with *mixed media data types*, like digital video, and owes its origins to the one of the most common of all problems associated with computing: functional obsolescence. Designed during the initial generations of personal computers, the ISA bus is basically the expansion bus on a PC into which users plug *expansion boards* for purposes such as attaching peripheral devices (a *CD-ROM* player, for example) or enhancing machine performance (e.g., *accelerator boards*). Inasmuch as it was designed during the era of alphanumeric computing, the ISA bus has a very limited *bandwidth*, only 8 MHz or so. When trying to accommodate *multimedia applications*, such as *digital* video or *compound documents*, the ISA bus simply gets clogged up, creating a major performance problem. One of the most common responses to this problem today is the *local bus* solution, which bypasses the ISA bus, routing data through the bus that is attached to the computer's *CPU*.

ISDN: Stands for integrated services digital network, an end-to-end digital service that is standardized throughout the world. Among other accomplishments, ISDN may help do away with most (if not all) forms of *analog* transmission, which today is demanded by the (twisted pair) copper wire, *last-mile loop* of the telephone network. You might think of ISDN as a digital socket on the wall, just like the electric power socket, that transmits and accepts digital streams of bits. ISDN could be a kind of universal service for digital forms of information. Owing to its much greater *bandwidth* capabilities (carrying capacity), ISDN may become the transmission network for a variety of *interactive multimedia* services.

ISO: Stands for the International Standards Organization, a group composed of the national standards organizations of its member countries. As the name implies, the ISO seeks to establish worldwide quality standards. The ISO has defined standards for data communications, most notably, the ISO model for *OSI* (Open System Interconnections).

Isochronous distribution: From the challenging world of networked video, this term refers to *digital* forms of audio and video that are guaranteed to arrive at the same time. It is a strategy for networking video that separates the audio and video channels from other data transmissions to avoid the interference that leads to errors and a lack of synchronization.

ITD: Stands for interaural time differences, a technical term that comes to us courtesy of the rapidly advancing world of *3-D sound*. ITD is one of the key *HRTF*s (head-related transfer functions) and refers to the obvious fact that sound which originates from one side of the head (as opposed to coming from directly in front of or behind the head) will reach the listener's ear facing the sound source. ITD is used to perceive sound direction and has become a critical element of efforts to create realistic sound environments in *virtual reality* systems where the participants are permitted to move around, thus changing the orientation of their heads.

IVD: Stands for interactive video disc, and is a term that, historically, has become associated with a particular *platform strategy* for delivering interactive video. It refers to a *platform* that combines a personal computer with a *laserdisc*. As such, it also refers to the first generation of interactive video platform. Most industry experts believe that the laserdisc is destined for technological extinction and that *CD-ROM*, or some other type of all-digital media, will come to replace it for delivering interactive video.

Silicon Valley is about entrepreneurship, making bets, taking risks. Hollywood is about playing the field, taking your 10%.

—Hollywood executive, commenting on the clash of cultures taking shape with the advent of multimedia technology

Jaggies: This slang term refers to *aliasing*, perhaps the most widely recognized *artifact* of *digital* media. This distorting effect is most evident on low *resolution* displays, where the outlines of objects take on a jagged appearance that silhouettes the square shapes of the *pixels* that form their boundaries with the rest of the image. In a low resolution picture of a mountain range, for example, the edge between the mountains and the sky is apt to appear jagged as a result of possessing this artifact.

JBIG: Stands for Joint Bi-Level Image Experts Group; this standards organization is related to, though much less well known than, *JPEG* (Joint Photography Experts Group) and *MPEG* (Motion Picture Experts Group). It was formed to address issues related to compressing "one-bit," bilevel, black-and-white-images such as a fax machine might send or a digital *scanner* might create from a page containing black text on white paper. The standards that emerge from this group will serve the industry segment focused on the convergence of fax, copier, and laser print technologies.

JFIF: Stands for *JPEG* File Interchange Format, an image file format based on the *JPEG* (Joint Photography Experts Group) standard for *compression* and *decompression* of images.

Job aids: From the world of *instructional design* and *CBT* (computer based training), these are relatively small, *granular* devices designed to prompt user performance relative to specific, job-related tasks. An *instructional designer* may develop job aids, also known as quick-reference aids, to avoid the time and expense required to develop memorized responses.

Joystick: This remote control device for a computer, which looks and operates much like the gearshift for a car, is often used in video and arcade games. As *home interactive media* come of age, variations on the joystick, such as *CD-I*'s so-called "thumbstick," are apt to become increasingly popular.

JPEG: Stands for Joint Photography Experts Group and has come to be synonymous with the *compression* standard for still images devised by the same organization. This compression technique relies upon *DCT* (discrete cosine transformation), as do many of the other most common *codecs* (e.g., *MPEG* [Motion Picture Experts Group] and *H.261*). JPEG is an *intraframe*, as distinct from an *interframe*, codec, meaning that it deals with compressing single frame sources of content, rather than motion picture sources. While the actual compression achieved depends on the frequency content (or colors) of the compressed image, *compression ratios* in the vicinity of 20:1 are typical for JPEG encoding.

Juke box: This is an increasingly prominent form of mass storage device often used for *image processing* systems, wherein multiple CDs or digital tapes are held in separate slots on a carousel or elevator type of container, with individual storage units being brought under the read head by some form of robotic device as the information it contains is requested by users. In today's market, it is not uncommon for this form of *near-line storage* device to have as much as one *terabyte* of storage capacity. Even with systems this large, access times do not typically exceed 10–100 seconds.

Jump cut: From the world of film and video, this term refers to *edit points* between camera *shots* that change the scene of action either between extremely different or extremely similar shots.

*Somewhere in my education I was misled to believe
that science fiction and science fact must be kept
rigorously separate. In practice they are so blurred
together they are practically one intellectual activity,
although the results are published differently, one kind
of journal for careful scientific reporting, another kind
for wicked speculation.*
—*Stewart Brand, Author of* **The Media Lab**

Kaleida Labs: Established in 1991, this joint venture of computer giants IBM and Apple was created to execute the mission of developing standards for *multimedia* products that span the personal computer, consumer electronics, and communications industries.

Karaoke: Now one of the more popular applications for musically oriented *CD-ROM* titles, this term refers to any entertainment product whose primary purpose is that of inspiring the audience to sing along. The better systems, which might be found on videotapes, *laserdiscs*, or, of course, CD-ROM, display the lyrics, as well as possibly even graphics and/or video clips.

Key frame: A term used in conjunction with *motion compensation* forms of video *compression*, a key frame is a base *frame* that has not been temporally compressed, but rather serves as a base against which the change, or delta, elements of subsequent frames are measured.

Key grip: From the world of film production, this term refers to the individual who manages the *grips*, who are the people responsible for moving equipment, props, costumes, and the like.

Keywords: With regard to *hypertext* systems, keywords represent a subclass of *link* where a word is highlighted, or in some way denoted as special. By clicking on that word, the user is taken to an item of information associated with it. The most common example occurs where clicking on a keyword opens a text window in which that word is given a dictionary-style definition. However, keywords are used for many other purposes, especially those related to connecting (linking) one document section with a related section of another document. A prime example of this is where clicking on a name keyword takes one to biographical information about the named person located at some other place within the hypertext system. Keyword is a term also frequently used in the related area of *text search and re-*

trieval, where it refers to terms that are drawn from a document owing to their assessed value for characterizing or summarizing the overall content of the document. In this search and retrieval context, keywords are placed in some form of header record offered up to the search engine as a more compressed, and therefore more efficient, item to be scanned for matching the document's content against the user's interests.

Kiosk: One of the major early applications for *interactive multimedia*, kiosks make use of multimedia technology by encasing the necessary delivery platform in some sort of architectural structure. Typically deployed in stand-alone fashion, i.e., without any human accompaniment, most kiosks hide everything from the user but the computer screen and employ *touch screen* technology to enable interaction with their programs. The building or campus directory is a typical example of how kiosks are used.

Kinesthesia: This is the sensation of movement or strain in muscles, tendons, or joints. This physical sensation is the goal of most of the *high-intensity amusement attractions*.

Kludge: This is a slang term for an awkward and unsophisticated implementation of technology. Early interactive video workstations were, for example, often patched together by joining incompatible devices never intended for such use. Walks through early computer trade shows (circa the early 1980s) would typically yield for the acute listener frequent grumblings about what "kludgey" systems these interactive video workstations were.

Knowledge engineering: This is the art of building *expert systems* by working with subject matter experts to codify their knowledge.

*. . . there is so much worthless information available to
each of us that intelligent pre-sorting of it, whether
performed by people or by a machine, is an
increasingly critical service.*

—W.R. Johnson, Jr.,
VP, Telecommunication and Networks,
Digital Equipment Corporation

Ladder of challenge: A concept stolen from the world of academe, this term refers to a common gaming strategy whereby as soon
as a player masters the challenges presented by a game at one level,
the gaming logic automatically upgrades the difficulties of the challenge to a new and heightened level. The purpose of this logic, of
course, is to sustain interest and induce the player (also covetously
viewed as a consumer) to stay with the present game, rather than
moving onto that of a competitor. Fortunately, this concept has also
been extended into the realm of *educational software*, where it is used
to produce what are called "adaptive learning systems," which are
programs that attempt to match the level of academic difficulty to the
learner's demonstrated level of skill and knowledge.

LAN: Stands for local area network, a widely used term which refers
to data communications networks that span a physically limited geographic area (less than 10 km); are implemented using some type of
switching capability and high *bandwidth* communications on a relatively inexpensive medium such as coaxial cable; and are owned by
the user, as opposed to using public (e.g., *public switched telephone
network*) communications facilities. With the onset of *multimedia*, a
great deal of pressure is being placed on the LAN producer community to add both greater transmission bandwidth and greater central
(server) storage capacity.

Laser: One of the dominant technologies of the information age, a
laser is a device that generates light in which all of the photons are
exactly in step and produce a coherent beam. Laser light has one
wavelength and is more easily controlled than other kinds of light.

Last-mile loop: This term refers to the *transmission media* that
make up the final segments of the telephone and TV networks, i.e.,
those low *bandwidth* segments that actually connect the global and
national networks to our homes. For a long time, the last-mile loop
has been viewed as a prohibitive bottleneck with respect to deliver-

ing high bandwidth, high-quality media services such as *picturephone* and *movies-on-demand* into the home. In the phone system, the bottleneck is that last bit of copper wiring that connects the *Public Switched Telephone Network* to our residences. With regard to cable TV, the last-mile roadblocks are the long cascades of amplifiers that run from the cable company's transmission headquarters to the home, boosting the signal every quarter-mile or so, and frequently introducing all sorts of electronic *noise*. Traditionally, media futurists have believed that it would take a massive investment in residential *fiber optic* connections to make the likes of point-to-point interactive video and *HDTV* (high definition television) possible. However, recent innovations in *compression* technology have paved the way for possibly using the existing stock of last-mile media to carry at least the first generation of *home interactive media* into our living rooms.

Large format scanner: This is a type of *scanner* used for scanning engineering drawings and other large documents too big for standard *sheetfed* and *flatbed* scanners.

Laserdisc: This term refers to a form of *optical storage* that is very much on the wane. Most industry critics believe that it is being replaced gradually by *CD-ROM* technology. Like CD-ROM, laserdisc stores information in an optical format, i.e., one that relies on patterns of *pits and lans* burned into the disc surface, and that is read by a head that is sensitive to the reflectance values that occur when a laser beam is bounced off of that storage surface. Unlike CD-ROM, which employs an all-*digital* format, laserdisc stores its information in an *analog* format. Hence, laserdisc is not nearly as compatible with the computer environment as is CD-ROM.

Latency: With reference to *virtual reality* (*VR*), this is a measure of the time between when a person moves in a virtual world and when the computer governing the virtual world registers that movement. In systems that are primarily visual—as most VR systems are today—this term is closely associated with *frame refresh rates*. Obviously, the key to success in displaying the computer-generated imagery that these systems rely upon is low latency and high frame refresh rates.

LBE: Stands for location based entertainment, which is the primary use of *surrogate travel* technologies for entertainment purposes. This term is now being applied to the theme park uses of surrogate travel, such as those embodied in virtual rides and *IMAX Theatres*.

LCD: Stands for liquid crystal display, a rapidly evolving form of computer display. LCDs are popular with users and manufacturers of small machines owing to their low power demands and light weight. LCDs differ significantly from *CRT*s (cathode ray tubes), the most common form of video playback device, because they are light modifiers, or valves, rather than light producers. They typically consist of two small panes of glass, between which are a vast array of cells, also referred to as *pixels*, which contain a liquid crystal substance. When no electrical current is sent to an LCD pixel, the crystals are oriented in a particular direction, blocking light from passing through and thereby causing that pixel to remain dark. When a small electrical current is sent to a cell, the crystal's orientation is altered, allowing light to pass. The patterns formed by these electrically manipulated pixels are what create the images we see on an LCD screen.

Learning styles: From the world of learning theory—and, more recently, from *instructional design*—this term is used to describe a classification scheme that is based on the realization that people learn in widely varying ways. One group of people may learn better, for example, by working through related tasks with other people, while others may be better able to master the same content by reading from an instruction manual in solitude. Some people learn more from what they hear, while others excel in learning from what they see. Being able to determine learning styles by observing learners using a particular piece of *educational software* is one of the more ambitious goals of contemporary *instructional design*. Progress in this area of research will serve the larger goal of individualizing *multimedia* content relative to the specific needs of the user.

LED: Stands for light-emitting diode, a device used widely for a broad number of applications in the world of computing and electronics. LEDs are basically transmission devices, in that they emit pulses of light energy in response to various sorts of stimuli. They are usually coupled with *photosensors*, which serve to convert light energy to electrical energy to be used, for example, to create the logical, *digital* patterns of computing devices.

Levels I-IV: Refers to levels of interactive *videodisc*; see *Videodisc levels*.

Life quality: As Walt Disney was pushing the world of cartoon *animation* to new levels of quality with his feature films (e.g., *Snow White and the Seven Dwarfs*), this term emerged in the press to describe the effect his obsession with realism and detail had on audiences (and critics). For example, he was reputed to have sent all of his animators through seminars and coursework in animal anatomy in advance of the making of *Bambi.*

Light pen: This handheld device detects light emitted by elements comprising the picture on the screen. It can, for example, detect the presence of lines or points.

Linear: As in "linear video," this term refers to the dominant mode for producing media for at least the last several centuries. In fact, not since the oral storytelling tradition waned as our primary mode of delivering socially sanctioned stories has the linear tradition received any considerable threat to its hegemony. However, with the apparent imminence of *interactive* media, that unchallenged dominion is now in doubt—and the implications are potentially staggering. To understand these implications it is necessary to examine the ingrained habits of mind that dictate the behaviors of those who produce linear media. For example, with linear, all *segue*, or branching, decisions— such as what scene follows another, or when a particular scene should end and its successor begin—are left entirely under the author's (director's) control. With interactive, most of these branching decisions are transferred to the user, who now becomes a participant in a medium that can be characterized as a form of shared authorship. The **big** question that is raised by this impending challenge to linear media is just this: will the same people who have made a living (a fortune, actually) making linear media be well suited to producing interactive? Think about it.

Line driver: From the world of *data communications*, this term refers to a signal converter that conditions a signal to ensure reliable transmission over an extended distance.

Line level inputs: From the world of audio production, this term refers to inputs made to a recording device that originate from another electronic source, such as a tape deck, VCR, or CD player. This form of input is often contrasted with *microphone level inputs*, which originate from natural sources and, as the name implies, are captured to electronic storage through a microphone.

Line segment: In *vector* graphics, this term refers to the portion of a line bounded by *endpoints.*

Link: With regard to *hypertext*, this term has a quite specific meaning. It refers to an *icon*, or other visible *hot spot*, that makes a connection between one location in a hypertext system and another location. Links are based on some sort of association between the origin and the destination. The icon that denotes a link is usually styled to represent the conceptual basis of that connection. For example, in a geographic portion of a hypertext system, a magnifying glass icon might be used to indicate the availability of a *zoom* link, i.e., a link that shows some portion of a map in greater detail.

Linked list: Is a data structure in which each element points to the next element.

Lipsynch: From the earliest days of film and TV, lipsynch refers to the synchronization of lip movements on screen with the vocal sounds of the soundtrack. Lipsynching confronts a renewed challenge in the world of *digital video*, where techniques such as the *interleaving* of voice and image on *disk* must be used in order for the computer to access these two disparate, memory-hungry forms of data quickly enough and in close enough proximity to one another to achieve the desired synchronization effect.

Local bus: From the world of processor design, this term refers to an emerging tweak of standard personal computer architectures designed to speed the processing of the massive amounts of data that accompany *multimedia applications*. A number of local bus designs have come to the market in an effort to address the processing demands of multimedia technology, the two most dominant to date being *VESA*'s (Video Electronics Standards Association) *VL-bus* and Intel's *PCI* (Peripheral Component Interconnect). Local bus circuitry speeds the processing of media-intensive data types by transferring data directly to the system processor using a broader data path so that faster throughput can be achieved than on the traditional system bus of PCs (e.g., the 16-bit *ISA bus*). In all likelihood, the local bus will be remembered as a momentary annoyance and minor footnote in the computer's transformation from being just a computational machine to being an *interactive multimedia* machine.

Localization cues: This term is used with respect to *3-D sound* to describe the localizing effect created when sound arrives at one ear before the other. These cues enable human listeners to create an audio picture of their environments.

Lofting: This term refers to an interactive graphics technique in which the third dimension is obtained from a 2-D representation. A good example of lofting would be the creation of a 3-D image from the elevation contours contained in a topographic map.

Logical assets: As opposed to the *media assets* of a *multimedia application,* this term refers to the branching, performance assessment, and other software design features that, taken together, supply a program with its sense of having intelligence. Generally speaking, in today's multimedia market, high-end gaming and *simulation* programs possess the strongest logical assets.

Long-document-handling features: In the early days of desktop publishing, most of the programs advertised under this moniker were ill-equipped to handle large documents such as books or magazines or lofty proposals; they were better suited to handling the company newsletter. However, with time and market pressure, these programs have taken on a set of features that makes them well qualified to work with large or long documents. These features include automatic tables-of-contents, automatic *back-of-the-book indexes,* facilities for chaining multiple documents, and the like. The appearance of these features represents a maturation of the electronic publishing industry. The next major push for this industry segment will be the features associated with ERD (electronic reference documents), such as *hyperlinks* and full-text search.

Long shot: From the world of film and video, this term refers to a camera shot with a vantage point relatively far from its subject. An aerial view of a cityscape would be a prime example of a long shot. This type of shot has been most commonly used at the beginning of movie scenes to establish the locale or atmosphere. The long shot is often held in contrast to the *close-up,* which is used to provide intimacy between subject and viewer.

Lossy compression: Refers to a group of *compression* techniques that sacrifice exact reproduction of data for better compression. A common example of a lossy compression technique is the *MPEG* (Motion Picture Experts Group) standard for motion video compression, which achieves ratios on the order of 100:1, all the way up to 2,000:1, but sacrifices quite a bit in terms of image quality. A second common example is the *H.261* standard, used for *video teleconferencing.*

Luminance: The intensity, or brightness component, of an electronic image. By itself, luminance creates an image in black, gray, and white. With color television, it is combined with *chrominance* to create a color image. Because the human eye is more sensitive to luminance than it is to chrominance, when it comes to *compressing* color digital images, more is done to reduce the chrominance content of the image than is done to eliminate the luminance information.

LV-ROM: This term stands for laservision—read only memory, a *laserdisc* format developed by Philips UK in conjunction with a number of other media and computer interests in 1986. The format accommodates *analog* video, *digital* audio, and digital data.

Technology is sporadic. As in the history of optics, it may take thousands of years to realize a theory.
—*Douglas Leebaert,*
Professor, Graduate School of Business,
Georgetown University

Magnetic positioning systems: This term refers to the primary position-sensing technique used in *virtual reality* (*VR*) research today. The underlying concept of these systems is simple. Electrical current sent through a coil of wire generates a magnetic field oriented along a single axis. Conversely, when a coil of wire is exposed to a magnetic field, an electrical current is generated which is proportional to the field's strength. The closer to the axis of the magnetic field, the greater the electric charge generated. Then, if you mount three coils of wire at right angles to each other and feed them electrical current, the coils create magnetic fields along three axes. And if you move a second three-coil set through these magnetic fields, it produces three distinct electrical charges depending on its position and orientation. It is then possible to process these values mathematically to provide position (x, y, and z) and orientation (roll, pitch, and yaw) information about the sensor. All of this magnetic magic makes it possible for a VR system to track the movement of objects through a virtual world. The first, best known example of this three-coil, magnetic system is the *Polhemus Tracker*.

Magnetoencephlamography: Perhaps one of the longest words in the English language, this term refers to a futuristic, perhaps frightening form of computer input now being contemplated in some research labs. Based on medical brain scanning, the concept is that scientists will be able to measure the electromagnetic signals coming out of your brain and match them with a map of what previous brain scans revealed. One of the hopes is that we might be able to teach computers to recognize certain types of brain activity. Going beyond this, it is theoretically possible that particular thoughts create distinct patterns of brain activity, and that the equivalent of *MIDI* (musical instrument digital interface) *wave tables* could be filled with recorded thought patterns such that the computer could read the human mind. Scary thought.

Markup tags: Used by *tagging languages* such as *SGML* (standard generalized markup language) and *HTML* (hypertext markup language), markup tags enable users to embed specialized publishing and document formatting characteristics within documents.

Mass deployment: This general term is now gaining a very specific meaning: it is coming to represent that awaited moment in our national future when we convert our communications infrastructure—our *NII* (National Information Infrastructure), if you will—from one dominated by the traditional *analog* set of technologies to one governed primarily by *digital* technologies. When this occurs, all of the now-anticipated forms of information and entertainment—such as *VOD* (video on demand), the *virtual mall*, even the *personal newspaper*—will move from the status of blue sky to reality.

Mastering: This term is used most commonly in reference to a critical step in the process of producing a *CD-ROM*. As the word implies, it refers to the process of creating the disc from which all others will be produced. It involves the burning of *pits and lans*—the CD equivalents for binary data—into the photoresistent surface of the master disc.

Matte: From the world of traditional film and video, this production tool is essentially a mask. There are two types: the female mask, which is the character or object photographed over a black background; and the male mask, which is a silhouette of a character or object shot on a white background. When applied to the realm of *DVE* (digital video effects), this term refers to the *two-plane effect*, in which a defined area of the *front plane* is made transparent, revealing the image on the *back plane*.

MCC: Stands for Microelectronics and Computer Technology Corporation, a consortium of American high technology firms established in 1982 to share technological innovations for the purpose of warding off the competitive onslaught of Japanese firms. Located in Austin, Texas, the founding corporations of MCC include Digital Equipment, Motorola, National Semiconductor, Advanced Micro Devices, Honeywell, Martin Marietta, and Bell Communications Research.

MCI™: This term stands for Media Control Interface, and it refers to a *multimedia* software utility in Microsoft *Windows*. It is used to provide standard methods for accessing the various devices that one associates with multimedia delivery platforms, such as *CD-ROM*, *laserdisc*, and the like through the *Media Player*.

Media assets: As opposed to the *logical assets* of a *multimedia application*, this term refers to the video, audio, and text elements that together convey the media production value of a program.

Media integrators: This term refers to the low end of software tools used to build *multimedia* presentations. When compared against the high-end *authoring systems*, media integrators seek ease of use as their primary goal. Examples in today's market include Macromedia's Action! and Interactive Media's Special Delivery.

Media Lab: Founded in 1985 at MIT by Jerome Weisner and current director Nicholas Negroponte, this center receives fame for the research it conducts on the future of communications technologies. The founding concept of the Media Lab was a belief in the inexorable merger of three previously separate and distinct industries: broadcast and motion picture, print and publishing, and computers. The center is funded mostly by grants from corporations and governments, all of whom hope to see the future of communications 30 or so years down the road.

Media Player™: This is a software utility in Microsoft *Windows* that is the main interface to the *MCI*. It utilizes VCR-like buttons to control remote devices, such as the *CD-ROM* player on the *MPC* (multimedia personal computer).

Memex: In 1945, Vannevar Bush wrote an article entitled "As We May Think," and many people hold it out as the inaugural work of the information age. In that article, Bush described a machine, which he referred to as a memex, that could be used to browse and make notes in a voluminous online text and graphics system. The memex contained a large library of documents as well as personal items such as notes, photographs, and sketches. This imaginary machine was to have several screens and a facility for establishing a labeled *link* between any two points or nodes in the library. The memex is an obvious ancestor of the concept that we today refer to as *hypertext*.

Memo field: From the world of database design, the memo field is a design feature that enables users to place fields in records that can receive data of widely variable size or length. With traditional database design, data fields have a maximum length specified in the database's data dictionary. For example, a name field might be defined in the data dictionary as having a fixed length of 30 characters.

This means that the designer of that database anticipates that no name will exceed 30 characters in length. Virtually all of the fields specified for the typical database possess this type of length specification, which provides pre-determined structure to the data and makes it easier to manage. The memo field was introduced to account for the increasing tendency for users to want to add information to a database that is of considerable length, and that varies in size, so that it is nearly impossible to anticipate size with any degree of accuracy. The first such incidents of this must have been "memos" that people wanted to add to data records, as in adding a memo to an accounts receivable record that explains why a particular customer has been extended credit. With the advent of *mixed media data types*—of audio, image, and video—the need to add information that varies widely in size/ magnitude is going to grow dramatically. Thus, to many the memo field is viewed as a point of entry for extending the capabilities of traditional database management tools and systems into the age of *multimedia*.

Menu: Perhaps the most basic element of graphical user interface (*GUI*) design, the menu is a pulldown list of functions available in a software application.

Metadata: Is information about a data file that is also part of that file. Typical examples would be the name of the file, the date of generation, statistical information about the data, and so forth. As *mixed media data types* and their assorted *codecs* and media handling routines proliferate, this sort of information will become a critical portion of the media file's metadata profile.

Methodology: In the world of computing, a methodology is a defined, structured approach and process to developing a software application throughout its life cycle. A typical process involves analysis, design, evaluation, development, installation, and maintenance. Within these phases, various roles (players, such as the *instructional designer,* the programmer, and the *information designer*) interact and perform specified activities to create process deliverables (i.e, documents that define and describe the application as it is in the various stages of its development, such as the requirements document or the design statement) that will eventually culminate in the application itself. It is hoped that developers of *multimedia applications* and *hypermedia applications* will follow a methodology to help ensure product *usability*.

Microphone level inputs: Refers to forms of audio input that originate from natural sources and are captured to storage through a microphone. This term is often contrasted with *line level inputs*, which refer to inputs that originate from other electronic sources, such as VCR, tape deck, or CD player.

Microwave: Refers to the following: 1) radio transmission which uses very short wavelengths; 2) a high *bandwidth* facility that provides line-of-sight radio communications and that requires repeater stations to be placed every 40 km or so because of the curvature of the earth's surface.

MIDI: Stands for musical instrument digital interface and represents one of the most powerful early innovations in multimedia technology. MIDI is both an interface used for connecting MIDI instruments and a music description language that reproduces instrumental sound (just as *PostScript* by Adobe Systems is a page description language used to create printed and other graphic output). The technology is based on the analytical decomposition of sound into its fundamental and electronically reproducible elements. There are two types of MIDI synthesizers, the devices used for creating electronically generated music: *FM synthesizers*, which use oscillators to reproduce sound waves; and sampled sound or *wave table* technology, which uses digitally recorded samples of instruments. Commands from the MIDI description language tell the synthesizers what to play. MIDI devices assign different instrument sounds to different channels and use those channels to play back or record MIDI songs. Because MIDI devices use a symbolic representation of sound which then generates a synthesized version of that sound on the fly, rather than the space-hungry, digitized equivalent, this technology represents a powerful form of audio *compression*. Using MIDI, an hour of stereo sound can be stored in less than 500K.

MIPS: Stands for millions of instructions per second and is the standard measure of processor speed in the computing world. In the early 1990s, personal computers are equipped with microprocessors that operate in the 20 MIPS range. These speed levels, though impressive, will need constant improvement if the personal computer is to be successfully migrated into *interactive television*.

Mix: In film and video, the mix is a recording session during which all the tracks for dialogue, music, and sound effects are combined onto a single master.

Mixed media data types: This phrase has emerged as another way of referring to the realization that information processing must now be inclusive of the nontraditional, high *bandwidth* sources of data—namely, audio, image, and video.

Mode: This very general—some would say overused—term refers to "one among several alternative methods of operation." Being a classificatory term, each mode has some characteristic or set of characteristics that sets it apart from another mode.

Model sheet: Used extensively in the world of cartoon and feature *animation*, this is a group of drawings showing various views of a character, designed to show the animators and assistants how the character is to be constructed. In many respects, the model sheet illustrates an *object oriented* approach to animation, inasmuch as it isolates the characters as objects from their immersion in a story.

Modem: A contraction for modulator-demodulator, this term refers to a *data communications* translating device that links a computer to a telecommunications network (usually the *public switched telephone network*). A modem converts the *digital* signals of a computer to *analog* signals for transmission over the telecommunications network, and then converts those analog signals back to digital when they arrive at their destination. It is generally believed that as we enter the age of multimedia, the demand for modems may wane as all-digital transmission media gradually replace the older stock of analog devices. This trend will be precipitated by the immense demand for carrying capacity levied by the *mixed media data types*, such as image and video. Modems are simply not equipped to handle the mammoth files associated with mixed media.

Modular Windows™: A subset of the popular Microsoft *Windows* graphical environment manufactured by Microsoft, this product is aimed at the emerging *CD-ROM* player TV accessory market. It is designed to be controlled by a TV viewer wielding a remote control, and thus offers larger screen fonts and has a different look and feel than its parent, Windows. An early user of Modular Windows is Tandy's *VIS* (Visual Information System) player, which is being sold through Tandy's Radio Shack stores as a direct competitor to the Philips *CD-I* system.

Moire effect: This term refers to a noticeable pattern of wavy, regularly spaced spots that results from the nearly parallel alignment of the axes of two superimposed dot screens. In the world of color printing, this effect is considered highly undesirable because it reduces the clarity of the printed image.

Morphing: A special effects technique of fairly recent vintage, morphing is the now familiar visual process whereby one object blends into another. Now abundantly used in television, whenever one sees an object such as a face blend quickly and seamlessly into another object, such as another face, the technique being used is that of morphing. Drawn from the word "metamorphosis," this technique is based on very simple principles. To create a morph, first, the beginning and ending *key frames* are selected. Each point in the first key frame is associated with a point in the last key frame. The artist also selects a number of points between these two bookend key frames, then specifies the number of *frames* over which the transformation will occur from beginning to end. Obviously, the more points that are selected for use with this *inbetweening* tool, the finer the transition.

Mosaic: This is a popular, *public domain* graphical user interface (*GUI*) standard graphical front-end to access information on the *Internet*.

Mosaic effects: From the realm of *DVE* (digital video effects), this term refers to a family of effects that are used to coarsen a video image. These techniques are typically employed as a method for fading out of a scene and are most effectively used when the fade coincides with the psychological effect of losing attentional focus, such as when someone is losing consciousness. There are two dominant mosaic effects. The first, *pixel repeat, zooms* in on a portion of the screen, but without providing any additional detail. The result is that the portion of the screen that is enlarged in the zoom comes to appear increasingly coarser, or out of focus. The second technique, known as *pixel hold*, retains the whole screen (does not zoom) but creates a granulated look by taking the color and tone (*chrominance* and *luminance*) of one *pixel* and extending it to neighboring pixels. Typically, this process is continued until the whole screen seems to break up into a set of increasingly hazy squares.

Motion compensation: This term refers to a breed of video *compression* techniques that compress across video frames by saving only the differences between them. The *MPEG* (Motion Picture Experts Group) standard is a prime example. Motion compensation *codecs* are also referred to as *interframe codecs*.

Motion-control photography: One of many technical innovations created by George Lucas' Industrial Light & Magic, this term refers to a family of products that use computers to provide precision control of camera movement. This technology is used, for example, to create multiple exposures of the same scene, such that various special effects can be laid down on that scene in a seamless fashion.

Motion-JPEG: One of the most popular *codecs* available today, it serves as the core codec for Apple's *QuickTime*. Motion-JPEG (Joint Photography Experts Group) is an *intraframe codec*, which means that it is symmetrical and can, for the most part, be performed on the fly (in *real time*).

Motion parallax: An anomaly of the human visual system, this term refers to the phenomenon that occurs as we move our heads from side to side; objects closer to us appear to move faster than objects that are farther away. This perception is caused by the fact that the images of closer objects are larger and move across our retinas faster than the images of distant objects. This phenomenon can be put to dramatic effect by creators of visual media, often by simply getting objects in the visual field of action to move.

Motion platform: One of the outstanding new features of *high intensity amusement attractions*, motion platforms are used in conjunction with high resolution video systems to create an immersive sense of motion associated with the action being portrayed in the video or graphic part of the system. As the name implies, the motion platform actually moves in conjunction with the video, artfully using a relatively small amount of movement to create for the audience an amplified sense of motion. The most popular and effective uses of motion platforms are found in our country's high visibility theme parks (e.g., Universal Studios and DisneyWorld both in Orlando, Florida).

Mouse: Aside from the keyboard, the mouse is currently the most common computer input device. It is a handheld device that inputs coordinate information and is chiefly used as a "pick device" for selecting items from among *icons*, screen *menus*, and the like. The technology for the mouse was first developed at Stanford Research Institute in the 1960s and was later integrated into the seminal interface research that occurred at *Xerox PARC* in the 1970s and '80s. The principle behind mousing is a simple one: a small ball is placed inside a device that is rolled on a table. Sensors measure how far the ball has rolled forward, backward, or side-to-side, and computer *algorithms* translate these movements into horizontal and vertical coordinate movements of an on-screen *cursor*.

Mouth action: This refers to the numerous shapes the mouth must take when speaking. With an *object-oriented* approach to *animation*, these shapes are stored in an object library, available to be inherited (with appropriate modifications, of course) by any character.

Moviemap: A subtype of the *surrogate travel* genre, moviemaps are used to enable people to travel the roads and byways of geographically remote areas. The early examples were created by, first, actually filming movement (by foot or by car) through the target geographic area, and then by digitizing these travel segments and placing them on some form of *optical storage*, most commonly *laserdisc*. Points within the moviemap where users can change direction, e.g., turn down another street, are represented in the moviemap by simple *branchpoints* that enable the various street segments to become (seamlessly, one hopes) connected to one another for the purposes of simulating movement. The tedium of capturing a city's geobase of street segments on film is apt to give way in the future to terrain modeling systems that are integrated with geographic information systems to enable dynamic and automated rendering of virtual pathways through the target city. The *Aspen Movie Map*, created in 1978 by MIT's Machine Architecture Group, represents the proof-of-concept prototype of the moviemap.

Movies-on-demand: Made possible by the rapid expansion of the channel *bandwidth* available to cable operators, this media service makes it possible for cable viewers to order up films at their own leisure. The full implementation of this service is projected to give viewers access to vast libraries of film offerings (e.g., the complete MGM library) and, therefore, to severely undercut, if not make completely obsolete, the VCR and the home video rental industry.

Moving viewpoint commands: One of the emerging primitives of *interactivity*, moving viewpoint commands are a subtype of interactive *branchpoint*. As the term suggests, these branchpoints enable participants to change what occupies their field of vision as they move through a particular scene. With the more immersive forms of interactive story, i.e., with *virtual reality*, these commands will be effected by sensors that correspond directly with the participant's own body movements (e.g., through the technology of the *DataSuit*). Consequently, they will obtain high levels of sophistication with respect to the *code of resemblance*.

MPC: Stands for multimedia personal computer, and represents an increasingly important market specification set forth by the *Multimedia PC Marketing Council* of Washington, DC. Now in its second generation (MPC II), the first generation of the standard was published in 1990, the second in 1993. Its goal is to encourage the adoption of a standard multimedia computing platform, which, of course, stands to benefit hardware and title manufacturers as well as consumers. The council grants a distinctive MPC certification mark to all hardware manufacturers who meet the functional requirements of the specification. In summary, the minimum requirements of Level 1 were as follows: 386SX *CPU*; 2 MB of RAM; 30 MB hard drive; single-spin *CD-ROM* drive with 150 KB *transfer rate* and *CD-DA* outputs; VGA monitor (640 x 480, 16 colors); and *MIDI I/O, joystick*.

Most experts agree that this standard is simply not powerful enough. In fact, most of the recent multimedia titles have zoomed past this specification. The 1993, Level 2 standard is much more robust and includes the following specifications: 486SX, 25 Mhz CPU; 4 MB of RAM; 65,000-color graphics at 640 x 480 *resolution*; 160 MB hard drive; double-spin CD-ROM drive with 300 KB transfer rate; *CD-ROM-XA* ready; and *multisession*-capable MIDI I/O, joystick. Given the rapid pace of the multimedia market, it would not be unexpected to see MPC III soon.

MPEG: This acronym, which stands for the standards committee known as the Motion Picture Experts Group, has become synonymous with one of the early favorites to become a dominant *codec* for delivering *digital video*. In contrast to its close cousin, *JPEG* (Joint Photography Experts Group), the MPEG standard is an interframe, or motion compensation, codec. Like all codecs, MPEG seeks out redundant information that can be removed from a data stream. Because it is an *interframe codec*, MPEG seeks out redundancies that occur between frames in a video stream, as well as those that occur within single frames (as is the case with *intraframe codecs* like JPEG). If it is a sure sign of viability when a standard moves into its second generation, then the MPEG standard is doing quite well. The first standard, originally just called MPEG, but now being referred to as MPEG 1, provides a level of image quality that has been likened to the VHS standard of our VCRs. Technically speaking, the MPEG 1 format, which was finally blessed by its committee in 1993, is capable of presenting a quarter-screen picture at a *resolution* of 352 x 240 *pixels* at the *NTSC* (National Television Standards Committee) standard *frame rate* of 30 frames per second (*fps*). While full screen implementations of MPEG are common, they are actually *interpolated* from the original quarter screen data. This first round of the standard is considered most appropriate for presentation on *VGA* monitors and for use with *CD-ROM* titles. The second iteration of the standard, MPEG 2, is expected by many to become the digital transmission standard for the broadcast cable industry. In fact, most industry analysts expect that the 50+ million cable subscribers in the U.S. will convert to digital *set-top boxes* with MPEG 2 decoders by the turn of the century. The MPEG 2 standard will bump the resolution of MPEG to 720 x 480, thereby achieving a full television-quality standard.

MSC: Stands for MIDI show control, a language extension to the *MIDI* (musical instrument digital interface) standard that provides for the computer control of a variety of equipment systems used in live performance and large audiovisual productions. Motorized stage equipment, pyrotechnical effects, various audio devices, lighting systems, and *videodisc* players are just some of the devices that have been brought under the control of the MSC language. As envisioned by its authors, MSC will provide strong assistance to the traditionally harried board operators responsible for launching complex sequences of on-stage events in precise order and with precise timing.

MSCDEX: This combination acronym-contraction stands for Microsoft *CD-ROM extensions*. It is a program that enables the MS-DOS operating system to "talk" to a CD-ROM drive.

Multidrop line: Also commonly referred to as a "multipoint line," this term refers to a single communications line that is connected to two or more stations. The most obvious examples of a multidrop line are the telephone and cable connections that provide phone and TV services, respectively, to the residential market.

Multimedia: Is the umbrella term that has been coined to cover all of the synergistic uses of text, voice, music, video, graphics, and other forms of data to enhance the computer's role as a communications device.

Multimedia applications: Though the first years of this decade have witnessed an explosion in what are being called multimedia titles, few have stopped to question what type of content denotes a *multimedia application*. We offer the following three-part taxonomy as a tentative starting point for defining the array of multimedia applications: **1) Structured Pathways:** these are largely training applications—often called *tutorials*—that tightly constrict the user's movement through a series of interactive presentational sequences designed to convey a specific set of learning objectives. This genre of multimedia is most often used with regard to content that requires a large measure of rote memorization. *Drill and practice* programs for grade school math and end user training for software applications are two common examples of this type of multimedia. It is best employed with learners who bring very little base knowledge to the learning experience, and therefore require that the *scope and sequence* of the content be laid out for them. **2) Exploratory:** probably the most common type of multimedia title coming onto the market today, this type of program lies on the opposite side of the learner continuum from structured pathways in that it works best with users that are already quite familiar with the content. The exploratory category is best typified by programs that are termed *hypertext* or *hypermedia*. It provides a navigational interface to large volumes of *hyperlinked*, or relationally associated content. Electronic museums, electronic encyclopedias, online help systems, medical databases, and *surrogate travel* programs are all examples of exploratory multimedia (i.e., hypermedia). This type of program is fairly easy to build in that it does not demand sophisticated software logic. Exploratory programs rise or fall on the merits of two factors: the desirability or appeal of their content, and the quality of their navigational interface. **3) Gaming:** this is the most demanding of the three from the standpoint of software design. Gaming multimedia programs succeed by providing an engaging context in which users are challenged to achieve one or more well-specified goals (e.g., find the buried treasure, slay the appropriate villains, earn the imaginary fortune). Well-constructed games provide abundant feedback and are highly interactive. Most games inspire repeated use by implementing what educators call the *ladder of challenge*: once the player has obtained mastery at one level of challenge, the program automatically upgrades that challenge to a heightened level of difficulty. Though games are frequently scoffed at by those in the corporate world, a deeper look would reveal that the much-respected business simulation is, in fact, based on the same software design principles as games—the only substantive difference between the two is that the simulation is placed in a job context with real world variables and feedback systems.

Multimedia applications have their roots in standard training and education courses with or without exercises, *CBT* (computer based training) programs for education and training, and video games, simulations, and stories for fun and entertainment.

Multimedia database: This term has emerged in the nomenclature to pay witness to the fact that most database applications are making it possible to embed *mixed media data types* in their traditional database records. The most commonly cited example of this is a personnel database, where the employee picture is attached as part of the employee record.

Multimedia PC Marketing Council: This is a nonprofit organization incorporated as a subsidiary of the Software Publishers Association. Using the multimedia PC standard set forth by Tandy Corp. in 1990, this council of 11 members established the standard of what constitutes a *multimedia* personal computer. As a way of enforcing this standard, the council makes available to all hardware vendors the option of licensing the *MPC* (multimedia personal computer) trademark, which thereby stands as a validation that any workstation thusly trademarked has achieved the level of technical sophistication demanded by the MPC standard.

Multiprocessing: This term refers to an emerging trend in personal computer design to incorporate more than one processor. Often confused with parallel processing, which denotes many small, identically constructed processors working simultaneously, in parallel, multiprocessing refers to the somewhat different notion of a computer with two or more specialized processors. In the age of multimedia, multiprocessing will play an increasingly important role, as manufacturers discover that the most efficient way to handle the various forms of encoded media—text, audio, image, video—is to supply each with their own specialized processor. This is the approach that the Electronic Arts offshoot, 3D0, has taken in designing its home interactive multiplayer of the same name. The design approach of 3D0—which may replace the *CPU*-oriented designs of today's personal computers—is to allocate to the CPU the function of "babysitting" a number of other processors working independently on processing the sound, graphics, and animation. The 3D0 design also incorporates a number of *DMA* (direct memory access) channels, which further reduce the processing load of the CPU by making certain that the movement of the various media files operates in a near-independent fashion.

Multisession: This term refers to the ability of a certain breed of write-once CD player to be able to record data during multiple sessions. The technology is essentially analogous to the append function familiar to database applications, wherein the physical placement of new data is located just beyond the existing data. With write-once, multisession CDs, this is the **only** place that new data can be placed, because once a portion of the CD's surface is burned with its digital pattern of *pits and lans*, there is no currently viable technology for "re-recording" these surfaces. However, multisession is considered a significant step forward, inasmuch as most CDs are single session, meaning that any disc surface that is unused during the mastering process shall remain forever wasted. The Kodak Photo CD technology is the best known early example of multisession CD.

Multi-threading: From the realm of operating system design, this feature makes it possible for several processors to run the same code simultaneously. A feature like this is critical to many high-end *multimedia applications*, where the volume of data to be handled creates bottlenecks on most standard systems.

The prospect, then, is that the intelligence of the human participants in a conversational medium will dominate that of the computer for the foreseeable future.

—Tim Oren,
Advanced Technology Group,
Apple Computer

NAPLPS: Stands for North American Presentation Level Protocol Standard and is pronounced "naplips." This standard is used for sending computer graphics over the television industry transmission infrastructure. It appeared over a decade ago, and though it is still used by the major online services, such as Prodigy and America Online, it is considered to be seriously out of date. Blocky graphics, slow transmission, lack of built-in support for mice, and no audio are just some of this standard's shortcomings. The *RIP* (Remote Imaging Protocol), created by TeleGrafix of Huntington Beach, California, is a more up-to-date standard that is attempting to bring these online services up to the graphic user interface (*GUI*) standards that characterize modern PCs and (especially) *MPC*s (multimedia personal computers).

Narrowband: Used in contrast to the term *broadband*, this word describes a transmission channel that has a relatively low carrying capacity, or amount of *bandwidth*. It is typically used to describe channels with voice grade bandwidth (4khz) or below.

Narrowcasting: In contrast to the traditional, mass-market, television network broadcasting predominant before cable television, this term describes media services targeted towards relatively small, specialized vertical market segment/interest groups. ESPN and A&E are prime examples. Narrowcasting is projected to continue as a powerful trend into the information age as transmission *bandwidths* for media services—and the resulting number of available channels—continue their unabated expansion.

Natural language processing: This term refers to a branch of *artificial intelligence* that specializes in programming computers with the ability to carry on normal, human speech. This branch has become tightly connected with the technologies associated with speech recognition (or *voice recognition*).

Navigation: A term that has found its way from seafaring origins to the world of *interface design* and *hypermedia*, it has become a popular design concept associated with building comprehensible structures when assembling large amounts of information into mixed media databases (*hypermedia*). Building the navigable *interface* is, for the present, one of the great challenges and research foci of the early stages in the age of *multimedia*.

Navigator: This term has been offered to describe an emergent software that searches and manipulates content on various databases. Perhaps the outstanding feature of a navigator is its ability to self-navigate the network, seeking out the most appropriate information items from the numerous public information databases.

Near-line storage: From the world of data storage, this newly minted term refers to a transitional form of storage between online and off-line media. It differs from online in one simple way: data is not processed directly from near-line devices. Rather, data is migrated from an *online storage* device to a near-line device when it is not needed and brought back to the online device when needed. Near-line can be distinguished from off-line storage such as traditional magnetic tape systems in two ways. First, the media onto which the files have been placed is continuously and immediately available (or nearly so) to the end user. There is no need for personnel to fetch and mount the media. Secondly, no system administrator intervention is required to save files or to retrieve them from storage. Examples of near-line storage include the optical *juke box* and the *tape autoloader*. In the age of multimedia, where all forms of storage will be under ominous pressure to increase capacity, this hybrid form of storage medium is apt to gain wide popularity, if only as a stopgap measure until higher capacity forms of online storage are made available.

Network operating system: Now a staple of the software world, a network operating system is that body of software features that enables computers to communicate with one another.

Neuro-Baby™: Created by Naoka Tosa of Fujitsu Laboratories in Japan, Neuro-Baby is a computer-generated 3-D character programmed to learn by using voice-input and neural network software. It reacts to the tone and frequency of a person's voice, and, for example, might cry or become angry if a person were to speak loudly to it. As such, this cutting edge technology represents one of the earliest attempts at the creation of an artificial personality.

NII: Stands for national information infrastructure and is the officially sanctioned term of the Clinton administration for the so-called *information superhighway.* If the vision is on target, this composite infrastructure of *fiber optic,* coaxial, and *wireless* transmission facilities, plus the machine intelligence to manage it, will play very big in the future of multimedia. The emerging medium of *interactive television,* for one, will be utterly dependent on the viability and vitality of the NII.

Noise: In the media industry, this term refers to the interference a signal picks up as it is transmitted along an electronic circuit. "Static" on telephone lines and "snow" on TV screens are two common examples of noise. From a broader perspective, and originating from the lofty heights of information theory, noise refers to any random or unintentional forms of information that get embedded in a message and become distracting, or otherwise degrade the quality of that message.

Noise gate: Used by audio engineers, this device makes it possible to erase all sound that registers above or beneath a specified level.

Noninterlaced video: This is a high quality form of video offered by many video digitizers, wherein the original, *interlaced video* signal (a signal painted on the screen in two passes) is buffered into memory and merged into a single screen image before being displayed on the monitor. A near-synonym is *progressive scanning.*

Nonlinear video: This term is used in the video industry to describe the *random access* abilities afforded the producer when working in the *digital* format. Frequently used as an off-line tool, nonlinear video editing is a process whereby video is *digitized* in *real time* and stored on a hard disk. When video is placed in this digital format, the editor can go to any single point in the digitized video sequence without having to rewind or fast-forward through other material. You might entitle the story associated with this term: "Hollywood Discovers Random Access."

NTSC: Stands for National Television Standards Committee and is used most commonly to refer to the U.S. color video standard. This longstanding broadcast standard is represented by 525-line screen running at a rate of 60 fields/30 frames per second and at a broadcast bandwidth of 4 MHz. Most people in the multimedia industry equate this acronym not only with the standard per se, but also with the level of image quality that is associated with television broadcasts.

NTSC safe colors: For those who are creating graphics on computer for eventual transfer to some form of television broadcast, this
term refers to a set of constraints that limit the selection of colors to
those that reproduce well on video.

NVOD: Stands for near video on demand and represents one of the
earliest interactive products to be offered through *interactive television*. Most industry analysts view NVOD as a temporary precursor to
true *movies-on-demand*, or *VOD*. The service will be characterized
by movies staggered on multiple channels with enough copies always playing so that viewers will never wait more than just a few
minutes for their selection to start.

NVRAM: Stands for non-volatile random access memory and refers to a typically small portion of computer RAM that is kept from
losing its *digital* patterns when the computer is turned off by some
form of battery. NVRAM is used to hold data of high priority, such as
password information or key last-usage data. With the growing importance of long-play video games, NVRAM will be used increasingly to *bookmark* the progress of particular gaming sessions so that
users can have the liberty to turn off their machine without having to
restart a possibly involved game when they return.

Artificial realities will have the same relationship to the real one that our homes have to the natural environment. Our homes are abstract spaces, partly defined by economics but primarily by our aesthetic sense. **—Myron Kreuger, Author**

Object-oriented programming: This is the new philosophy of programming. Rather than segregating software procedures from their associated data, as has been typical of the programming discipline for the bulk of its history, object-oriented programming encapsulates procedures and data into tightly structured entities that the industry now calls "objects." Though there are many benefits to this change in approach to software engineering, its most notable advantage is that it promotes the re-use of code. This is an enormous leap forward for the software industry, which has been historically characterized by the re-invention of almost every algorithmic wheel, ad nauseum. Now, in the Valhalla promised by object-oriented programming, programmers build libraries of objects which can be passed on to both their colleagues and their heirs. Though the impact of object-oriented programming is global to the entire software industry, it has a very specific advantage within the multimedia industry: software simulations are far more easily coded when using an object-oriented approach. In fact, one of the original programming environments to enforce the various rules and constraints of object orientation was a language called "Simula," which was invented to aid in the creation of simulations by encouraging programmers to write pieces of encapsulated code (objects, of course) that simulate objects in the real world.

OCR: Stands for optical character recognition, which is conceptually one of the most attractive and efficient methods for converting printed text to machine-readable character codes. An optical character reader scans a typewritten or printed document, stores it as a *bit-mapped* image, and then converts the letter shapes based on some form of pattern recognition into *ASCII* codes. OCR is far from being a perfected technology, owing to the difficulties associated with pattern matching against the broad range of font sizes and styles that make up our canon of printed materials. Hence, the typical functional specification for an OCR device will include its average error rate.

Off-line compression: Refers to an expensive, *CPU-intensive* form of *compression* that typically requires users to send their source video to a service that uses more sophisticated and time-consuming *algorithms* than are typically tenable on a PC. Off-line compression is the high-end, expensive part of the *codec* equation and is also described as an *asymmetrical codec* because it makes the compression side of handling digital video much more time consuming and expensive than the *decompression* side.

Off-line editing: The first of two phases involved in video editing, the second being *online editing*. During the off-line phase, the *editor* reviews footage, makes edit decisions, prepares a *rough cut*, and compiles an *EDL* (edit decision list). As *desktop video production* approaches, many production houses today are relying entirely upon PC-based video editing tools to carry them through the off-line phase.

Off-line storage: A venerable form of mass data storage, off-line is distinguished from *online* and *near-line storage* in that it requires human intervention to make its store of contents accessible to users. By far, the most common form of off-line storage is magnetic tape. Typically, these tapes are stored on racks, and when a particular tape is needed, an operator retrieves and mounts the tape on a reader that is online to the computer system. Obviously, off-line is impractical for any type of data needed on a frequent or regular basis, and so is primarily used for archival storage.

OLE: Stands for Object Linking and Embedding and refers to Microsoft's utility for *Windows* designed to make interapplication data transfer easy to manage. Put succinctly, OLE is intended to enable different applications to communicate and share information. In practice, this translates into the ability for users to construct *compound documents*, because, for example, OLE makes it possible for a user to embed a digital video movie in a word processor, without, of course, requiring that the word processor have any native video capabilities. Briefly, OLE is designed to work in such a way that it is up to one application (called the source document) to take the responsibility for the overall structure of the compound document, while the other, contributing applications participate by owning sections of the structure. Once the user has created a link to, or has embedded something from another application, that user need only double-click on a particular section to invoke its parent application.

Online editing: This is the second of two phases involved in video editing, the first being *off-line editing*. During the online phase, the *EDL* (edit decision list) is loaded into an editing system that controls the playback and record decks and automatically assembles the final production by dubbing the video and audio sequences selected from the playback deck onto the record deck. For most broadcast quality productions, producers still rely upon the high-end equipment found only in traditional video production suites. The day approaches, however, when even online editing is done using a PC.

Online storage: This is the most immediate form of long-term (permanent) storage. A file storage medium must meet two criteria to be considered "online." First, data must be processed directly from the medium; that is, it must be directly accessible to the computer's internal memory (RAM). Second, there should be no operator or user intervention required to access the medium. In today's world, magnetic disk is still the most common type of online storage, owing to its relatively large capacity, and fast access and data transfer speeds. As multimedia continues to exert its voracious appetite for mass storage, however, the hegemony of magnetic disk is increasingly threatened by optical disc and magnetic tape, two forms of storage that can be configured as online media, though they both suffer from decisively slower access and transfer speeds than those of magnetic disks.

OPAC: This acronym stands for Online Public Access Catalog, which is a part of our emerging *information superhighway* that provides a place where schools, libraries, media centers, and other institutions can hook up via *modem* to obtain information on current news, scan the contents of electronic encyclopedias, etc.

Optical fiber transmission: This term refers to the increasingly critical technology that makes possible the rapid and relatively distortion-free transmission of information through fine optical fibers. With this transmission medium, digital data is transmitted as a series of on-off pulses of light representing bits of information.

Optical juke boxes: These are otherwise known as *juke boxes*.

Optical memory: This general term is used to describe forms of storage that rely upon the fundamental of light, rather than magnetics, to record and retrieve *digital* information. *CD-ROM* and *laserdisc* are the two most common forms of optical memory. This type of memory is known for its much greater capacity, a feat made possible by the use of high-precision *laser* beams; but suffers in reputation for its slow *transfer rates* and lack of writability.

Optical printer: From the world of film and video production, this is a machine that is a combination of a projector and a camera. Generally speaking, it is used to combine live action and animation and also to make fades, *dissolves,* and *wipes.* These devices are also capable of creating split screens, skipping frames and superimposing text on film, and rotating shots and creating multi-exposure scenes. Optical printers are the devices most responsible for creating all sorts of special effects in the *analog* video world. As we move toward an all *digital* world, however, the importance of these machines may eventually wane.

Optical storage: By all indications, optical storage may rapidly become the dominant storage medium of the era of multimedia technology. Optical discs offer two advantages over other forms of mass storage: they have large storage capacities; and they are removable, providing users with access to many discs per drive. Both of these advantages owe to the fact that optical storage devices use a *laser* instead of a magnetic field to make marks on the medium. Given the vast storage requirements demanded by *multimedia applications* (video, audio, image), optical storage may grow in parallel with the adoption of multimedia technology in general.

Orange Book: Related to the *Red Book* and *Yellow Book* standards for *compact disc,* this term refers to the latest set of standards for how information is to be organized on compact discs. The Orange Book defines the standards that enable the user to write audio and/or data to the disc. There are two parts to this standard: 1) Compact Disc-Magneto Optical (CD-MO), where data can be written, erased, and re-written, and 2) Compact Disc-Write Once (CD-WO), where data can be written, but not erased.

Organic video effects: This emerging class of *DVE* (digital video effects) simulates natural phenomena as a way of transitioning from one video shot or scene to the next. Examples include breaking glass or pouring liquids.

OSI: Stands for Open Systems Interconnection and is the name given to the model defined by the *ISO* (International Standards Organization). This data communications model contains seven layers used for comparing and defining computer network architectures. Its primary purpose is to promote standards for data communications throughout the industry, thereby making it easier for buyers to create their own optimal solutions even though that strategy might lead them to buy from several different vendors.

Out of sync: This phrase is used to describe a sound track running either ahead of or behind the picture.

Output devices: This general computer term refers to devices that draw, print, photograph, or otherwise display the information generated by a computer.

Outtake: In film, this is a scene rejected by the director.

The kinds of tasks that computers perform for us require that they express two distinctly anthropomorphic qualities: responsiveness and the capacity to perform actions.
—*Brenda Laurel, Author*

Packet: From the world of *data communications*, this term refers to a way of organizing data for transmission in which the target data (the actual information that the user is concerned with sending) is placed between header and trailer information. These headers and trailers identify key attributes of the enclosed, or "packetized" data, including the address of the packet's destination and its proper sequence relative to any other packets it must be re-combined with at the destination.

Packet switching: With respect to *data communications*, this form of transmission is favored for its flexibility when compared against its most common rival, *circuit switching*. Packet switching works by breaking data down into small chunks called *packets*. Because these packets contain addressing and sequencing information, they make it possible to break large files into relatively small units that can be routed across the network over different pathways depending upon the ever-changing and shifting availability of *bandwidth*. Thus, packet switching accommodates peak loads in one part of the network by re-routing packets over alternate pathways, or combinations of paths. Owing to the presence of sequencing information in the packets, some packets can even arrive at their destination before their predecessors, because the intelligence of a packet switching system will simply re-sequence the packets into their original order before turning the data over for processing at that destination. Because of this flexibility, packet switching is a very popular way of handling data communications. However, when it comes to transmitting the extremely large and time-sensitive files associated with digital video, packet switching is often untenable because the processing overhead and network irregularities associated with routing and re-assembling the packets can cause disruptions in the video stream.

Paint systems: This is the generic name for computer art systems that produce *bit-mapped* graphic images. They generally are pixel-oriented, and the artist uses them to create pictures by setting *pixels* to specific color values. Most paint systems are driven by some form or combination of *pointing device* (e.g., *mouse, graphics tablet*), and provide, at a minimum, functions for changing brush size and shape, changing and merging the colors provided by the systems' standard *palette*, and cutting, pasting, and merging one *bit map* with others. Paint systems are often held in contrast to *draw systems*, which are designed to manipulate *structured graphics* (also called vectorized graphics), which are mathematically represented objects such as lines, boxes, circles, etc.

PAL: Stands for phase alternating line and is the TV signal encoding counterpart to the North American *NTSC* (National Television Standards Committee) standard. PAL is used in Great Britain, most of Europe, Africa, Australia, South America, and China.

Palette: With reference to graphical user interface (*GUI*) design, a palette is a collection of small symbols, usually enclosed in rectangles, which offers the user a quick, visually cued method for switching between a host of related functions. The symbols used to represent the various functions can be icons, patterns, characters, or drawings that stand for their respective operations. This term is also used in its more traditional sense with *paint systems* to refer to the particular mix of colors that are available to the computer artists as they create a piece of computer art.

Pan: Short for *panorama*, this term refers both to a shot where the camera sweeps across a given area, thereby giving the audience a panoramic view of the film subject; and to a shot where, in contrast to a *zoom*, the camera pulls away from its subject, thereby placing that subject in its larger social or natural context. As a form of cinematic language, the pan is often used at the beginning or end of a major film segment to place the subject against the larger backdrop of its setting. Increasingly, both forms of panning are becoming a part of desktop video systems, which means, of course, that they can be achieved with regard to a particular visual subject by merely issuing a single command.

Parallel processing: Perhaps the next generation in computer design, parallel processing refers to a form of processing where more than one processor is devoted to executing the same program simultaneously, or in parallel. Based on a half-century history of computing, we have come to think of the *CPU*—the brains of the computer—as a single, serial processing device. Although this single device has undergone a steady increase in size and speed, it is still a serial processor, which means it can only execute one instruction at a time. Rather than focusing on the throughput capacity of a serial processor, advocates of parallel processing insist that a wiser direction for many applications is that of having many small processors work in parallel. With the huge file sizes and *codec* processing requirements of *digitized* media, parallel processing seems ideally suited for many of the computing tasks associated with *multimedia*. In fact, many of today's chip developers are hard at work creating the next generation of chips for the multimedia era, and many of their efforts are focused at creating "on-chip parallelism," where groups of small processors team up to do such inherently parallel tasks as *decompressing* a screen's *pixel* map of incoming *digital* video.

Parallel protocols: This term describes the emerging standard for multimedia networking in which two network protocols co-exist on the same physical network. Historically speaking, there have always been the *contention protocols*, which handle the *bursty traffic* associated with traditional alphanumeric data. More recently, and with the appearance of *mixed media data types*, there are the stream management protocols now associated with the large, continuously flowing streams of data necessary to play compressed digital video or other high-*bandwidth* audiovisual data types.

Parallel transmission: This term is used to refer to a mode of data transfer in which all eight *bits* of a *byte* are transmitted simultaneously over parallel communication lines (such as the ribbon cable found inside many computers). This form of transmission is typically held in contrast to serial transmission, where data are communicated over a single communication line one bit at a time.

Parse: From the realm of software engineering, this term refers to the very common practice of scanning a list or sequential file of uncertain length, one character or element at a time, to determine its contents. Thus, for example, the common word processor accessories known as spell checkers typically work by parsing the text files created by users in an effort to seek out misspelled words.

Party-line games: This is a projected form of interactive game that will be played over a network by two or more players.

PAS™: Stands for Performance Animation System, which is an *object-oriented* software toolkit developed by SimGraphics that enables developers to create *real time* character-*animation* applications.

It is a prototype authoring tool for creating *digital puppet* applications.

Pass-through video: This term refers to a way of presenting video on a computer in which the video signal is not handled by (or integrated with) the computers graphics subsystem, but rather is simply passed through to the computer's monitor in its original *analog* format. Pass-through video is the simplest form of computer-related video technology.

Patch: With respect to *wave table synthesis*, which is the highest quality technology now associated with *MIDI* (musical instrument digital interface) synthesizers, this term refers to one of the individual sound recordings that occupy the synthesizer's table of sounds. Most patches represent recordings of musical instruments, but, owing to the 128-patch size of the *MPC* (multimedia personal computer) standard, most wave tables include noninstrumental sounds such as applause, gun shots, and such esoterica as the "space voice" sound. The group of sounds that go into making up a particular wave table are often referred to as that player's patch set.

Pattern recognition: This term refers to the recognition of shapes and patterns by machine systems. As computing becomes increasingly visual, this form of machine intelligence will continue to take on a correspondingly heightened importance. Ultimately, the computer may be able to recognize individual faces, and thus be able to recognize people by sight.

PBX: Stands for private branch exchange, a relatively high-end piece of communications hardware designed to manage large numbers of telephonic connections, usually between the denizens of a single office building and the rest of the world. This term has gained renewed popularity, because the device that it describes is being used as an analogy for *data communications* hardware that is now coming to market for use by cable operators to offer *movies-on-demand* services (hence, *video PBX*) to their residential clientele.

PCI™: This term stands for Peripheral Component Interconnect and represents an open standard for *local bus* developed by Intel. Like other local bus technologies, PCI has been developed to help eliminate the inevitable bottlenecks that occur on traditional *ISA bus* personal computers when they attempt to move *mixed media data types* between the computer and its peripherals.

PCX: This venerable graphics file format is a *bitmap*, or *raster file* format that was originally the native format of the PC Paintbrush graphics development program. Paintbrush is a program now owned by Microsoft, and it is still offered as a utility program to all who purchase a license to MS-DOS or MS *Windows*—a fact which, of course, accounts for its widespread use. Owing to both its age and its position in the mainstream of desktop computing, the PCX format has been revised numerous times over the years to keep pace with the continual enhancement of PC displays.

PDA: Stands for personal digital assistant and represents a broad class of handheld devices that many critics believe represent the next logical progression of the personal computing revolution. These devices will rely heavily on *wireless* forms of transmission, and will certainly grow to increasing levels of *multimedia* capability as they evolve. The Apple Newton is one of the early examples of a PDA. They provide a form of *data communications* that is free from the spatial constraints of the computer or the telephone, enabling users to carry on data processing activities anywhere they happen to be.

Pen plotter: This is a type of electronic drawing, or "plotting," device that works by moving a robotic pen carriage over a recording surface (paper, for example). There are basic types of pen plotter: *flatbed* and *drum*.

Perceptual asymptotes: A term coined by the French film theorist Andre Bazin, it refers to the process by which various media continue to improve and refine themselves in terms of the amount of information they deliver until they reach a point at which they exceed the human capacity to process that particular type of information, at which point there is no further need to improve the technology. The classic modern example of a perceptual asymptote has to do with CD audio, which, at a *sampling rate* of 44 MHz, has refined itself to the point that exceeds the capacity of the human ear to discern any further enhancements. Long since gone, Bazin was a true visionary, foreseeing the general tendency for all media to continuously add capability.

Perfect sound: This term was coined in the world of audio engineering to describe manufactured sound that cannot be distinguished from real sound, or copies of an original that cannot be distinguished from that original.

Performance animation: An outgrowth of research efforts in *virtual reality*, this term refers to a form of *animation* wherein the performance of the animated character is tied directly to the *real time* movements of an actual human. The technique relies upon human performers outfitted with special motion-tracking devices used to drive all of the animated character's movements and expressions, including all of their mouth movements.

Performance support system: Though it has not quite earned the status of an acronym (PSS) yet, this term is gaining ground as a concept for how to electronically structure an organization's information and training resources. A PSS is a computer based system that provides on-the-job access to integrated information, advice, and learning experiences, thus improving worker productivity. Owing to their expansive goals, PSSs have numerous components, and, in fact, are starting to spawn their own vocabulary: they include advisory systems, *hypermedia* information bases, and libraries of *tutorials* and other indexed learning experiences. The central dream of PSS is to offer embedded, or just-in-time training, giving workers just what they need, nothing more than they need, and all of this at precisely the moment they need it.

Performance tracking: From the world of *educational software*, this term represents a concept that scales up from simple *answer analysis* (the learner answered a questioned correctly, or not) all the way to complex systems that track performance over long periods of time and across broad spans of curricula. In most cases, performance tracking is achieving by simply recording the learner's responses to various questions, and then by subjecting the accumulation of those responses (even if only to one question) to some form of analysis. With gaming software, tracking is a bit more indirect than it is in instructional situations, but basically operates by assessing, and then recording how well the user is responding to the game's central challenge. In many respects, the high end of performance tracking is akin to creating a database of someone's school transcripts and test results. The difference, though, is that by converting this, or any far-reaching span of performance data, into a machine-readable format, it makes it possible for an *instructional designer* to build sophisticated instructional systems that perform such tasks as *strand management* (where specific content, and styles of presentation for treating that content, are matched to the user's diagnosed needs). This, in turn, helps the designer deliver on the long-sought promise of individualized instruction—courseware that analyzes learner need and prescribes instructional sequences that are specifically suited to meet that need. In large measure, performance tracking must be considered one of the frontiers of *interactive multimedia* and *instructional technology* because it represents the vanguard of software engineering efforts that seek to understand in considerable detail the needs of specific users.

Persistence: A term used frequently in the domain of *object-oriented programming*, it refers to the ability of objects to persist through multiple sessions; for example, if data created during the running of a program does not last (persist) after the program session is terminated, then that data does not possess the characteristic of *persistence*. In contrast, data that does survive between sessions is persistent.

Persistence of vision: From the realm of human perception, this term refers to the illusion of smooth, continuous motion that people experience when viewing *animation* or *video* that is created when the sequence of *frames* is played back rapidly enough, and the differences between individual images is small enough.

Personal newspaper: Like *personal television*, this concept was developed at the *Media Lab*, courtesy of its founder, Nicholas Negroponte. Now a popular concept for the next *interface paradigm* (beyond the *desktop metaphor*, that is), the personal newspaper exploits the familiarity of the newspaper to present information in headline-and-column format that has been tailored to the individual's needs. As now conceived, the tailoring will be done by *agents*, software programs that self-navigate the *information superhighway* in search of information items that meet the needs and preferences of the individual. In its full-blown future—if that ever comes to pass—the contents of the personal newspaper will be *multimedia*, with the actual delivery medium for any given piece of information being determined by which one is best suited for that particular piece. Thus, for an essay written by, say, Tom Wolfe, the delivery medium would be plain old text; for an item that reports some sort of natural disaster, any video footage that is available would naturally be employed, and would be shown in the type of window now used by the traditional newspaper for still images (aka, photos).

Personal television: A concept invented at the *Media Lab*, this is a future version of the television projected to operate by culling from public media sources just those items that are of personal interest to the viewer. The device will be programmed with an individual's information and entertainment needs and preferences. It will possess a soft copy of one's media profile. This information will be used to scan the mass of public media sources to construct an individual's personal viewing menu.

Phase modulation: Is modulation in which the phase of an otherwise continuous carrier signal is modified (shifted) based on the data value to be transmitted.

Phong shading: This is one of the high-end forms of polygon shading associated with computer generated graphics. Use of this technique can create extremely realistic computer images.

Phosphors: These are a class of substances that give off light when acted on either by radiation or by certain chemicals. The term is also used to describe the picture elements in most televisions, which use this technology for creating the visible picture that we see on our TV sets.

Photosensor: This device is capable of converting light energy to electrical energy. A common use of photosensors is to serve as the conversion mechanism that links *fiber optic* transmission to computing devices.

Phototexturing: From the world of computer graphics, this sophisticated graphics technique is used extensively in *DTM* (digital terrain modeling) and works by draping real photos and satellite imagery over *polygon*al terrain data. It is heavily used for adding realism to simulations that incorporate a substantial amount of terrain scenery.

Physics-approximate simulation: Is a form of computer simulation wherein models of the real world are created from a library of *algorithms* based on Newtonian Physics. The term was coined by Marvin Minsky, considered one of the fathers of *artificial intelligence* and a visionary with respect to the future of technology.

Pick-up: From the world of audio engineering, this term refers to one of the most common and simplest of recording devices, an electromagnet that captures acoustic vibrations and converts them to electrical signals.

PICT: This is a standard *bit-mapped* graphic file format for the Apple Macintosh.

Picturephone: Most communications experts believe that this term represents the next phase in remote, point-to-point, human communications. Early prototypes are appearing that transmit *quasi-video* (very small screen sizes at very low *frame rates*).

Picture planes: In seeking to understand how *multimedia applications* manipulate the screen, it is important to realize that most programs make use of a set of picture planes, arranged one behind the other. Today's standard is four planes: At the frontmost position is the *cursor plane*, a small area of up to 16 x 16 *pixels* that holds the current position of the *cursor*. Behind the cursor are two image planes, known, respectively, as the *front plane* and *back plane*. These are the two most active and important planes, are used for executing most *DVE* (digital video effects), particularly the large subclass of digital effects known as *two-plane effects*. At the backmost, behind these two center planes, is the lowermost plane, typically referred to as the *backdrop*, which usually holds items such as screen background colors.

Pinna: This anatomical term refers to the soft, shell-like mass of skin that surrounds the ear. Psychoacoustic research in the area of *HRTF* (head-related transfer functions) has determined that the pinna plays a major role in the listener's perception of the direction from which sounds are emanating. Consequently, efforts to digitally encode and create *3-D sound* have begun to take stock of this role, often referred to as the "pinna effect."

PIP: Stands for picture-in-picture, a term that represents the migration of software *windows* concepts from the realm of personal computing to the world of television. Simply put, PIP is the appearance on a television screen of more than one channel at a time, a feat made possible by the creation of an on-screen window that overlays a portion of the current channel and plays host within its confines to a second channel.

Pistol grips: This is a new form of input device being employed in prototypical interactive movie theaters whereby the interactive moviegoer can vote on such issues as plot outcome.

Pits and lans: For better or worse, the evolution of optical technology has ensured that these two terms are bound together for all time. They describe the way in which binary (*digital*) information is encoded onto the surfaces of *optical storage* media. Simply, pits are microscopic holes that are etched into the surface of an optical platter, while lans are areas that remain flat because they are not so etched.

These two surfaces represent the binary data of the digital world because when a laser beam is shone off of a pit it bounces back as a different reflectance value than when that same laser beam is shone off of the flat surface that is a lan.

Pixel: This term was first coined to describe the smallest unit of a video screen and is a contraction of the phrase "picture element." With respect to video screens, the term refers to the small dots which, when taken altogether, make up the visual image that appears on the screen. The term's use has been recently expanded to describe the smallest elements of any system that represents data in the form of 2-D arrays of visual information (e.g., fax machines, copiers, laser printers). The term is typically used to describe the *resolution* or image quality of such devices (e.g., 480 x 640 pixels for full *VGA* monitors).

Pixel hold: From the world of *DVE* (digital video effects), this term refers to one of two types of effect that are known together as *mosaic effects*. Pixel hold works by extending the color and tone (*chrominance* and *luminance*) from one pixel to its neighbors in a process that continues until the screen appears to break up into a gathering of extremely coarse and hazy blocks.

Pixellation: One of the primary *artifacts* of digital forms of video, pixellation is the mosaic-like effect obtained by *zooming* in on portions of a *bit-mapped* image.

Pixel pusher: This is the insider term for a computer graphics artist.

Pixel repeat: From the world of *DVE* (digital video effects), this term refers to one of two types of effect that are known together as *mosaic effects*. Pixel repeat works by *zooming* in on a portion of the screen, but without providing the additional detail needed to keep the on-screen image well focused. Thus, as the target portion of the screen continues to be enlarged, the image itself appears to be getting coarser, or more out of focus.

Pixel thinning: Is a technique for compressing an image—thereby reducing its *bandwidth* requirements—by systematically discarding certain classes of *pixel*.

Platform: Also referred to as "Delivery Platform," this term means the combination of hardware and software components that are assembled to deliver some sort of *multimedia application*. Because the industry is still so young, single devices that integrate all of the devices in a way that is transparent to the user have yet to appear. Thus, for most multimedia applications it is still necessary to build a platform by assembling components, such as high resolution monitors, *joysticks,* and *CD-ROM* players. In time, most industry experts believe that one or more single-device, integrated solutions will emerge. In fact, most believe that the *interactive television* (ITV) will be just such a device. When the ITV appears, we may no longer have to bother with this term.

Platform strategy: Owing to the volatility in the *multimedia* hardware and software markets, most sane developers of *multimedia applications* undertake to devise a platform strategy very early in their design process. This strategy will specify the *platform*, or range of platforms, that the planned product will be able to run on.

Plug-and-play: High on the lexical scale of wish fulfillment, this term refers to the notion that getting a PC peripheral to operate as advertised should demand no more effort than that required to pull the device out of its box and plug it into the computer. As most PC users would attest, this is hardly the case. Compatibility problems riddle the PC industry, and often the most difficult part of acquiring a new peripheral—say, a laser printer, a *CD-ROM* player, or a *scanner*—is just getting the _____ thing to work in the first place. To achieve the dream of plug-and-play, PC hardware and peripheral devices must be automatically configured by the operating system. The Macintosh environment has typically been credited with doing a better job of this than the PC (MS-DOS), a tendency which owes to the stronger enforcement of software and interface standards that Apple can enforce because it controls the manufacture of both the hardware and the operating system. The lack of plug-and-play as an industry characteristic will be a nagging obstacle to the evolution of the *multimedia* market.

Plug-in module: Often, well-constructed, or just plain popular software packages attract further development from third party software developers, who seize the opportunity to enrich the target package by building some set of functions that that program is missing. For example, a *paint system* that is well received and popular might, for some unknown reason, be missing a good library of *fill* patterns (e.g., *radial fills, gradient fills*, etc.). A smart third party software developer might take advantage of this opportunity by filling that gap with a good library of fills, even before the original software manufacturer does. When this occurs, the gap-filling piece of software is often referred to as a "plug-in module," indicating that the customer can simply plug the expanded functionality into the existing package without worrying about any compatibility problems.

PLV: Stands for production-level video and refers to one of two standard video file formats that comprise Intel's *DVI* (Digital Video Interactive) technology. PLV is a high-quality format that relies upon an *asymmetrical, interframe codec* that, like the *MPEG* (Motion Picture Experts Group) standard, demands a time-consuming and expensive encoding process. PLV stands in contrast to *RTV* (real-time video) the inexpensive, *intraframe* portion of the DVI codec canon.

Pointer: A widely used programming technique, a pointer is a statement within a computer program that "points" to the location of another statement. Pointers are employed abundantly in such data structures as *VTOCs* (volume tables of contents), where they are used to point to the starting addresses of the files located on a particular storage device. In *hypermedia* programs, the *hyperlinks* that connect one portion of the document to another are, essentially, pointers—they point from the origin of the hyperlink to its destination.

Pointing device: This computer input device enables the user to directly manipulate objects on the screen. The *mouse* has been the standard graphical user interface (*GUI*) pointing device, but *trackball*, graphic pen, and laser gun are all additional examples of this increasingly popular and important method of interacting with the computer.

Polhemus Tracker™: This is one of the first, and still most popular, forms of *magnetic positioning systems* developed for use with *virtual reality* (*VR*) systems. Created by Polhemus Navigation Sciences of Colchester, Vermont, this device uses a form of magnetic position sensing to enable virtual reality products to track the movement and position of VR users (cybernauts) as they move about within their virtual worlds.

Polygons: With reference to computer graphics, especially those at the high end where *virtual reality* devices and *CAD* (computer aided design) applications dwell, this term refers to a 2-D image segment manipulated in various ways (through shading, for example) to make up images of 3-D objects. For example, a 3-D cube is made up of six flat squares. Each one of these squares is a polygon. Obviously, the more polygons a particular image uses, the more realistic it looks. However, as is typical with the cost-benefit downside of most computing applications, the more polygons one uses, the longer it takes to create the image.

Polyphony: With regard to *MIDI* (musical instrument digital interface) synthesis (the dominant sound technology of the *MPC* [multimedia personal computer] standard), this term refers to the number of individual notes that a particular player is capable of playing simultaneously. Often referred to as the number of *voices* (e.g., 24-voice polyphony), the larger the polyphony, obviously, the richer the sound.

Portability: Used frequently in the field of software engineering, this term refers to a desirable feature of software systems wherewith the system can be easily migrated, or "ported," from one platform to another. This feature is desirable because it eliminates or reduces the considerable expense associated with re-programming products to run on every popular platform in the market. The widely acclaimed move to *object-oriented programming* is at least partly motivated by this programming discipline's ability to accommodate the feature of portability.

Position tracking: Refers to a family of technologies being developed under the banner of *virtual reality* (*VR*) to keep track of the positions and orientations of users as they interact with the VR system. These technologies include techniques that make use of mechanical, ultrasonic, magnetic, optical, and/or *image extraction* sensors.

Postchannel world: This term describes the belief that in the near-future our TV networks will be comprised of so many channels—will be capable of carrying so much video *bandwidth*—that the concept of an individual TV broadcast channel will become obsolete. Rather than being subject to the constraints of a viewing schedule prescribed for them by distant network executives, the viewing public will be afforded the luxury of viewing whatever they want, whenever they want it.

Post-production: In the traditional world of film and video production, this term refers to that phase of the product development cycle that covers all of the manipulation of the video after it has been produced or shot. Thus, this large segment of the development cycle covers all of the editing and the addition of all special audio and video effects (for example, *DVE* [digital video effects] such as the fades and *dissolves* that appear between, and link scenes). It is a common saying in the film industry that all of the filmmaking activity that occurs in advance of post-production is as nothing more than the making of raw clay, and that the real artistic shaping of the film occurs during that post-production phase. Up until now, the post-production phase of filmmaking has required the use of relatively expensive facilities and equipment, usually located in what are called "post-houses." The current flood of all-digital, *desktop video production* tools is all but threatening to cannibalize the post-production industry by making the most sophisticated forms of editing and DVE available to artists at a fraction of the costs associated with traditional *analog* facilities.

PostScript™: A page-description language that serves much the same role for documents that *MIDI* (musical instrument digital interface) serves for music. PostScript was developed by Adobe Systems and has now become the defacto standard for page description languages. The value that it brings to the market is that it is a type of display list placed in a certain format that PostScript-compatible printers, regardless of brand, can read. By instructing the printer through code where to place its ink, a printer can recreate any image, and any font without having the font loaded into memory.

Post-symbolic communications: This phrase, originated by *virtual reality* visionary Jaron Lanier, describes a near-future form of communication in which the maturation of the various technologies surrounding virtual reality will make it possible for communicating parties to share ideas with one another, not so much by talking about the world, but rather by manipulating objects in a shared virtual world. Lanier also refers to this form of communication as "reality conversations."

POTS: Stands for plain old telephone service, still the backbone of the modern communications system.

POV: Stands for point of view, a term that describes the vantage point from which an act of communication is witnessed or perceived. Thus, in a film, POV typically refers to the positioning of the camera relative to the subjects being filmed. With literature, POV may mean much the same thing as it does with regard to film; that is, the physical vantage point from where the reader should imagine seeing a scene. But the term may also refer to a more abstract notion, such as a particular political point of view. However, when used as its acronym, the term usually refers to the physical vantage point for viewing a scene or situation. POV has always been one of the fundamental artistic considerations in building a piece of video or film. This lofty status should not change—in fact, it may actually grow in prominence—as we enter the era of interactive forms of entertainment.

PowerPC™: This term refers to a multi-vendor family of desktop computing products introduced in 1994. Based upon a RISC (reduced instruction set computing) processor designed by IBM and fabricated by Motorola, and on an operating system developed by Apple, the PowerPC is intended to provide significant competition against the long domination of the personal computer market by machines based on the Intel 80 x 86 processors. Because the RISC architecture has been responsible in the early nineties for some of the more powerful graphics workstations, the PowerPC's primary allure is its facilitation of *multimedia applications*.

Prediction: In the world of video *codecs*, this term refers to a form of *motion compensation* in which a *frame* is constructed during *decompression* from the difference information between the original frame (determined during the *compression* process) and the preceding *key frame*.

Preference tracking: A close cousin to *performance tracking*, this concept drives software engineering efforts to create programs that understand the emotional preferences of the user. Examples of this might include programs that monitor preferences for style of TV programming (e.g., westerns vs. whodunits, violent vs. nonviolent programming), purchasing preferences, social styles, etc. The purpose for tracking preference is, of course, to then use that data to match system resources to the needs of the user. In the emergent phenomenon of *home interactive media*, preference tracking will serve as an *enabling technology* used to help deliver on the promise of *personal television—smart TV* that knows the user's likes and dislikes and uses that information to build individualized evenings of entertainment.

Pre-production: In the world of film and video, this term refers to that part of the development phase that lies in between the completion of the scripts and the commencement of the video shoot (also called *production*). Once a script is approved for production, the development team must first perform a number of preparatory functions before launching into the very expensive process of shooting the field footage. They must, for example, break out the scripts, identifying the characters, the props, the sets, and the locations. Then, if locations are to be involved in the shoot, they must scout for the best site(s). Also, they must conduct casting sessions, select the cast, and perform a large number of tasks associated with estimating and controlling the budget. En toto, these preparatory activities are referred to as "pre-production." Because most *multimedia* budgets are still quite constrained when compared against those that are available for the typical film project, much of the video placed in multimedia titles is actually *stock footage*, rather than originally produced video. This course of action eliminates the labor intensive and costly activities required by the pre-production and production phases.

Problem-based learning: From the realm of *instructional design*, this term describes an emerging school of thought that says that people learn best, not by deliberately studying educational materials, but by applying concepts and skills to the task of solving specific problems. This premise has major consequences for how the computer is employed as a teaching tool. The dominant, early model of computer based instruction has been the study, or *drill and practice,* model. During the late eighties and early nineties, schools spent considerable funds on integrated learning systems, which are dominated by the drill and practice model of instruction. The reliance on this model reflects, not so much a deep-seated belief that the study model of instruction is the secret to effective pedagogy, but rather a capitulation to the relatively easy nature of programming drill and practice programs, which amounts to little more than programming a succession of multiple choice style questions. Advocates of the problem-based approach to learning oppose the extensive use of integrated learning systems and are promoting a move to problem-solving, game-oriented programs that go much further in terms of engaging the learner. Educational software is likely to move in this direction in the near future, and away from the drill and practice paradigm.

Procedural knowledge: From the world of *artificial intelligence*, this is the form of machine knowledge responsible for modeling the sequence and nature of task completion. This form of machine knowledge draws heavily upon, but is independent from, declarative knowledge.

Proclamation 66: Considered a landmark case in the history of educational technology, this legislative act by the state of Texas has made it possible for Texas school districts to purchase instructional multimedia products with funds that hitherto were limited to the acquisition of standard textbooks. To many, this act represents a break-through in thinking about what constitutes a "textbook."

Production: In the world of film and video, this term refers to that most exciting of phases in the development process during which the director says "lights, camera, action." It is the phase that lies between *pre-production* and *post-production*, and it is the penultimate act of film creation in which the actors and crew are assembled, and the original field footage is shot.

Production chart: With reference to the production of a film/video/animation, this is a form that shows the status of every scene in the picture during the various stages of production.

Progressive scanning: The standard form of scanning for today's television is termed *interlaced* scanning, which means that it takes two complete passes of a TV's *CRT* (cathode ray tube) electron gun to paint a single image on the screen. When a single screen image of *NTSC* (National Television Standards Committee)-quality TV is transmitted, it is actually transmitted in two separate *frames*, each one containing every other line of the 525 *scan lines* that make up a television image. Thus, one frame will contain all odd scan lines (1, 3, 5, etc.), while the very next frame contains the even lines (2, 4, 6, etc.). This interlaced method is motivated by the need to conserve *bandwidth*. Progressive scanning is the more natural, but much more bandwidth-intensive technique whereby one frame equals one screen image. It is called progressive scanning because each scan line is followed, not by its next odd or even cohort, but rather by its next, and closest relative. Thus, scan line 1 is followed by scan line 2, which is followed by scan line 3, etc. One of the competitors for the *HDTV* (high definition television) standard is recommending a progressive scanning method of transmission. This form of scanning eliminates many of the typical *artifacts* of normal TV broadcasts, such as inter-line flicker and certain distortions associated with rapidly moving objects. The penalty, of course, is that with progressive scanning, a transmitted image in the video stream requires twice as much bandwidth as is required by an interlaced image.

Project Jedi: This is a project being undertaken by Lucasfilm with the goal of changing the way that movies get made. The primary intent of the project is to convert from a process that, historically, has relied entirely upon analog technologies, to a process that relies entirely on digital technologies. It is believed that the outcome of such a conversion will make possible unprecedented levels of ability to manipulate the visual image for artistic purposes.

Prototype community: The costs of software development tends to be high. So too are the costs of creating high-quality media. When you combine the two—which is exactly what you do when you build interactive multimedia—the costs can be very high. Thus, it behooves multimedia application and hypermedia application developers to create early prototypes of their programs, and to test them on at least one representative sample of their target market. This is no easy chore, because it involves organizing a willing and qualified community of users (viewers, gamers, or whatever). When such a community is organized, the organization who did the organizing tends to view them as a considerable asset and seeks to use them for extensive testing, perhaps of more than one product or system. The term "prototype community" is now being used to describe this community of users upon which prototypes are tested.

Psychoacoustics: From the increasingly prevalent world of 3-D audio, this term refers to an academic discipline that concerns itself with the human perception and interpretation of sound. Most of the recent advances in the digital encoding of *HRTF* (head-related transfer functions) have grown out of research in this field.

Public domain: Any item of electronic content (media or software) that is free of any copyright, trademark or patent restrictions is said to be "public domain." In the coming age of multimedia, where so much of our information will be assembled from myriad, and previously unrelated sources (e.g., from stock footage, clipmedia, etc.), the need and demand for sources of public domain content will be intense.

Public switched telephone network: Also commonly referred to by its acronym, PSTN, this term refers to the massive telephone infrastructure to which everyone has common access rights. When someone wants to send information over a channel that is **not** private, they must access and use the PSTN. Thus, if someone is using a *LAN* (local area network), or a direct private line, they are **not** using the PSTN. But in almost every other conceivable case in which communications is occurring between geographically separate entities, they are making use of the public switched telephone network.

Pulse code modulation (PCM): PCM is done by *sampling* a waveform at a constant rate (*sampling rate*) of thousands of times per second to convert *analog* audio to *digital* audio. The minimum standard *MPC* (multimedia personal computer) samples sound at 11,025Hz with 8 bits per sample, and plays back waveform audio at 22,050Hz with 8 bits per sample. The sampling rate needs to be double the highest frequency of the sampled sound to produce the "Nyquest" frequency sound standard.

Purging: In traditional data processing, this term refers to the very necessary process whereby files that have outlived their usefulness are removed—are purged—from the system's storage devices. Purging can be accomplished through either manual or automated procedures. Most automated procedures base their decision to purge a particular file or piece on information on the criterion of lack of use. In other words, if a file has not been accessed for a pre-determined period of time, it is judged by the system to no longer be of use, and it is therefore eliminated from the system. In the era of multimedia, where file sizes are going to mushroom in order to handle the *mixed media data types*, the need to purge files in a logical and consistent way is apt to grow in importance.

Px64: This is a popular *videoconferencing* standard developed by the *CCITT* (Consultative Committee on International Telephone and Telegraph). It is primarily a *codec* (compression-decompression) standard, and facilitates the transmission of audio and video data over copper or fiber channels.

Users and developers will start with conventions that they understand—television, books, films, computer games, computer-aided instruction—and then discover new ways to use the multimedia technology environment.
—SueAnn Ambron, Apple Computer, Inc.

QHY: Stands for quantized high-resolution Y, a term that refers to a technique that elaborates on the *DYUV* (delta luminance color difference) *compression* scheme. QHY works by enhancing the *luminance* (or Y) signals of the image and interpolating it between the *chrominance* and *luminance* values already stored as a DYUV image. Wherever luminance varies greatly between two DYUV *pixel* values, QHY interpolates a correct value to achieve the effect of a sharper image.

Quantization: In the process of *ADC* (analog-to-digital conversion), quantization is the step that immediately follows sampling and is responsible for providing *digital* media with the binary-encoded numeric values that capture some or most of the properties of the original sensory signal.

Quasi-video: As computing makes the painful transition from the alphanumeric forms of data to the higher *bandwidth* versions of data—audio, image, and especially video—it is being forced to render these presentational media in a compromised format. With regard to video, which has the highest bandwidth of the three, there have been three basic avenues of compromise. The first has to do with screen geography. Since all forms of *digitized* visuals are translated into a *pixel* format, and since each pixel represents some amount of memory requirement—the basic element of size, insofar as the computer is concerned—the size and corresponding memory requirement of a piece of *digital* video is directly proportional to the amount of screen space it is projected on. Thus, many digital video applications are limited to a certain size *window*, so as to control the overall amount of computer data that must be moved through the system to create the motion picture. The second area of compromise has to do with *resolution*, i.e., with the number of pixels that must be represented to display a given image. Obviously, the lower the resolution, the smaller the amount of data that must be employed to represent the image. Thus, lowering the resolution is another way of lowering the memory and processing requirements associated with displaying video. Finally, the third factor of compromise has to do with how many frames per second (*fps*) are used to represent the motion picture. For television, the standard is 30 fps. In the first half of the '90s, however, most makers of video hardware and software still find this frame rate to be a bit daunting. As a result, many "video files" are stored and played back at lower frame rates, the most common hovering in the 10-15 fps range. Taken together, these three compromises represent what many in the multimedia industry are referring to as the "quasi-video" of computing. It is important to note that, with time and the inexorable advance of hardware and software, the compromises of quasi-video will likely go away (and with it, the term).

Queue: In the computer world, this term refers to a group of items waiting to be acted upon by the computer. The arrangement of items determines the processing priority.

QuickDraw™: Introduced with the initial Apple Macintosh in 1984, this is Apple's library of software tools for developing static graphics. It made the *PICT* file format an industry standard for graphics files.

QuickRing™: The *local bus* standard for Apple Macintosh, it is capable of moving up to 350 MBps, making it one of the fastest local bus standards in the industry.

QuickTime™: Introduced in 1991, this is Apple's library of system software tools for creating time-based data—audio, animation, and motion picture. At the heart of QuickTime, as with any motion-enabling software, is a *codec* (responsible for data *compression-de-compression*), and so it seems inevitable that QuickTime will be compared against *DVI* (Digital Video Interactive), *MPEG* (Motion Picture Experts Group), and other codecs. QuickTime has three major components: The Movie Toolbox, which makes it possible to play, edit, and otherwise manipulate the time-based data; The Image Compression Manager, which is the high level interface to QuickTime's codec; and the Component Manager, which is largely responsible for interfacing QuickTime resources to external system resources.

Stalking the future is a curious game.
—Nicholas Negroponte,
Director, The Media Lab at MIT

Radial fill: From the world of computer paint systems, this term refers to a type of *fill* in which a pattern is projected from a center outward in all directions.

Radio button: An *interface* element common to graphical user interfaces (*GUIs*) based on the *desktop metaphor*, radio buttons are typically placed in groups of three or more. Their principal distinction as a mode of selecting program functions is that they are mutually exclusive: you can only select one of them. Their name derives from the obvious metaphor with the dials on a radio.

RAID: Stands for redundant arrays of inexpensive disks and represents the latest incarnation of magnetic disk storage. This new form is gathering wide appeal among *multimedia* developers because it offers much higher capacities than traditional magnetic storage, and yet offers the far greater data transfer speeds that have always characterized magnetic as compared to optical disc (e.g., *CD-ROM*). Through a process called *file striping*, this form of storage also provides the desirable feature of redundancy, wherewith the failure of one disk in the array does not cause any loss of data because each file is duplicated on the other disks in the array.

Random access: Of longstanding importance as a central concept in data processing, this term is often defined in terms of its opposite: *sequential access*. With information that is stored on a sequential access device, *access times* are typically longer because one has to pass over everything that intervenes to access the desired information. Tape storage is the classic example of a sequential access device. If you are at the end of a tape—one of your VHS tapes, for example—and want to access something near the beginning, then you must rewind the tape, searching all the while, until you get all the way to the front of the tape to reach the information you want. In contrast, random access means that you can access any single piece of information as easily as any other piece of information, regardless of where any of it is stored on the medium. Disk storage is considered the classic example of a random access device. This random access capability is made possible by the use of directories, which enable read heads to find out the address of the desired information, and then move directly to that location.

Raster file: As opposed to a *vector file*, a raster file is an image file generated either by using a paint program or by scanning an image. A raster file is stored in the form of a *bit map*. This is literally a "map," or two-dimensional array, of the display image containing the location of each *pixel* and its representative grayscale or color characteristics. Raster images are noted for their brilliant colors and high *resolution*, but also for their unwieldy size and resistance to flexible manipulation (e.g., resizing). Vector files, in contrast, are generated by *draw programs* and are laid out on the basis of mathematical equations, or "vectors."

Raster image processor: Providing the bridge from electronic content (e.g., *ASCII* data) to image (e.g., *bit map*), this device transforms the encoded representation of a character into the desired pattern of *pixel* marks so that it may be laid down on paper. The quality goal of a raster image processor is to take the encoded character and transform it into a pixel pattern that captures that character's typefont, style, size, and orientation as accurately as possible.

Raster-to-vector conversion: In the workaday world of *multimedia applications*, there is frequent need to convert image files from one format to another. Raster-to-vector conversion is one of the most difficult of these conversions, demanding a great deal of the conversion software. This process requires the software to detect the presence of geometric shapes in a *bit-mapped* image, and then convert those shapes to *vectorized* or mathematical representations. Typically, this is done with a trace function that literally traces and redraws the image with mathematical vectors of the lines, shapes, and objects that make up the image.

Ray tracing: This technique is used for creating realistic computer images by tracing rays from viewpoint to light source, which is, of course, the reverse of light rays. In other words, this technique traces the path of light as it bounces off of reflective surfaces. It calculates both hidden surfaces and *shading*. However, it tends to be *CPU-intensive*, requiring a relatively lengthy processing time for each image that is generated. The high cost in terms of CPU cycles is, however, offset by the high value that ray tracing provides to a graphical image. It is a technique that is used primarily to give computer generated images a very realistic and subtle sense of lighting.

RBOC: Stands for Regional Bell Operating Company, a type of corporate entity that was established as a result of the 1984 anti-trust suit that broke up the AT&T Bell System. There are seven RBOCs, or "baby bells" as they are sometimes called: Ameritech, Bell Atlantic, BellSouth, Nynex, Pacific Telesis, Southwestern Bell, and US West. The legislation that broke up the system prohibits the RBOCs from providing video services into their local market areas, but these restrictions are under severe legislative scrutiny and may be lifted at almost any time. In any event, the RBOCs are busy at the work of forming alliances with *CATV* (cable) operators, and are expected to become major providers of *multimedia* services as we enter the *Age of Interactivity*.

RDS: Stands for radio data system, an innovation recently imported from Europe to the United States that offers interactive services to radio listeners through an FM *subcarrier* channel. Haled as the first major innovation in radio technology since the introduction of the FM signal in 1961, RDS will offer services such as a small screen to display printed information like the station's call letters, the name of a song and its artist, traffic and weather bulletins, and possibly even advertising. Additional features will include the ability to search the dial by format, rather than by station; a *hand-off function* for cross-country drivers that automatically switches to a stronger station for a broadcast being aired nationally (e.g., National Public Radio); and, the ability to automatically interrupt any station with an emergency announcement, such as a weather warning.

Real time: This refers to an operating mode for computers under which data are received and processed, and the results returned so fast, that the process appears instantaneous to the user. Real-time modes are usually described in contrast to *batch* systems, where data are accumulated over time, and then submitted for processing all at once, often during late night hours when the real-time processing load placed on the computer system has diminished. As more and more of the processing load moves to managing the *user interface* in concert with the rise of *multimedia applications*, the pressure will grow on hardware/software to provide systems that feature real-time performance.

Rear-projection: A form of projection system that has grown very popular in corporate America, rear-projection provides for significantly larger display areas than are feasible with conventional video monitors. Rear-projection works by reflecting the video image off of a mirror which stands behind a special screen onto which the image is cast. The use of this type of system for marketing and other corporate presentations has done a great deal to foster the speaker-support segment of the multimedia industry.

Recognizer: From the world of *OCR* (optical character recognition), this term refers to a process that is the opposite of rasterizing. The recognizer takes the *pixel* image pattern of a character on a document, identifies the particular character that it represents, and then assigns it the appropriate computer code. In the PC domain, a recognizer converts a character stamped on a paper document into its appropriate *ASCII* code.

Red Book: This term refers to the original compact disc format standard established by Philips and Sony for digital audio, also known as CD-DA (Compact Disc—Digital Audio). When one buys a music CD at a retail center, a sure bet is that the disc has been pressed in accordance with the Red Book standard.

Redlining level: In the world of digital audio, this term refers to the amplitude of the loudest sound that a digital system is capable of expressing. For an audio engineer, the trick is to keep all events in the sound track beneath the redlining level of the digital system that is being used.

Refresh rate: This is the rate at which the electron beam of an *RGB* (red, green, blue) monitor scans the screen, thereby restoring (refreshing) the image. Most computer displays—and TVs under the *NTSC* (National Television Standards Committee) standard—refresh the screen every 1/60th of a second.

Remediation: From the field of learning theory, and more recently, from *instructional design*, this term refers to a teaching strategy that seeks to address learning deficiencies directly, rather than working on learning strengths. With the various forms of computer based learning (e.g., *CAI* [computer aided instruction], *CBT* [computer based training], *educational software*, etc.), remediation is often used in direct response to an incorrect answer to a question.

Render: One of the most *CPU-intensive* of all computer processes, rendering is the penultimate phase in the creation of 3-D graphics and animation. Prior to rendering, a graphics artist will create a 3-D model, which is, in essence, a wireframe representation of the graphical object (a chalice, for example). Once this model has all of the shape and size attributes the artist wishes, the rendering process will be launched. This process involves removing all of the jagged edges and hidden surfaces, followed by adding all of the object's shading attributes, such as texture and depth. Rendering is becoming an increasingly sophisticated aspect of multimedia production, and, along with the *compression* of motion pictures, represents one the strongest forces pushing chip manufacturers to build faster processors.

Rendering engines: Are hardware/software systems powerful enough to generate illusion-sustaining landscapes, buildings, etc. An example of a rendering engine would be *DTM* (digital terrain modeling). The future of rendering engines is clear: they will play a role as one of the key automata involved in the creation of realistic settings for virtual reality and interactive fiction products.

Re-recording: With regard to filmmaking, this term refers to one of the penultimate phases of post-production, where the final sound track is "re-recorded" from its various components, which were either separated from one another at an earlier time so that they might receive individualized attention (e.g., the various voice tracks in a dialogue), or were recorded separately in the first place (e.g., the film's musical components). During this final *mix*, many things are done to perfect the audio track, such as balancing volumes, adjusting the pitch of the voices or sounds (treble/bass balance), and perhaps adding some special effects (e.g., a telephone filter, which, obviously, makes a voice sound as if it is being heard over a telephone). As with so many aspects of media production, this process has a great deal to benefit from the *digitization* process, because it leads to the ability to analyze, separate, and recombine sounds, all on the same platform, and all without the traditional concern for handling many different types of physical media. The maturation of such technologies as *MIDI* (musical instrument digital interface) and *DSP* (digital signal processing) ensures that the process of re-recording will soon be done entirely within the domain of a computerized system.

Resample: This process is undertaken to adjust the *resolution* of a digital image to match the capabilities of the current hardware platform. Resampling down discards *pixel* information in an image. Conversely, resampling up adds pixel information through *interpolation*.

Resolution: In its most general sense, this term refers to the fineness of the detail represented by any form of media—audio, image, video, or even such exotic forms of media as tactile feedback. The most common use of the term today occurs with regard to the images shown on a video or computer display, where they are measured as a number of discrete elements per area—for example, *pixels* per square inch. The higher the number, the better the resolution and the higher the quality of the image.

Resolution independence: This term refers to a highly desirable capability for computers to be able to output media—audio, image, video—at any *resolution*, regardless even of the resolution at which the original media was captured or *digitized*. This term is nearly synonymous with *scalability*.

Retinal imaging: One of the more futuristic of new media devices being contemplated today, this technology represents the art of painting an image directly onto the retina of the eye. One strategy for doing this is for the computer to steer a low-powered laser beam around the retina, thereby activating rods and cones in the desired patterns and intensities.

Reverb: Short for "reverberation," this audio engineering term refers to the natural echo that accompanies almost every sound as it bounces off of natural objects in the listener's environment. Because sound recordings that lack reverb are perceived as thin and unnatural, much effort is made by audio engineers to add this dimension to their finished work.

RGB: Stands for red, green, blue and represents the most widely used representation of video images, wherein the constituent pixels are defined by their respective red, green, and blue color components.

RIP™: Stands for Remote Imaging Protocol, a standard for transmitting computer generated, *mixed media data types* over the television transmission infrastructure. It is created by TeleGrafix of Huntington Beach, California, and is intended to replace the longstanding *NAPLPS* (North American Presentation Level Protocol Standard) by making it possible for online services to transmit a much more media-rich form of content.

RLE: Stands for run length encoding and refers to a commonly used strategy for compressing data, especially data with black-and-white images, like those associated with paper documents. RLE works by counting the number of consecutive *pixels* that have the same visual value—such as occurs with the proportionally large white spaces in most documents—and then stores only the location and "count" of these consecutive pixels. This is in contrast to *bit-map* images, which supply the numeric, or digitized, value of each and every pixel in the image. It is important to note, however, that many RLE algorithms start with bit maps as their primary source of input, and then "compress them down" by parsing, counting, and then saving all of the segments in the bit map that possess consecutive pixels with the same digital characteristics.

Rolling demo: From the world of *multimedia applications*, this type of *hypermedia application* is used almost exclusively in marketing situations, such as show or retail floor exhibits. With rolling demos, a sequence of screens/video segments is programmed to flow from one screen/segment to another with little or no need for human intervention. These demos are typically used to display key product characteristics and features. Their primary benefit is, of course, that they do not require the expensive services of a salesperson, and so can be left unattended at shows or in stores. Most rolling demos provide a feature that enables users to break out of the pre-programmed sequence, and take direct control of the program's *media assets*.

Room tone: From the world of audio production for film and video, room tone represents the natural sound of any location (e.g., the low buzz and china-clinking of a restaurant crowd, the machine-murmur of outside traffic). Room tone is used instead of blank film or tape for spaces in between sound takes, because every location has a sound, whereas film and tape do not. In the age of multimedia technology, an abundance of audio *clip media* is becoming available to provide a library of such sounds to video producers.

Rotoscope: In the world of feature animations, this is a machine made to project filmed images *frame* by frame onto the surface of a drawing board. The image is traced onto animation paper and used by the animator to achieve lifelike movement. In a sense, rotoscoping is a form of *data capture* for animation.

Rough cut: From the world of filmmaking, this term refers to one of the first phases of the post-production process wherein the director/editor team put together their first pass at building the finished movie. They do this by sequencing together an initial selection of takes and shots from the production phase. Depending upon many factors—e.g., the skill of the director as reflected in his choices during production—the rough cut will be either close, or rather distant from what the finished film will look like. Many of the more sophisticated electronic video editing products, such as Adobe's Premiere, make it possible for film developers to prepare their rough cuts entirely in a *digital* format. This means that, rather than coping with the problems associated with a potentially large and cumbersome number of *sequential access* video tapes, the editing crew can work entirely in *random access* or *nonlinear* mode. Of course, this also assumes the presence of some rather large storage devices, including a sizable volume of erasable media.

RTF: Stands for rich text format, a Microsoft file formatting standard that grew out of the Microsoft *Windows* software developer's kit. It was designed to enable software developers to create help files to accompany their software. Specifically, RTF enables developers to embed elements of document structure, such as table of contents, index entries, *hyperlinks*, etc. Many popular word processing packages now support the RTF standard.

RTOS: Stands for real-time operating system and refers to operating system(s), or OS components, that operate quickly and efficiently enough to manage direct user interaction. With the increasing movement of computer applications into the workaday world of noncomputer professionals, and with the addition of high bandwidth (media) data types, the demands placed on operating systems to manage high volumes of information in real time will continue to grow. *CD-RTOS*, the operating system of Philips' *CD-I* standard for home interactive media, provides a good example.

RTV: Stands for real-time video, and refers to one of the two standard file formats that make up Intel *DVI* (Digital Video Interactive) technology. RTV is an inexpensive, *intraframe codec* in which both compression and decompression can be executed on the fly and stands in contrast to *PLV* (production-level video), the more expensive, *interframe* portion of the DVI codec canon.

Rubberbanding: In this line-drawing technique, an "elastic" line is extended from one or more point(s) to wherever the screen *cursor* is located. This feature is used with many paint systems to enable an easy and flexible way for artists to re-shape objects.

The computer de-routinizes, and routine is a sedative to the mind. The general relegation of trivial tasks to the mechanical periphery is perhaps the most explosive phenomenon of computerization.
—Douglas Leebaert,
Professor, Graduate School of Business,
Georgetown University

Sample rate converters: Because there are now so many forms and modes and standards for *digitizing* the various media (audio, image, video, etc.), there is often a need to convert a signal from one sampling rate to another. *Sample rate* converters perform this function, and therefore can be said to be part-in-parcel of a *scalable architecture*. The need for sample rate conversion commonly arises when transferring a digitized signal from one system to another. For example, an audio signal recorded at 48 kHz on a professional *digital* tape deck may have to be converted to 44.1 kHz for storage on a CD. Another obvious example has to do with digital telephone systems where, in order to carry the low-quality 8 kHz standard of the *public switched telephone network*, (PSTN) digital audio from almost any other digital source must be down-converted.

Sampling: The first step in any form of *DSP* (digital signal processing), this process is responsible for converting the continuous, *analog* forms of signal known in the real world of nature to the discrete-time, binary forms of signal employed in the world of *digital* computing. In the process of *ADC* (analog-to-digital conversion), sampling precedes the step known as *quantization*, whereby the discrete-time signal obtained by sampling an *analog* signal is converted to a binary-encoded numerical value that captures some or most of the natural signal's properties.

Sampling rate: This refers to the number of times per second that digitizing circuitry measures an *analog* signal to produce a *digital* value. With regard to digitizing various sources of media, this critical variable is virtually synonymous with quality, because it expresses the resolution at which *ADC* (analog-to-digital conversion) takes place. The higher the sampling rate, the finer the quality of the *digitized* media.

Saturation: A technical characteristic of color, saturation refers to the purity of a color. Rich, intense colors are thus said to be highly saturated, while dull or diluted colors are characterized as not being very saturated. For example, pink is a low-saturation red.

SBCELP: This acronym stands for an emerging standard in *voice coding*. The SB is short for Lernout & Hauspie Speech Products of Belgium, the firm responsible for developing the coding technique; while the CELP stands for code-excited linear prediction, an acronym that captures the essence of the technique's algorithmic makeup. SBCELP is routinely capable of creating voice compression ratios in the range of 30-to-1, and possesses a *codec* that requires about 12 *MIPS* (millions of instructions per second) of computational power for compressing the voice signal, and about 1.5 MIPS for decompressing the same signal. Numerous low cost *DSPs* (digital signal processors) are now available that can perform these *codec* tasks.

SCADA: Stands for system control and data acquisition and represents one of the emerging, large scale applications for multimedia technology. SCADA centers look like the War Room at the Pentagon. They feature large video displays and are connected to the world by abundantly equipped *broadband* communications facilities. Geographic Information Systems (*GIS*) that present *real time* sources of data on brightly colored maps are perhaps the most common form of *enabling technology* used in conjunction with SCADA. Picture this: a fast food mogul stands before a GIS displaying real-time sales data and joyfully shrieks at the realization that there is a flurry of cheeseburger sales in Delaware.

Scalability: A term of increasing importance in the world of computers and multimedia, scalability refers to the ability of a given technology to scale up or down in capability in conjunction with the differing capabilities of the technologies which surround and support it. For example, when used with reference to the balkanized world of video *codecs*, this term refers to a computer's ability to optimally adapt a *digital video* stream to the *data rate* of the playback system it finds itself working on. If, on the one hand, the playback system has superior resolution (e.g., *SVGA*), then the codec should scale itself up so that the compressed image is decompressed to play at this high-quality resolution. If, on the other, the playback system has antiquated display technology, the codec should decompress the image to play at the lower level of resolution.

Scalable architecture: This term refers to any product designed so that buyers can upgrade their initially purchased items without having to replace those items. This term can be aptly applied to the personal computer market, where it is possible to upgrade one's initial purchase by, for example, adding internal memory chips, attaching new peripheral devices, or even by replacing the machine's motherboard. In contrast, the television has, for the most part, failed to make scalability a part of its design: if a family has a black-and-white TV and now wants color, they must simply buy a new color television set. This term is much in vogue now, because as the industry contemplates the inevitable merger of the television and the computer, there is much hope that this new device—the *interactive television* or *smart TV*—will feature a scalable architecture. Looking ahead, this architecture is expected to make it possible for television owners to do such things as add new disk storage so that they can download more programming or simply add more flatbed screen cells so that they can watch a bigger screen.

Scan converter: Also referred to by the longer phrase "video scan converter," this device helps to convert video signals from one format to another, mediating format differences primarily between the worlds of TV and computer video. Unfortunately, this increasingly intense interface between the analog world of traditional media production and the digital world of computers is based upon a significant technical difference in the way the video signal is handled. For TV, the format has remained the same in the United States since the NTSC (National Television Standards Committee) standard was set for color television in the 1950s. In contrast, for computers, the standard seems to change with every new release of every make and type of computer, which means, of course, almost daily. When converting an image from computer to television formats, for example, a scan converter must change the image from *digital* to *analog*, and from *noninterlaced* to *interlaced*, plus it must match the *refresh rates* between the two. So long as the analog and digital worlds co-exist in nervous parallel, the market for scan converters should remain a strong, but complex one. Bring on the *teleputer*.

Scan head: Is the part of a *scanner* that optically senses the text or graphic as it moves across the page.

Scan lines: These are the parallel lines across the video screen along which the scanning spot travels from left to right when projecting the video information that makes up the picture on the TV screen or monitor. *NTSC* (National Television Standards Committee) standard video systems produce 525 lines on a screen.

Scanner: This term refers to a data-capture device that creates a two-dimensional, bit-stream image of the object being scanned. Most commonly, scanners are used to *digitize* paper documents. The primary function of a scanner is to translate paper documents into electronic *pixel* or *bit-mapped* images. Typically, the scanning process involves reflecting light off of the target object in such a way that it can be captured or converted to *digital* data. The subcomponent within a scanner responsible for converting the light to digital data is the *CCD* (charge coupled device).

Scientific visualization: This emerging field uses computer graphics to create visual models of physical processes and numerical data. Ranging from literal translations of nature, such as a visual, cross-sectional model of a volcanic eruption, to highly abstract renderings, such as a color-coded, *heat-mapped* depiction of a stock portfolio over the course of a trading session, scientific visualization is an approach or a process that makes it possible to distill huge amounts of numeric data into a single image or a series of images over time in animations.

Scope and sequence: From the hallowed halls of academe, this term refers to a significant step in the design of any educational program. It has become quite popular with *instructional designers*, who use this step to lay out the scope of the content to be covered in a particular piece of *educational software* (*courseware*), and to specify the most desirable sequence(s) in which that content should be experienced by the learner.

Screen candy: This insider term refers to little visual rewards placed within an interactive program to dazzle the user.

Screen capture programs: This term describes a family of software utilities, commonly used by multimedia developers in particular, which are used to quickly capture the current contents of the computer screen. These programs typically work by creating a snapshot, or *bit-map* of the current contents of the screen, and can usually be enacted by some form of simple command, such as a two keystroke combination or command sequence.

Script-X™: One of the mission-specified projects of *Kaleida Labs* (the joint venture between Apple and IBM), Script-X is a multimedia authoring language. It enables developers to create applications for multiple platforms. As envisioned, Script-X is to *multimedia* what Apple *PostScript* is to desktop publishing.

Scroll bar: From the world of the *desktop* graphical user interface (*GUI*), the scroll bar is a common *interface* element used to change locations within a document. Typically, the scroll bar is a rectangle having on each end an arrow in a square box indicating direction of movement within the document. Inside the scroll bar is a scroll box, which is the item that the user drags to move within the document.

Scrolling: A common technique in computer user *interface design* whereby all the displayed information on the screen is moved at once, either vertically or horizontally.

Scrolling game: This is a somewhat pejorative term that has been used to label the dominant genre of video games in which the player-controlled protagonist is moved across the screen from left to right, encountering a succession of obstacles as different backgrounds scroll by.

SCSI: Stands for small computer standard interface and refers to a very important set of standards that was established to control the way that peripheral devices of virtually every kind (scanners, storage devices, printers, etc.) are connected to personal computers. Pronounced "scuzzy," this 8-bit, parallel standard makes it theoretically possible for any device, such as a *CD-ROM* player, to attach to any personal computer, provided of course that both have been equipped with a SCSI interface.

SECAM: Stands for Systeme Electronique Coleur Avec Memoire and is the counterpart to the North American *NTSC* (National Television Standards Committee) standard for encoding TV signals. SECAM is used in France, Russia, and Eastern Europe, and makes use of 625 *scan lines* and runs at 25 *frames* per second (*fps*).

Seek: This term is used most often in the *digital* world to refer to the positioning of a read head on a mass storage device in the correct location to read a particular file or a particular piece of information.

Seek time: This term represents a performance measure used most commonly with disk storage devices. It measures the time it takes for the disk read head to pick up from its current location and move to its next. Obviously, seek time is controlled in large measure by how close the data from one read is relative to the next read. Thus, seek time as an official performance measure is usually recorded as an average over several types of read.

Segue: Industry jargon from the world of video production, this term is used to describe the transition from one major theme, scene, etc., to the next.

Sensorama: This was one of the earliest prototypes of virtual reality. Developed as prototype arcade game in the mid-1960s by Martin Heilig, it was one of the first examples of a multisensory simulation environment that provided more than just visual input. This prototype featured a binocular viewing optics system, 3-D binaural sound, simulated vibration cues, wind simulation, and a chemical smell bank that generated simulated smells borne into the user's face by the wind simulator. The premise of the game was a first-person-viewpoint motorcycle ride through New York city.

Sequence: Is a series of scenes that make up a definite episode in a story.

Sequencer: In the word of *MIDI* (musical instrument digital interface) sound production, this term refers to a program feature that enables a composer or sound engineer to move musical and other sounds around, i.e., to rearrange them into the desired sequence. In many respects, the sequencer is highly analogous to the cut-and-paste features found in word processing programs and *paint systems*.

Sequential access: Of longstanding importance as a central concept in data processing, this term is often defined in terms of its opposite: *random access*. With information stored on a sequential access device, access times are typically longer than with a random access device. Tape storage is the classic example of a sequential access device. If you are at the end of a tape and want to access something near the beginning, then you must rewind the tape, searching until you get to the front of the tape to reach the information wanted. In contrast, random access means that you can access any single piece of information as easily as any other piece of information, regardless of where any of it is stored on the medium. Disk storage is considered the classic example of a random access device. This random access capability is made possible by the use of directories, which enable read heads to find out the address of the desired information, and then move directly to that location.

Server: A term usually associated with *LAN* (local area network) and database technologies, a server is centralized repository of shared database information. In a typical LAN configuration, the server is the largest machine in the network, and generally manages the network (plays host to the *network operating system*), as well as playing host to the network's largest collection of shared objects. Attached workstations make requests to the server, which then *downloads* the requested information to those workstations.

Set-top box: This term is fast becoming the center of one of the great technological debates of our time. While it is widely accepted that the computer will converge with the television in the long run, it is not at all certain which of these two venerable devices will win out in the near term. That is to say: we all know that the computer is becoming more like the TV, that it can now show TV-quality images, and that it can, in fact, be rigged with an *expansion board* that makes *pass-through video* possible; and, we all know that the TV is being made smarter all the time, and that, in fact, there are boxes that we can attach to the TV which, in effect, provide it with most, if not all of the intelligence of a computer. These boxes are now being called "set-top boxes." They actually have quite a history, going back at least to the beginning of the video game industry, when companies like Nintendo and Sega were placing *CPU*s in their game machines, but avoided calling those devices by any name that might suggest the presence of a computer out of fear that any computer-like device would cause a phobic reaction among their buyers. Nevertheless, these set-top boxes have CPUs, and so have the essential ingredients of a computer. Moreover, their technical make-up is advancing rapidly, and with products like the 3D0 player, are approaching the power of a full-blown *desktop* computer. Thus, we have a controversy: will the set top box become so powerful that it eliminates the need for a personal computer?, or, will the personal computer take on so many media capabilities that it will eliminate the need for a separate presentational device like the television?

SGML: Stands for standard generalized markup language and is the leading standard among *tagging languages*. It uses special character sequences called *markup tags* to embed control information within streams of text data. These tags work by separating text to be processed in a specialized way—text to be boldfaced, for example—from the remainder of the text stream. The specific rules for how to interpret the various markup tags specified under SGML are set forth using *DTD*s (document type definitions). The greatest weakness of SGML today is that it has no facilities for handling nontext data. Consequently, it is not presently suited for handling the *mixed media data types* of *compound documents*.

Shading: Is one of the fundamental techniques for creating highly realistic computer generated graphics. Shading occurs when a light source is added to the visual environment created by the computer. When this happens, areas that fall away from the light source are shadowed, and areas closer to the light source are highlighted. The problem with shading is that it tends to add significantly to the computational load, thereby slowing *frame refresh rates* significantly in most contemporary systems. *Gourad* and *phong* are two techniques that represent the high end of shading.

Sheetfed scanner: This type of *scanner* has fixed sensors and light sources. The documents are fed past the light sources like a fax machine. This type of scanner is generally used for high-volume applications, though there are now some small, personal-use models available.

Shot: From the world of filmmaking, this term refers to the smallest logical unit of a film—to the fundamental unit of filmmaking. A shot represents the span of time in a film during which a single camera *POV* (point-of-view) is sustained. Obviously, shots vary widely in duration. Though moving from one shot to another has typically been considered an aesthetic decision to be governed entirely by the filmmaker's artistic goals, with the advent of digital processes, it is increasingly a decision that has significant technical and practical implications. The most powerful motion picture *codecs* (*compression-decompression* programs) work on the principle of finding and eliminating redundancy in successive frames of a film. To the extent that a piece of film moves in a hurried fashion, jumping quickly from one shot to the next, a codec will have a difficult time achieving a high *compression ratio* because—on average—there will not be much redundancy over the groups of frames that make up the film. In contrast, films with a lazy pace (from the standpoint of how they are edited), featuring lots of extended shots where the camera stays focused on the same objects for long periods of time, are ideal for achieving high compression ratios because they will possess a great deal of visual redundancy (also called *temporal redundancy*).

Shot list: From the world of filmmaking, this term refers to a list of the shots that must be executed based on the *blocking* of the scene in the director's mind. As such, it is one of the more important planning documents that goes into the making of films, scene by scene. With the use of *authoring systems* that possess *time-line* interfaces, the links between the shot list and the finished shots can be automated, thus making it possible to automate at least the first phase of editing a picture together. This, of course, assumes that the finished shots have all been *digitized*.

Shovelware: Some jaded jargon from the realm of *hypermedia*, this term refers to disks loaded with so much poorly organized information that the user, seeking to *navigate* that information, is lost in an electronic maze.

Shuttle: From the analog world of tape, this term refers to use of the fastforward and rewind features of a tape deck to search for some specific part of a video. While users are locked into this sequential access search mode, the picture must be visible so that they are able to have "visual hits." The pain and agony of shuttling is one of the reasons why many feel that *nonlinear, random access*, all-digital video is the wave of the future.

Signal: In the world of *digital* media, signal refers to physical properties of sensory information that change with time, especially those associated with the electromagnetic spectrum. Thus, in speaking about *DSP* (digital signal processing), it is customary to speak of the "voice signal" or the "video signal," etc.

Signal processing: This is a near-synonym to *DSP* (digital signal processing).

Signal reconstruction: This term is roughly synonymous with *decompression* in that it describes the reconstruction of an *analog* signal from its digitally encoded, compressed counterpart.

Silence function: Often available with *digital audio production systems*, this function eliminates all sources of ambient sound and other unintentional noise in an audio track by enabling the audio editor to simply force all values in the selected passage to zero.

SIMNET: Short for simulated network, this program represents the first serious effort at creating a networked *virtual reality* simulation, also referred to as *cyberspace*. SIMNET is a networked virtual battlefield funded by *DARPA* (Defense Advanced Research Projects Agency), and developed at the Institute for Simulation and Training at the University of Central Florida in Orlando. It enables geographically dispersed players to wage war with one another on a simulated and shared battlefield. It thus provides a prototype of the role of *equitagonist*. Each standalone simulator is in the form of a tank and contains a copy of the world database, including the terrain and the virtual representations of all of the other simulators in the conflict.

Simulation: This term refers to an increasingly popular form of *multimedia application*, used most often for providing educational experiences in the most realistic contexts possible. Simulations are based on the same goal oriented, highly interactive design principles as video games, except they typically place the gaming challenge within some real-world, job-relevant context. Flight simulators, simulations of the stock market, and war games are three fairly obvious examples of this highly sophisticated form of multimedia.

Simultaneous-interpretation telephone: Conceived by Koji Kobayashi, former head of Japanese corporate giant NEC, this term refers to a telephone system that provides real-time, machine-generated translation between languages, thus making it possible for individuals to conduct a free and normal conversation even though they do not understand one another's language. Though this technology has yet to be achieved, it is commonly thought of as one of the key *enabling technologies* of the global village.

Sine wave: Is a continuously varying, repeating signal characterized by amplitude, frequency, and phase; the sine wave is the primary mathematical symbol for analog phenomena, which include, of course, analog media.

Sliders: From the world of *interface design* (not baseball), this term refers to a type of on-screen control *icon* used to control functions— like sound volume, for example—that vary along a scale of values, rather than just being subject to an on-off determination, which is a toggle switch.

Smart TV: One of the many emerging synonyms for *interactive television*, this term underscores the necessity for televisions to take on machine-based, or processor-based intelligence as they become interactive.

Smell-o-vision: This is industry slang for a loser technology. It refers back to an early 1960s attempt at virtual reality in which the authors tried to incorporate smell as a form of output. Obviously, it did not work out.

SMPTE: Stands for Society for Motion Picture and Television Engineers, a professional society that has been responsible for establishing a number of standards for motion picture and television equipment.

Snap-to grid: One of the many *accuracy aids* now used in computer graphics programs, this term refers to an underlying, and often transparent grid that works to force alignment of objects at a microscale within a graphics development environment. Thus, for example, this tool is often embedded in *paint systems* so as to force alignment of bullet points and other forms of lettering that the artist would normally want to have a common vertical or horizontal edge. Every once in while, this otherwise useful tool can get in the way by forcing alignment where the artist wants rough edges. As with most software features, though, the artist can typically circumvent this problem by simply turning off the snap-to grid feature, or by making adjustments to the spacing between elements of the grid.

SNR: Stands for signal-to-noise ratio, which is a measure of quality for any form of digital signal. For example, with regard to audio, where this ratio is most often used, SNR refers to the clarity of sound in relationship to ambient noise.

Soft robot: A term coined in 1984 by Alan Kay, it refers to much the same software design concept as does the term *interface agent*. A soft robot is a computer based agent that represents a system made up of software routines. When given a goal (by a human user), this system is capable of carrying out the details of the appropriate computer operations and of asking for, and receiving advice in human terms when it gets stuck.

SONET: A *CCITT* (Consultative Committee on International Telephone and Telegraph) standard that defines a number of levels of *digital telephony* service over *fiber optic* transmission lines. SONET is often associated with the backbone of the American communications network and ranges in carrying capacity from 1.544 megabits per second (Mps) up to 2.4 gigabits per second (Gps).

Sound placement DSP: This technology permits audio producers to position apparent sound sources anywhere in space around prospective listeners: front, back, left, right, above, below. Based on digital signal processing (*DSP*) technology, sound placement DSP is a foundational technology for creating the 3-D, surround sound systems critical to the success of many *high-intensity amusement attractions.*

Sound-space resolution: This term is used to describe how many sound source positions can be simulated in a *3-D sound* system.

Spatial: When used in conjunction with the world of video *codecs*, this term refers to actions that are performed on an individual *frame*. In this sense, spatial is nearly synonymous with the term *intraframe*. Spatial is often used in contrast to *temporal*, which refers to codec actions that are taken over the span of two or more frames, and in this sense, the contrast between spatial and temporal techniques is synonymous with the contrast between intraframe and *interframe* modes of *compression.*

Speckles: From the world of document and image scanning, this term refers to any dots or gray patches found on scans, faxes, or copies. They represent a form of background noise.

Specular light: Is directional light from a specific source that reflects directly off the surface of an object without entering it. This form of light is a key concern of advanced graphics programs which are seeking to create increasingly realistic visual representations of the world.

Speech font: A projected future technology for multimedia, wherein one is able to use sophisticated *text-to-speech* and speech synthesis technologies to shift between different styles of computerized speech (e.g., male/female, bass/alto, etc.) with the same ease and flexibility characteristic of changing fonts in today's word processors. Imagine a day may soon come when you request that your computer speak to you in the voice of Humphrey Bogart or Lauren Bacall.

Spline: From the realm of *3-D animation* and modeling, this term refers to one of the fundamental elements upon which most commercial animation packages are based. A spline is a mathematical representation of a curve. Spline-based graphics are, therefore, pictures built from numerous mathematically defined curves.

Split bar: From the world of graphical user interface (*GUI*) design, this term refers to the bar, or separation marker that splits one *window* from another. Thus, for example, if a user has opened up two documents and has made both of them visible on the screen at the same time, with one in each of two windows, respectively, the bar that separates those two windows is called the "split bar."

Sprites: From the realm of computer *animation*, a sprite is a small image, stored in libraries of such images, movable under program control. In many respects, sprites are the computer animator's version of a subroutine library, representing reusable graphical elements. Sprite libraries normally range in content from character sets used in representing text on screen to sets of characters used in animating computer games.

Square: In the realm of *DVE* (digital video effects), this everyday word takes on the specific meaning of a *two-plane effect* where the image on the *front plane* becomes a square opening or closing, revealing the image on the *back plane*.

Stand-alone system: This term is used to describe a self-contained computer system not connected to either a network or a larger computer.

Star topology: From the realm of computer networking, this is one of three dominant network topologies. The other two are ring and *bus*, and both of these differ from "star" in that they connect all of the workstations on the network over a single transmission line. In contrast, star topology features a separate transmission line for every workstation, and all transmission lines emanate from the *server*. Star topology is on the ascendance because it is the only one of the three topologies well suited for handling the large, continuously flowing streams of data characteristic of multimedia applications.

Steadicam: From the world of filmmaking, this relatively recent invention is a device that makes it possible for the camera to make rock-solid, "steady" shots, even when mounted on something moving, such as a plane, a roller coaster, or even the shoulder of a person who is running. In many instances, the steadicam has been used to create for the film viewer the sense of being "in" the movie, of being, as it were, in the shoes of one of the characters. This ability to place the viewer in the action will have growing significance as filmmakers turn to interactive cinema as an artform. Thus, whether or not the steadicam continues to be of practical use in our technological future, it should at least be remembered for the technical goals it successfully achieved.

Step frame: This term refers to a feature of certain video manipulation devices, such as frame accurate tape decks and *laserdiscs*, which permits the user to move backwards and forwards in the video stream one *frame* at a time.

Stereo pairs: These are pairs of overlapping images shot by cameras from slightly different vantage points for the purpose of creating stereoscopic, 3-D forms of visual media.

Stereoscopic glasses: By rapidly displaying slightly offset images alternately in both lenses, these early *virtual reality* devices create for their wearers a 3-D illusion. In the future, these devices may become as light and unobtrusive as eyeglasses, with increasing resolution and separation accuracy.

Stereoscopic vision: Is the sensing of a single 3-D image by binocular vision of two perspective images generated from different vantage points.

Stock footage: In the world of filmmaking, this term refers to film footage that represents commonly used scenes, or filler, such as trains, planes, or automobiles in transit. These scenes can be acquired from companies that collect and sell such categorized film segments as their core business. Stock footage houses provide filmmakers with catalogs that provide an indexed listing of the contents of their libraries. By making use of these libraries, filmmakers can decrease the cost of making a particular film by an amount commensurate with what it would cost to shoot the scenes they buy as stock footage. Given the high costs of original film production, the savings from using stock footage can be considerable. Many of these stock footage firms are now digitizing their libraries, laying them down on CD, and thereby broadening their markets by a considerable degree to include the growing number of *desktop video producers*. In the emerging multimedia industry, these newly digitalized vendors of *clip media* are being referred to as "content vendors." It is possible to visualize a day when commercially successful films will be comprised entirely of stock footage, or clip media segments—artfully stitched together.

Storage place: This term is used in the context of describing the storage feature of a highly literate form of multimedia such as an art gallery *kiosk*. The term represents the shift in perception of electronic storage from that of a physical or logical phenomenon to that of a cultural phenomenon. Like the burial place of archaeological concerns, it is a relatively simple futuristic leap to imagine that our children's children will remember their ancestors by storing their media representations—a video biography, for example—rather than, or in addition to, some form of their physical remains.

Storage virtualization: This term refers to the ability to make storage devices appear as if they have unlimited capacity. A network-implemented concept, this is done by transparently migrating inactive files through a series of "migration steps" to servers located (theoretically) anywhere across a network. The steps for implementing storage virtualization are controlled by network administrator-defined rules, which are transparent to users.

Store and forward: This term describes a commonly offered data communications service, wherein data messages (broadly defined) containing address information about their destinations are temporarily stored, and then later transmitted on toward their respective destinations. *Voice mail* and e-mail are two common types of store and forward service.

Storyboard: A term co-opted into the interactive field from the world of film and video, it refers to a piece of panel material on which is placed one or more sketches that present the look and feel of a proposed screen or story sequence. Storyboarding has become an integral part of the planning of any program that has a significant visual component.

Story cube: This term is a play on the linear video design term *storyboard*, and it represents a design presentation tool used by interactive designers to provide a high level, graphical representation of the structural aspects of their programs.

Storymercials: Many analysts and industry pundits have wondered upon the problem that will face advertisers when our prospective *information superhighway* makes all forms of entertainment available on demand, potentially eliminating the one-minute advertising slot altogether, creating a form of TV in which all channels would be operated like the contemporary premium (pay per view) cable channels such as Showtime or HBO. One idea that has surfaced is that products will become "embedded" in the entertainment, illustrating their benefits by virtue of how they are used by a story's protagonists. The term being offered to cover this idea is that of "storymercial."

STP: This term stands for shielded twisted-pair, an expensive, high-end form of *transmission media* used in networking data applications that require high levels of capacity and reliability.

Strand management: From the realm of *instructional technology* and *educational software*, this term refers to the body of design principles that electronically organize and sequence the flow of educational segments that students experience as they move through a program. In well-designed programs, the strand management logic is governed by software routines that track and assess performance and learning styles so as to match the learner's knowledge, skill level, and learning preferences to appropriately designed educational sequences. When this occurs, the educational software can be accurately credited with obtaining the long-sought dream of individualizing instruction. Though the concept of strand management has been around for years, its implementation has been very difficult and expensive to achieve. The biggest barrier has been the costs associated with creating a large and rich enough library of educational segments so that the software can be truly responsive to every learner's needs. Programs that possess strong elements of strand management are commonly referred to as "adaptive learning systems." They can adapt on the fly to whatever problem or deficiency the learner exhibits. As a concept with wide transferability, strand management has much to offer to producers of sophisticated video games and other types of interactive entertainment.

Streaming data: This refers to any data with a time component, such as *digital* audio and video.

Stream management: From the world of computer networking, this term is on the rise, as it describes a type of service demanded of any network management system that would manage the flow of the large, continuously flowing streams of data that characterize *digital* video and other high-*bandwidth* sources of audiovisual data.

Stretch target: This term from the business management school of process innovation refers to projects that enable the sponsoring organization to stretch their current capabilities in a dramatic fashion. As organizations large and small begin to implement such enterprise-wide multimedia solutions as *performance support systems*, they will, by definition, be setting stretch targets for themselves.

Structured graphics: This term refers to a way of describing an image using a set of simple geometric primitives. These primitives (e.g., lines, arcs, rectangles, ellipses, etc.) are the building blocks that construct the image. Structured graphics represent a distinct approach to treating visual data and are often referred to as *vector* graphics and contrasted with *bit-mapped* graphics. With structured graphics, the image is stored and drawn as an array of *pixels*. Thus, every pixel in an entire image is given a value that represents its visual characteristics (brightness, color, etc.). When high levels of image quality are sought (defined in terms of numbers of pixels and permissible colors), bit-mapped images can become large and difficult for a computer system to store and transmit. Bit-mapped graphics store the image itself; structured graphics store a set of instructions for drawing the objects that comprise it. This system saves considerable storage, and it is the chief advantage of this approach. Structured graphics, however, usually require complex display software, which must contain a module that can interpret the structured graphics instructions and draw the appropriate objects.

Student model: From the realm of intelligent *CAI* (computer aided instruction), a student model is a software component that records and maintains an information base on such learner characteristics as preferred learning mode and current level of skill mastery. A well-designed student model contains common student errors and misconceptions compiled by classroom teachers and cognitive scientists. The overall goal of the student model is to make interactive forms of training more responsive to the individual needs of the student.

Stylus: This pencil-shaped graphical input device is used with a *data tablet* to enter data and commands into some form of graphics software package.

Subcarrier: This term is used with reference to radio and television broadcasting to describe small portions of a given station's broadcast channel not used for radio or television signals, respectively. As we enter the age of interactive radio and television, this hitherto unused resource is now being viewed as a potential carrier of data signals; i.e., as a narrowband path along which users can interact with the broadcasting source to express such items as station content or format preference.

Submarining: This term refers to an artifact common to *LCD* screens in which the *cursor* disappears briefly during a rapid move. The problem is caused by the relatively slow response times of *pixels* in an LCD screen.

SUI: Stands for sound user interface and refers to an *I/O* (input/output) interface specialized for processing voice and other forms of audio. SUIs will become common components on *DSP*-equipped *MPC*s (digital signal processing equipped multimedia personal computers).

Superscalar: From the realm of computer processor design, this term refers to a feature present in many of the latest processors, including the Pentium line of microchips from Intel, in which two or more arithmetic operations are executed at the same time. Superscalar chips tend to have very high performance with respect to floating-point math, which is particularly important for graphics processing.

Surrogate travel: This is one of the first applications of interactive video and virtual reality to have rightfully earned the status of a multimedia genre. Simply put, surrogate travel programs are designed to create the illusion that users can move through geographically remote areas as if they were there. Common subtypes are the *moviemap*, wherein users can travel the streets and byways of remote territories, and the *walkthrough*, wherein users can navigate the rooms and hallways of simulated buildings.

SVGA: The acronym for super video graphics array, it refers to a high resolution *RGB* (red, green, blue) color monitor designed to support a PC Super Video Graphics display driver card. An SVGA monitor supports 256 colors in its highest graphics mode (800 horizontal *pixels* x 600 vertical pixels). This standard is set by *VESA* (Video Electronics Standards Association).

S-VHS: Stands for super-VHS, a high-quality extension of the VHS tape format for home video creation. This higher quality format provides for clearer images and high-fidelity stereo audio. Low cost standards like S-VHS advance the mission of lowering the barriers to entry into the realm of professional video production—and, by virtue of a quick leap of faith, into the realm of *interactive multimedia* creation as well.

S-video: Offering a higher quality signal that *composite video*, but a lower quality than *component video*, this mid-level format divides the signal into two channels: *luminance* and *chrominance*. It is also referred to as *Y/C*, where Y stands for luminance, and the C for chrominance.

Sword of Damocles: Credited with being the first ever head-mounted display, this device was created in 1968 by *virtual reality* pioneer Ivan Sutherland, while he was a student at Harvard University. This device got its name because it was hung from the ceiling by a large and ominous-looking arm that served as a mechanical *position tracking* device.

Symmetric multiprocessing: A term of growing significance in the computer industry, it refers to a type of operating system that works in a *multiprocessing* environment such that it allocates code to run on any free processor in the multiprocessor computer. Thus, it views all of the processors as being equivalent, non-specialized resources for performing the processing requirements of the system. Asymmetric multiprocessing systems, in contrast, typically contain specialized processors not equally adept at performing all functions, and therefore contribute in varying fashion to the tasks at hand. An asymmetric system, for example, might have a processor specialized in handling audio data and would not make use of this audio processor unless the application had audio content. Also referred to by the acronym SMP, symmetric multiprocessing systems are generally perceived to provide better overall throughput and greater availability than do asymmetric systems.

Sync: Short for synchronize, this term refers to the need to create a precise sense of unison between picture and sound elements in a video sequence.

Synthespians: Are computer-generated actors, especially prominent in animated forms of interactive fiction, who may perform the roles of *interface agents.*

System emulation titles: A genre of interactive, *CD-ROM* titles that seek to engage users in environments that simulate certain real world economic and/or physical systems. SimCity by Maxis, which engages users in a game where they, in effect, manage and build a simulated city, is considered the exemplar, or core example, of this genre.

The stammering newborn work will always be regarded as a monster, even by those who find experiment fascinating.
—Alain Robbe-Grillet, French Avante-Garde Novelist

Tactile acuity: Is a measure of the resolution of a *tactile feedback* device, such as VPL Research's *DataGlove.*

Tactile feedback: One of the new frontiers of man-machine communication, this form of "touch and feel" feedback is beginning to emerge from *virtual reality* research labs. It has to do with delivering feedback in a form perceived in a meaningful way by the human *haptic system.* The *DataGlove* and *DataSuit* developed by VPL Research are two early attempts at creating the tactile interface.

Tagging language: This is a general term for languages that make use of *markup tags* to impart complex formatting characteristics to text documents. They are essential to programs, such as desktop publishing systems, specialized in creating highly formatted documents. *SGML* (standard generalized markup language) is perhaps the best known example of a tagging language. Another example is *HTML* (hypertext markup language).

Tape autoloader: This emergent form of *near-line storage* makes use of robotic arms to move tapes between a storage area and a unit that reads from, and writes to, the magnetic tape cassettes. This type of alternative storage is gaining popularity, because it accommodates some of the enormous storage requirements of large-scale multimedia applications, such as *VOD* (video on demand).

Targa file format: Also commonly referred to by the three-character identifier "TGA," this term refers to file format standard for *bit-mapped* images that dates back to 1984. The format was established for using the Targa video board by Truevision, one of the first specialized PC *expansion boards* designed for enhancing the computer's ability to handle visual data.

Taxels: An obvious analog to the *pixels* of the visual display world, this term is a contraction for tactile display elements. Taxels are the fundamental units of *tactile feedback* and are used in various *virtual reality* devices, such as the *DataGlove*, to deliver "touch and feel" or *haptic* sensations to the user.

TDMA: Stands for time division multiple access, one of two emerging standards for digital *wireless* communications. TDMA is modeled after a popular method of data communications known as "multiplexing," whereby a single communication channel serves the transmission of several messages by time-dividing the message stream so that users take their turn in sharing the channel. The accepted analogy is that TDMA places everyone in the same room, but allows them to only speak one at a time and only in short bursts. Because it represents a new form of transmission capacity, TDMA—along with its sister technology, *CDMA* (code division multiple access)—is thought to be part of the solution to the emerging *bandwidth* crisis that is part-in-parcel of the coming age of multimedia.

Tear off menu: From the world of *interface design*, this term refers to a menu that can be removed from the menu bar and moved around the screen like a floating *window*. What makes it useful is that it remains fully extended, even after it has been detached, so the user doesn't have to pop it down every time a selection is needed. This feature is extremely popular with graphic artists when they are working with *paint programs*, because it enables them to, for example, move a color *palette* close to the object they are colorizing. In a more general sense, the tear-off menu is intriguing as an interface design element because it suggests a mode of interactivity in which objects carry with them, wherever they go, their own user-selectable options.

Teleconferencing: The audio precursor to *videoconferencing*, this term refers to a form of communication in which the *enabling technologies* of *POTS* (plain old telephone service) are exploited to allow three or more parties to engage in the same voice conversation.

Telemetry: This refers to the control of machine processes from remote locations. With the emergence of audio and visual recognition systems, this multimedia technology will play an increasing role in the remote control of all types of machines and processes.

Telephony: This umbrella term is used to describe the totality of technologies associated with the telephone.

Telepresence: A birthplace of many *virtual reality* (*VR*) products and concepts, these applications enable users to operate a VR interface to simulate and enhance their virtual presence in a remote, real-world location. The primary purpose of the technology is to enable remotely situated operators to receive enough sensory feedback to feel like they are really at the location where they are able to do different kinds of tasks. One of the first attempts at developing a telepresence visual system was done by the Philco Corporation in 1958. With this system, operators could see an image from a remote camera on a CRT mounted on their head in front of their eyes, and could control the camera's viewpoint by moving their head. A contemporary real-world example would be the use of telepresence technology to manipulate a deep-sea probe (perhaps to upgrade or repair a trans-oceanic cable).

Teleputer: George Gilder uses this term for the device he predicts will come to serve the function of *interactive television*. He prefers this word because it better captures the sense that this new communications device will embody the convergence of the television, the telephone, and the computer.

Telerobotics: One of the key components of *telepresence*, this term refers to the remote manipulation of robotic devices. Though useful in its own right, telerobotics can also be viewed as an engine of *multimedia applications*, because by fulfilling the goals of specific telerobotic projects, researchers often stumble across technological serendipities that have much to offer to the manufacture of *virtual reality* devices. One of the reasons for this is that some of the most interesting elements of telerobotics can be used to experience the world in ways for which humans are not equipped. For example, though human sight is not equipped to handle the infrared portion of the electromagnetic spectrum, researchers are capable of creating robotic sensors that can see infrared, and from that source, create a representation (e.g., a color-enhanced, partially transparent overlay) that can bring the representation within our visible spectrum.

TeleTact Glove™: This *virtual reality* device was developed at the National Advanced Robotics Research Center in conjunction with Airmuscle Ltd., both of which are located in the United Kingdom. This glove device is used in tandem with the *DAG* (data acquisition glove), developed by the same principles. The TeleTact is essentially a virtual reality, *force feedback* output device. When users wear this glove, it is capable of making their hands feel as though they are grasping any number of real world objects. The capability to do this results from a process where the DAG records *digitized* patterns of force feedback—each pattern associated with grasping a particular object under given circumstances—and where the TeleTact then becomes responsible for re-creating this force pattern in a process roughly analogous to the *DAC* (digital-to-analog conversion) that occurs with *digital* audio devices.

Teletext: One of the earliest attempts at providing multimedia services to the residential (consumer) market, teletext works by transmitting textual information over the same transmission channels that serve television. Largely considered a failed, "bleeding edge" experiment, teletext has been relegated in recent years to supplying public service types of information.

Template matching: From the realm of *OCR* (optical character recognition), this term refers to one of the most commonly used techniques for recognizing the characters that lie on the original, scanned document. It works by comparing a character with a stored template of the same character. Its primary weakness is that the system can only possess a library of templates with a finite number of font shapes, sizes, and styles. When there is a match, the system will generate the *ASCII* code for the character. When no match is found, the character must be submitted to manual recognition. This technique of template matching is often compared with *feature extraction*, a more powerful, but more expensive alternative for implementing character recognition.

Temporal redundancy: This term is frequently heard in *codec* technology circles, where it is used to describe the tendency for large amounts of information to be repeated from one frame to the next in motion picture sequences. This tendency is what makes possible a class of *compression* technologies, *interframe codecs*, that dramatically reduce the amount of visual information required to represent a particular motion sequence by capturing just those elements that change from one frame to the next.

Terabyte: This next level of *digital* storage capacity may cause eyebrows to raise, but only in degrees of diminishing astonishment. Once thought obtainable, or practical for that matter, only by the very largest organizations, a terabyte of information represents 1,000 *gigabytes* (or a million, million bytes). As organizations undertake more and more multimedia-oriented projects, such as the mammoth *backfile conversion* projects to transfer all of their paper documents into image data, the use of terabyte-size storage systems will become increasingly common. In today's market, most systems possessing this level of storage capacity come in the form of *optical juke boxes*.

Tertiary memory: This term is used to describe low-speed, high-volume memory, such as *optical juke box*, tape, and other forms of *off-line* and *near-line* mass storage.

Text search and retrieval: This term refers to the core of software competencies that have emerged from the field of software engineering over the years to define the manner in which items of information are sought for and found from within our culture's mass of textual documents (e.g., magazines, newspapers, etc.). This is a very important frontier for the entire information industry, because how we learn to organize, and then find textual items, will establish the scientific bases for how we organize and search for other forms of information. In general, an information retrieval system may be thought of as a form of structured memory where items are stored and then tagged or indexed for later retrieval. With text, most of which comes in the form of poorly organized documents (i.e., documents that were not composed with search and retrieval in mind), the longest standing method for organizing the contents for searchability has been that of appending to the document a header record, or summary file, and then filling that data structure with *keywords* that describe the contents. Thus, a header record appended to the contents of this book would undoubtedly contain entries such as "multimedia," "interactive," and the like. Using this method, at least some portion of the document is structured for search and retrieval; and, in any event, the presence of the header record obviates the need to search the entire document, which can be an extremely *CPU-intensive* and costly undertaking. Of course, the crux of indexing is whether or not the index entries successfully represent the contents. The issue is further complicated when we recognize that different groups and constituencies (lawyers versus college professors, for example) will define what is important in a particular document in entirely different ways. Suffice it to say that as we move into an era where it becomes increasingly important that other forms of media are effectively indexed, as is already becoming the case with *clip media* and *stock footage* libraries, the role of indexes and keywords will become one of the focal points of research for the information age.

Text-to-speech conversion: This emerging medium of the *MPC* (multimedia personal computer) relies upon *DSP* (digital signal processing) technology to process *ASCII* text, generate a phonetic transcription, and then produce synthetic speech. In other words, with this technology, the computer becomes able to "read" any document stored in the industry-standard ASCII format. This technology has been available for some time in such products as IBM's Primary Editor Plus, a word processor for children, which, among other things, is capable of reading back anything that the user has typed. Most existing systems provide rather crude, and obviously mechanical, interpretations of human speech. But as voice synthesizers become more lifelike, computers will increasingly communicate by speaking.

Texture mapping: A common feature in *paint systems*, this term refers to the mapping of *digitized* surface textures (e.g., a brick pattern) onto a surface.

3-D animation: From the high end of computer graphics, this term refers to a form of animation that relies upon the on-screen movement and interaction of 3-D objects. From a production standpoint, the creation of 3-D animation presents many thorny problems; the most significant of which is that it is both *CPU-* and memory-intensive, and it is therefore quite expensive and time-consuming.

3-D digitizing: This emergent, sophisticated form of data capture works to capture (*digitize*) the x, y, and z coordinates of a real object, thus creating a 3-D representation of that object which might be used later for creating, for example, a holographic image. The fundamental unit of information captured by 3-D digitizing is often referred to as a *voxel*, the 3-D version of a *pixel*.

3-D sound: This term refers to sound systems that produce convincingly directional, 360-degree spatial motion and support acoustics. The implementation of 3-D sound usually involves stereo earphones that make use of *DSP* (digital signal-processing) to deliver complementary audio signals that reconstitute sonic volume and motion.

Thresholding: From the world of document and image scanning, this term refers to a process used to create clean images from dirty, faded originals. The user sets a limit of contrast—a threshold—beneath which the *pixel* will be reproduced as white and above which it will be reproduced as black.

Thumbnails: This term refers to the image-based *icons* that are rapidly taking their place in the design and implementation of graphical user interfaces (*GUI*). The term was originally coined as way of describing their average, postage-stamp size, which is also about the size of a human thumbnail. This size is justified because it is large enough to make the visual contents discernible to the human eye, but small enough to conserve screen geography and memory consumption so that first generation *MPCs* (multimedia personal computers) can make liberal use of them. The most common example of a thumbnail is a postage-stamp sized image of the first frame in a video sequence, which is used to both represent and launch (by clicking on it, of course) that video sequence.

TIFF: Stands for tagged image file format, an industry standard for image files, originally developed by Aldus Corporation. This standard uses tags (i.e., labels) to define the structure of graphics images captured by digital *scanners* for processing.

Timbrality: With respect to *MIDI* (musical instrument digital interface) synthesizers—perhaps the key audio technology of the *MPC* (multimedia personal computer) standard—this term refers to the number of different instruments that a given MIDI device can play simultaneously. Obviously, the greater the number of simultaneous instruments, the more resonant the sound.

Timbre: Pronounced "tam-bur," this term refers to one of the key components in a musical sound. Typically distinguished from pitch and loudness, timbre establishes the distinguishing quality of a musical sound. With regard to many of the emerging and sophisticated *digital* audio production tools, timbre is an element that is typically isolated so that it can be more directly manipulated by the composer or audio engineer. *MIDI* (musical instrument digital interface) composition tools are particularly adept at manipulating timbre.

Time code: This term refers to a code embedded in a video sequence so as to facilitate editing and synchronization. Each frame in the video is given a time offset (or address) from the beginning of the sequence, thus enabling editors to specify precise entry and exit points from which to start and end scenes, respectively. In the soon-to-be-extinct realm of analog video, time codes are actually burned into a spare track on the videotape (see *BITC*), where they remain until the penultimate stages of post-production. In the rising realm of digital video, time codes will be just another digital element in the video data stream and will be responsible for enabling random access and the databasing of video content.

Time-line metaphor: This term refers to the most commonly used *interface design* for *media integrators* and other computer presentation systems. These interfaces use a columnar, almost spreadsheet-like structure, with the columns calibrated in terms of time slots. The rows represent the various media sources (audio-voice clips, music, image, video sequences, etc.). By using this specialized, time-based, tabular structure, the time-line metaphor makes it easy for *multimedia application* developers to synchronize a wide variety of media types by controlling their appearance, their activities, and their disappearance with reference to a shared timeline.

Time stamp: Is information added to a message, record, or other unit of data indicating the time at which it was processed by the system.

Title depth: This is a descriptive term that connotes one very important aspect of a *CD-ROM* title's quality: namely, its depth of content, which can be largely discerned from how many times the user is inclined to use it. A "shallow title" would be one that users discard after using only once or a few times and would therefore be characterized as having very little depth. In contrast, a title with depth will have, generally speaking, many layers of content and will inspire its users to re-use the program over and over again. Because it possesses a strong multiplay quality, The 7th Guest by Virgin Games is said to have excellent title depth.

Titling: Refers to the process of laying down text overtop of a video signal. Now an integral function in most desktop video systems, standard applications of titling include placing video text for company logos on advertising pieces, and producing titles and screen credits for movies and TV broadcasts.

T1 line: A digital telephone line—commonly used for distance learning, among other things—the T1 line is on copper wire and transfers digital information at the comparatively high rate of 1.544 megabits per second.

Torque: In the field of animation, this term refers to the twisting of parts of the body in contrast to each other. It is believed that by paying close attention to such relational aspects of body motion, animators are better able to create *life quality* in their productions.

Touch screen: A popular form of effecting human-computer interaction, especially with *IVD* (interactive video disc) applications, this technology makes it possible for users to interact with computer programs by simply touching designated *hot spots* on the screen. Touch screens work under much the same principle as the *mouse* input device, except that, rather than clicking on the desired hot spot, the user simply touches it with a finger.

Track: With regard to the storage of *digital* information, a track is a linear, spiral, or circular path on which information is placed. This term is equally applicable to magnetic and optical forms of storage. This term is also used in the film/video community to refer to any single component of a finished video, such as the sound track.

Track analysis: In film and video production, this refers to an examination of a sound track by the editor to determine exactly where various sounds occur.

Trackball: From the world of computer input devices, this device uses a ball that is free to move around within a fixed mounting. As the user rotates the ball, receptors inside the fixed mounting record the movement and translate it into on-screen *cursor* movements.

Transfer rate: In computing, this general term refers to the rate at which information is moved between any two devices, particularly from storage into RAM. Currently, an important transfer rate is that between *CD-ROM* and internal memory, because it represents a bottleneck, making it difficult for producers of interactive programs to create many of the effects taken for granted in the arena of traditional, *analog* video productions.

Transmission media: See *Cabling*.

Transponder: This device is used in satellites to receive a data communications signal at one frequency and retransmit the signal at a different signal.

Treatment: A term derived from the world of film and TV, it refers to a general or high level description of a proposed program, an outline of sorts. It is generally used as the first step in the business planning process to interest potential clients, programmers, publishers, etc.

Trucking: In film and video production, this term refers to the movement of the camera toward or away from the scene. "Trucking in" means that the camera is being moved closer. "Trucking back" means that the camera is being moved further back. These terms are near-synonyms for *panning* and *zooming*.

TrueType™**:** Developed by Apple Computer, this widely used standard defines a set of outline-based typefaces that are used to create display and printer fonts.

TSR: This software acronym stands for terminate-and-stay-resident, and it is used to describe programs that load themselves into memory with the intent of staying there. TSRs are typically represented by software utilities, such as *screen capture programs*, which developers, in particular, like to have at their disposal.

Turing Test: This refers to the now famous test described by Alan Turing in his justly famous 1950 article "Computing Machinery and Intelligence," wherein he proposed that the only way for a computer to prove itself to be truly intelligent (in the human sense) was if it could respond to the questions asked by a human interviewer in such a way that the answers would be indistinguishable from those that one would expect to receive from a human. In other words, a computer may finally be deemed intelligent when—and only when—it can carry on a normal conversation with a human being. As we progress further and further into the recesses of the age of multimedia, the ability for *interface agents* to pass the Turing Test may become a key industry success factor.

Tutorial: Borrowed from the world of academe, this term is used by *instructional designers* to refer to a form of *multimedia application* that seeks to pull learners through a highly constricted sequence of interactive experiences designed to convey a narrowly defined set of learning objectives. Software tutorials and *drill and practice* math programs are two fairly obvious examples of this type of *educational software*.

TV tuner boards: This category of board product enables the user to receive broadcast video and display it in a window on the PC monitor. This type of board simplifies the process of using the computer to view video segments because it causes the video stream to bypass the PC's internal graphics subsystem, playing it directly from its analog source (e.g., directly from a VCR).

TWAIN: This term refers to an emerging *interface* protocol that seeks to standardize the way various image capture devices, such as *scanners* and *frame grabbers*, are accessed by application software. As an example, any scanner that is TWAIN compliant can be directly accessed from within software that support TWAIN devices. Not to be confused with Mark Twain, the nineteenth century American writer.

Twitch and shoot fantasy: An obviously derogatory term, this phrase describes the dominant genre in the first generation of video games that focuses on violent themes and the user's ability to respond quickly to various forms of animated threat by merely blasting those threats to smithereens (or its electronic equivalent).

Two-plane effects: From the realm of *DVE* (digital video effects), this term refers to a broad family of effects used primarily to transfer from one screen to its successor. Fades and *dissolves* are common types of this effect. Two-plane effects are so-called because they operate on two visual planes, with the image held on the uppermost, or *front plane*, being replaced by the image held on the lower, or *back plane*.

Our methods of transmitting and reviewing the results of research are generations old and by now are totally inadequate for their purposes.

—Vannevar Bush,
Conceptual Pioneer of "Hypertext"

Ultrasonic position sensing: This is an emerging form of position tracking being used in *virtual reality* research. Basically, the technology works by placing some form of ultrasound emitter on an object (such as a human being) that is to move around within a virtual world. As the object moves, ultrasound sensors (microphones) keep track of its position by *sampling* the location of the transmitter.

Underlay: In the world of animation, this terms refers to a section of the background that is mounted on the *cel.* Adopting an object-oriented approach to animation, underlays, like other constituent elements of the animated world, can be stored in libraries for continual re-use.

Undo: An important graphical user interface (*GUI*) application menu choice in most quality applications, it permits the user to reverse the most recently performed user action. Utilization of this option fulfills the maxim: "to err is human, to forgive divine."

Usability: In the world of computer programming, this refers to that quality of an application which makes the software easy for the user to understand, learn, and use. By building in online reference and procedural information (ideally hypermedia in the realm of the information designer), and by building in online training information (ideally *CBT* [computer based training] and *interactive multimedia* in the realm of the *instructional designer*), into the design of a *graphical user interface* (GUI) design, the corporate application development team can achieve a depth of *usability* that fulfills the goal of making the application easy for the user to understand, learn, and use. As with software applications, so too are *multimedia* and *hypermedia applications* better if *usability* is built into their *interface design.*

Usability evaluation lab: In the early '80s, IBM Corporation began focusing its efforts on small systems development as well as developing complementary business application software to run on these platforms. In an effort to improve the *usability* of the software *interface design*, as well as the design of the supporting training and documentation materials, IBM devoted its efforts to building usability labs, not to test for software bugs or hardware human factors glitches, as had been previously done, but to evaluate how easy it was for a new user to understand, learn, and use the business applications. A team in Atlanta, Georgia, composed of M. Mehal, R. Autry, P. Smith, Dr. J. Morgan, and Dr. D. Leonard developed the IBM Atlanta Usability Lab, as well as a usability lab evaluation process for planning, designing, running, analyzing, and reporting evaluation results. From that seed, IBM and its business application customers began to think about and evaluate software from a *usability* perspective. Through another IBM Atlanta effort, the Multiples Marketing Program, IBM disseminated to its hardware and software customers the knowledge, expertise, and process for conducting usability lab evaluations worldwide. As a result, many companies now have *usability* labs in which end users, sitting in a control room, perform various tasks with the software in development, are observed by developers in an observation room and are filmed, interviewed, surveyed, and essentially brought into the development process solely to improve the *usability* of the software and its supporting materials. Quantitative data extracted includes tasks performed successfully, task performance time, number of errors, and error recovery time. Qualitative data extracted includes (through observations, written surveys, and interviews) evaluation subject preferences, problems, solutions, and overall emotional responses to the software. Hopefully, the usability lab evaluation process will also be employed for the development of *hypermedia applications* and *multimedia applications*.

User interface: A term that has gradually taken on great importance for *multimedia applications,* user interface refers to the point of contact between a human user and the contents of a computer system. Traditionally, this term was used to denote the devices through which a user would communicate with the computer, e.g., the keyboard, the *joystick*, etc. As the computer has become more knowledge-oriented and media-oriented, and as these devices have become more sophisticated (e.g., with the use of *tactile feedback* devices, such as the *DataGlove and DataSuit*), the role of the user interface and its design will continue to grow and expand in significance.

UTP: Stands for unshielded twisted-pair, a term that refers to the least expensive, lowest capacity form of *transmission media* used in the transmission of data. Formed by twisting pairs of copper wires—typically in groups of four—UTP is just one step above telephone cable. By twisting the copper wires, this technology reduces some of the electrical interference that can occur from proximity to motors, computers, etc. Owing to its low cost, UTP is a very popular medium for networking computers and is often cited as a difficult-to-hit, but desirable target for implementing networked *multimedia applications.*

Reading entails the possibility that we may formulate ourselves and so discover what has previously seemed to elude our consciousness.
—*Wolfgang Iser, Literary Theorist*

Variable-length records: This refers to a way of organizing a database such that the sizes of records containing the data need not be uniform. With the move to media-based forms of data (to audio, image, and video databases) the need for variable-length records will grow. One of the carryovers from the alphanumeric-only days now being adapted for this use is the so-called *memo field*. With a memo field, only the address of the record is stored in a fixed-length format. The content of the field is open-ended, and in fact, may be stored on a separate device from the one that holds its address.

VBI: Stands for vertical blanking interval, which is the black bar in between frames of a television broadcast. The limited *bandwidth* capacity of VBI has been used in recent times to carry the small amounts of control information associated with early attempts at interactive forms of television. Information transmitted through VBI is limited to text, simple graphics, and information for positioning on-screen objects. In the 1980s, *teletext* services offered news and other information through a VBI signal on broadcast television.

VDU: Stands for visual display unit, a very general term that refers to the now-diverse universe of video displays (e.g., *LCD*s, *CRT*s, etc.).

Vector: This term is used in the realm of computer graphics to refer to the mathematical representation of a geometric object contained within a computer image. Vectors are typically used to represent objects such as circles, arcs, and lines. Their use in this context reflects an effort to create an abstract representation of *digitized* images, thereby reducing the storage space required to handle visual forms of data.

Vector file: As opposed to *raster*, or *bit-map* files, vector files are made up of mathematical equations—also referred to as "vectors"—that provide an easily manipulated representation of an image. Raster files, in contrast, are typically large, because they are comprised of a *bit map* that possesses a value (or set of values) for every *pixel* in the image. Though they are more readily manipulated, vector files typically do not possess the high image quality found in most raster files.

Vector-to-raster conversion: In the everyday world of *multimedia applications,* where there is a veritable explosion of paint and image manipulation software tools, there is frequent need to convert files from one format to another. Vector-to-raster conversion is one of the easiest conversion processes to perform. This sort of translation effectively snaps a picture of a *vector* file and organizes it into a bit map.

Vertical correlation: Also referred to as "vertical redundancy," and closely related to the concept of *horizontal correlation*, this term refers to an element of redundancy present in most sources of visual information. If, for example, two *pixels* located next to one another in the vertical plane of a picture have the same visual characteristics (i.e., the same color and brightness), then they may be said to possess vertical correlation. This form of redundancy, like all other forms of visual redundancy, is important to the process of video *compression*. If a whole vertical string of pixels have the same visual characteristics (in a background depicting the sky, for example) then they may be compressed down to a simple mathematical formula that expresses the shared visual characteristics only once, but then also lists the number of consecutive pixels possessing those characteristics (a compression technique known as *RLE* [run length encoding]).

VESA: This is the acronym for one of the multimedia industry's leading standard setting associations. It stands for Video Electronic Standards Association, and it is represented by a set of software and hardware manufacturers with a common concern for establishing standards for graphic and video display adapter cards.

VESA VL Bus™: The VESA stands for Video Electronics Standards Association, and the term refers to an emerging standard for overcoming the bottlenecks associated with handling video on traditional PCs. The VESA VL Bus, which is featured on a number of *video adapter cards*, is a 32-bit *bus* capable of operating as fast as a CPU's memory access speeds. This standard is designed to enable faster operating speeds of video display and hard disk subsystems at affordable prices.

VFW™: Stands for Video for Windows, Microsoft's package of system and authoring software for integrating video files into Microsoft *Windows*.

VGA: An acronym that stands for video graphics array, it refers to the medium to high resolution *RGB* (red, green, blue) color monitor designed to support a PC Video Graphics display driver card. VGA is a display standard that was originally developed by IBM in 1987 for its PS/2 line of computers and supports 16 colors in its highest graphics mode (640 horizontal pixels x 480 vertical pixels).

VGA-to-NTSC boards: This class of *board* product takes the signal from a PC's graphics adapter and converts it to a *composite* signal (e.g., SuperVHS) so that it can be recorded onto an analog medium such as a videocassette. Some of these products also offer *genlocking* and overlay capabilities, making it possible for the user to combine PC graphics with the video before it is sent to the tape.

Video: Is a system of recording and transmitting visual information by converting moving or still images into electrical signals. These signals can be broadcast through high-frequency carrier waves or sent through cables on a closed-circuit.

Video adapter card: A family of *expansion cards* designed to enhance the PC's ability to manipulate video, these cards work by offloading many of the video processing functions from the *CPU* to the card itself.

Video bandwidth: One of the key components in measuring the tractability of a *multimedia application* (i.e., the ability to process the amount of information at an acceptable rate), video *bandwidth* is a measure of the size of a *digitized* video data stream. There are four major elements that go into determining video bandwidth: 1) the *aspect ratio* of the picture; 2) the scanning method (*interlaced* versus *progressive*, with the latter requiring twice as much bandwidth as the former); 3) the picture's repetition rate (i.e., the *frame rate*), which is usually expressed as frames-per-second, such as the 30 fps of *NTSC* (National Television Standards Committee) television; and, 4) the number of *scan lines* in each frame (which is the dominant component in determining the picture's *resolution*).

Video christmas card: This metaphoric term represents one of those future exemplars of how we may use the high *bandwidth* networks of the future to communicate with one another at holiday events or whenever. An example is when Dave in *2001: A Space Odyssey* by Stanly Kubrick receives a visual birthday greeting from his parents while he is on board the space ship headed toward one of Jupiter's moons.

Video dial tone: A concept associated with the *picturephone*, the video dial tone is functionally analogous to the telephone dial tone in that it provides the individual user with some sort of visual pattern which signifies that *bandwidth* has been made available for purposes of placing a video phone call.

Video dictionary: A subclass of *hypermedia applications*, this term refers to programs that feature the alphabetically organized collection of information items, primarily in the form of video clips.

Video digitizer: Typically, this refers to a board level product that accepts *analog* video input from standard video sources, such as VCRs, videocameras, laserdiscs, and cable TV, and displays it on the monitor screen, converting the signal into a binary (*digital*) file on cue. Some of these products display the video signal in its native *interlaced* format, where the screen is painted in two passes. Other boards offer a frame into memory before displaying it as a *noninterlaced* image, which offers the advantage of less flicker and more clarity.

Videodisc: Like the old format war that was fought between Betamax and VHS over who would be king (*the* standard, that is) in the VCR industry, the videodisc standard is often compared against *CD-ROM* as an alternative for delivering interactive forms of media. The videodisc standard is larger than CD-ROM (about the size of an LP album) and is double-sided, and its data rate and rotational speed are higher. However, it has one serious drawback that seems destined to cause it to go the way of Betamax. Though its control information is stored in *digital* format, its program information—the images and other media—is stored in *analog* format. Thus, its primary form of storage is at odds with the digital format of computers.

Videodisc levels: Videodisc has traditionally been divided into five levels of technology/interactivity, ranging from the modest interaction of switching the machine on and off, up through the sophisticated branching and presentation strategies allowed by integrated systems of *CPU* and disc player. Those layers are: **Level Zero:** Linear play of videodisc; i.e., those designed to play only videodisc versions of movies. **Level One:** A player with still/freeze frame, picture stop, frame and chapter stop addressability, and dual-channel audio, but with no programmable memory. All functions are initiated by manual inputs from the player's keypad. Picture stop and chapter stop codes are put on the disc during mastering. **Level Two:** A player with on-board, programmable memory. The player's memory is pro-grammed from information contained in audio channel two of a Level Two encoded videodisc, or is programmed manually from the player's keypad. Inputs are made from the keypad. **Level Three:** Any video-disc player controlled by an external computer. This is the level that characterizes the preponderance of programs termed *IVD* (interactive videodisc) programs. **Level Four:** A videodisc-and-computer system in which the videodisc is used to store computer-readable digital data as well as *analog* video and sound information. The videodisc player functions as an optical storage drive to the computer, as well as the source of analog picture and sound.

Video fax: This term is nearly synonymous with *movies-on-demand*, a term that refers to an emerging service, whereby consum-ers access movies of their own choice from a central database of films. The term video fax describes the technical process that controls how users make use of movies-on-demand services. After accessing the database of movies, and making a selection, the consumer waits a short period of time, while the *digital* form of the film is downloaded from the central database to their own *interactive television* playback unit. Thus, envisioned in this fashion, movies-on-demand may work much like the ubiquitous document fax does today: The entire con-tents of the document (movie) are transmitted and received before the user begins to consume any part of it.

Video PBX: Nearly synonymous with *video server*, this term re-fers to communications hardware that serves as the intermediary be-tween residential consumers and databases of video product. It is called a *PBX* (private branch exchange), because it operates much like a telephonic PBX in making large numbers of point-to-point connec-tions. In most cases, equipment worthy of this term is relatively high-end (e.g., mainframe) computing hardware owned and operated by the cable companies.

Video server: This term refers to a specialized portion of a *LAN* (local area network) set aside to handle the unique demands of pro-viding sources of *digital* video to LAN clients in much the same way as traditional LAN servers provide data and application services to those same clients. A video server must cope with the unique chal-lenges associated with the large, continuously flowing streams of data necessary to play compressed digital video or other high *bandwidth* audiovisual data types. These multimedia technology data types are time-dependent, and thus, in addition to requiring a continuous (un-interrupted) connection between client and server, possess several key differences to the traditional sources of data that move over LANs. These traditional sources are characterized by relatively small file sizes, and thus, possess the need for only momentary and intermittent dominance of the network channel capacity. As a consequence, most traditional LAN protocols are contention-based and are designed to handle a *bursty* flow of traffic over a shared transmission line on the network, where only one client-server or workstation-to-workstation connection is being accommodated at any given moment. Typically, these data conversations are so brief, that the individual users are unaware that their requests are being handled out of a queue. In con-trast, multimedia technology connections demand relatively long and continuous ones, and so are not well suited to the traditional network protocols. Instead, most video servers demand dedicated, point-to-point connections with each of their clients, an arrangement referred to as a *star topology*. Additionally, because the transmission resource (the wire connecting server to client, for example) is not normally a shared resource, the network protocols for networked video are not normally based upon *contention* schemes, but rather rely on conver-sational protocols more typical of *telephony*.

Videot: This is slang for a video game junkie.

Video teleconferencing, videoconferencing: One of the earliest and largest markets for *multimedia*, this application es-sentially applies the technologies associated with *picturephone* to group situations. Despite the relatively high cost of transmitting video in *real time*, video teleconferencing is viewed as being affordable when used to hold high priority, corporate-style meetings where face-to-face contact is seen as a critical element in the communications. Several standards have cropped up to encode the *quasi-video* signals that are typically used in video teleconferencing, the most notable being the *H.261* standard.

Videowall: Seen frequently at large trade shows, videowalls are large assemblages of monitors stacked together to form a single dis-play area. Typically, they are controlled by a computer, which does the work of taking a single image and splitting it up so that the picture can be spread across all of the monitors.

View: In the simplest sense, the term "view" refers to what is seen—that is, what is visible to the user—within a window on a graphical user interface (*GUI*)-based personal computer. But this term means much more. It is one of those tip-of-the-iceberg terms. Put simply, it is one of the most important and central concepts in all of *multimedia*. Moving on to one of its still-simple, but abstract meanings, a "view" is one way of seeing a particular set of data. Critical to the concept of a view is that there are many different ways of looking at the same set of data. Thus, for a simple table of numerical data—representing, say, sales figures listed by salesperson—one can take a view of that data which is the table itself, or, one can take a view that represents the same data in the form of a bar graph, or maybe a pie chart. One might also take that data and write a narrative around it, describing how the various salespeople are doing, based solely on the sales figures contained in the table.

The point is, there are many different ways to "view" the same information. As one addresses more complex datasets, where it is only possible to consider portions or summaries of the data at any one moment, then the concept of view takes on another dimension; that of scaling up or down relative to the object being considered. Thus, as one scales up, the view takes in a wider scope, but contains less detail. As one zooms in, the scope narrows, but the detail is increased. In a sense, the notion of "view" takes stock of the perceptual limitations of the human mind relative to the volume of information that can be considered at any moment in time. And this notion of presenting digestible views, within the context of a "view-generating system" that can switch flexibly and quickly between many different views, is a core concept, a sort of gestalt that drives the entire enterprise of *human interface design*, *GUI*, and *usability*.

Viewer polling: This is one of the prototypical forms of *interactivity* that is already being experimented with in anticipation of the coming of *interactive television*. As the term implies, viewer polling works by actively soliciting the opinions and attitudes of viewers. In today's technology context, viewer polling is conducted by using the telephone as the means by which viewers communicate their opinions back to the broadcasting source. Obviously, this is a contemporary *kludge* that uses two separate technologies. As envisioned for true interactive television, though, future forms of viewer polling will involve the user's direct interaction with the TV (by clicking on an on-screen *icon*, for example) which, in turn, will communicate back to the broadcasting source via some form of data *backchannel*.

Viewport: A term for programmers, it refers to a rectangular portion of the screen onto which the *window* and its contents are mapped.

VIMS: Stands for visually induced motion sickness, a unique form of motion sickness that is a result of some of the more powerful *virtual reality* entertainment environments. Almost exactly the opposite in cause from normal motion sickness, VIMS occurs when there is a compelling sensation of self-motion without any corresponding visceral cues. Research shows that this form of nausea tends to occur during a user's initial exposure to a particular simulation, especially in cases where there are many motion cues.

Virtual communities: This term describes subsets of Marshall McLuhan's global village, groups of geographically dispersed people who communicate with such intensity that they form what could be properly called communities. Obviously, these communities will make heavy use of multimedia technology, as the capacity of our public networks expand to accommodate the higher *bandwidths* associated with moving *mixed media data types* between remote locations.

Virtual mall: This term refers to one of the emerging visions for how interactive shopping will be presented as an *interface paradigm* once *mass deployment* of an all-digital, national information infrastructure occurs. Under this interface paradigm, the at-home shopper will fly through an electronic version of a mall, using the input device to steer and stop as the salivary glands of shopping dictate.

Virtual memory: This term represents one of the older software design technologies and perhaps the first use of the word "virtual" in the computer world. Virtual memory is a fairly sophisticated technique used in computer systems as follows. First, an application is divided up into discrete chunks. In most cases, these chunks are regular in size and are called pages. When an application is running, it typically uses only a few pages of the program in a given time frame. These active chunks are referred to as the working set of pages. Since only a few pages are being used at any one time, a large program can waste a great deal of memory in a system with inactive pages that may never be used at all. To ensure the efficient use of memory, a computer can be programmed to load only the working set of pages into memory and still be able to run the application, even though much of its code is absent from memory. If the application requires a page not currently in memory (for example, when branching to a different part of the program that lies outside of the code represented by the current working set), a page fault is generated by the computer hardware. At this point, the computer chooses a page not being used, swaps it out to hard disk, reads in the required page, and then continues executing the application. This process is totally transparent to both developers and users alike. Thus, since no "out of memory" error ever confronts either of these two groups, even though they may be working with extremely large program files, the computer appears to have a limitless supply of memory. This apparent extension of capability beyond what is real is what has given rise to the use of the term "virtual." In the era of multimedia technology, where an explosion of file sizes of all sorts will be upon us, expect virtual memory to be one of the more important forms of virtual for quite some time.

Virtual reality (VR): VR is primarily a real-time graphics and animation technology that immerses users into alternate worlds, ones that are intended to seem as real as the real world of nature. Through a combination of sensing and interface devices, and software, VR systems provide direct interaction with computer generated models. In its purest form, virtual reality is a computer generated, surrogate environment that allows users to experience the full sensory/tactile feedback of a place in space and time different from the one in which the user really is. Thus, virtual reality relies on many of same illusionary forces so critical to our various narrative traditions (e.g., the novel and the movie). Recently, there has been such an expansion in the uses and technologies associated with VR, that there are now all sorts of VR systems, ranging from *environmental VR* to *full immersion VR* to many different forms of partial VR. Taken as a whole, virtual reality should be viewed as the leading edge of *interactive multimedia* technology—potentially the most sophisticated, demanding, and engaging medium of the information age.

Virtual surreality: A term coined by the philosopher Daniel Dennett in his 1991 work, *Consciousness Explained*. Dennett joins a widening group skeptical of the various meanings implied in the term *virtual reality*. According to Dennett, the experiences one has while garbed in the paraphernalia of VR systems are at best something a user might imagine as real for only a short span.

Virtual VCR: This term was coined by those in the know about *interactive television*. Basically, it is a synonym to *movies-on-demand*, a term that describes one of the early interactive TV services, whereby the consumer orders a movie from a large menu of choices. The actual movies are stored on a large *video server*, located on the facilities of the cable operator.

VIS™: Stands for Visual Information System, which is Tandy's entrant in the home *CD-ROM* player market. Rather than being designed as a PC peripheral, VIS is more like Philips' *CD-I* system, in that it is designed as a television accessory. VIS makes use of a stripped-down version of Microsoft's *Windows*, known as *Modular Windows*, and is intended for use by couch potatoes wielding remotes.

Visualization for Planetary Exploration: This is one of the most prominent applications of *virtual reality* technology for purposes of exploration not yet undertaken. This project, being developed at NASA's *Ames Research Center*, involves taking topographical data generated from satellites and space probes to create 3-D models of portions of planet surfaces from around the solar system. The system will then make it possible for users to *fly* over mountains and down into valleys on, for example, the Martian surface. As better *rendering engines*, and more accurate data become available, the system is planned for *scalability*, such that one day people may be able to simulate flight through photorealistic versions of planetary surfaces.

Visual workbench: This term refers to a *human-factors engineering* application for *virtual reality*, whereby physical environments are modeled/simulated for purposes of conceptual trial-and-error. A contemporary example is provided by the University of Washington's Human Interface Technology (HIT) lab. HIT has developed a simulation of a new runway for SEATAC airport, complete with simulated sound, so that stakeholders can test out the impact of various design strategies.

VOD: Stands for video on demand and is nearly synonymous with *movies-on-demand*. Many industry critics see true VOD as still lying somewhere out there in the near, but as yet unobtainable future. Its immediate predecessor, *NVOD* (near video on demand), will make use of the rapidly growing *bandwidth* of the cable TV infrastructure to supply users with so many starting times for a particular film that wait times will never exceed a very short duration, say 10 minutes at the most. It's like a bus schedule where the buses are running with very high frequency. VOD will follow on the footheels of NVOD and not only allow viewers to pick out a program and choose just when they want to use it, but will also enable them to start, stop, and pause each program without affecting any of the other programs available to, or being viewed by others.

Voice: This everyday word has recently moved into the world of digital audio, where it has taken on the meaning of an independent channel in a multichannel, *digital audio production.* Thus, you may find it written in one of the trade journals that the sounds produced by a particular musical instrument, say a horn, make up one of the voices in a 24-voice production.

Voice annotation: A concept associated with *hypermedia applications* and the *compound document*, it refers to the practice of annotating reference documents with voice messages. Obviously, voice annotation is one application of voice *digitization.*

Voice coding: Refers to methods of digitally encoding and compressing voice signals optimized to the spectral patterns characteristic of voice. Techniques like *SBCELP*, developed by Lernout & Haupsie Speech Products of Belgium, are making 30-to-1 *compression ratios* for voice signals possible. Such medium-specific specialization in algorithm development is a reflection of the growing maturity of multimedia technology.

Voice grade: A term used to describe the relatively low quality audio signal that typifies dial-up telephonic communications. Voice grade has a relatively modest *bandwidth* of 3,000 Hz.

Voice mail: Though not usually thought of as such, this *store and forward* service is a precursor to the *compound document*, which may become one of the dominant forms of multimedia technology. Because they store messages in an audio format, and are typically controlled by computers, voice mail systems are clearly multimedia technology.

Voice recognition: A long sought-after goal of the computer intelligentsia, voice recognition is a form of user input whereby the computer is able to respond in a meaningful fashion to human speech. This form of input has long been held back by the lack of a thorough understanding of human speech, a scientific deficiency that has made it impossible for programmers to create the algorithmic foundations, often referred to as natural language processing, required by computers so that they might be able to "understand" normal, conversational speech. Today's voice recognition systems are confined to the use of fairly limited vocabularies. Most systems can only recognize vocabularies under a thousand words. These systems are based on a technology whereby the words spoken by a human are first *digitized*, and then submitted to a lookup function, which attempts to match the digitized instances of human speech against a table of stored speech patterns. It is expected that as our scientific knowledge of human speech progresses, the vocabularies supported by voice recognition systems will expand apace, ultimately reaching the long-awaited dream of continuous speech recognition.

Voomies: These are *virtual reality* movies designed to be experienced in a 3-D movie theater. According to industry rumor, the first voomies may be exploratory virtual realities, where audience members can move through the virtual settings (environments) and watch the action of the dramatic characters from whatever perspective they choose.

Voxel: This volume element can be thought of as the 3-D equivalent of a *pixel*. It is used, for example, to describe the spatial display elements in a 3-D visualization system.

VRAM: Stands for video random access memory and is pronounced *vee-ram*. It is a special type of memory used with high-end, high-performance *accelerator boards* to speed up the processing of visual (display) information in personal computers. Its most distinguishing characteristic, and the thing that separates it from standard dynamic RAM, is that it allows the computer to write new information to a memory location, even while the old information is being read.

VTOC: Stands for volume table of contents. This is a critical portion of any form of data storage disk because it includes the disk (or volume) name, copyright information, pointers to datablocks, sequence numbers in a multivolume set, and version numbers.

Historical accident has kept programmers in control of a field in which most of them have no aptitude: the artistic integration of the mechanisms they work with.
—Theodore Nelson, Distinguished Fellow
Autodesk, Inc.

WAIS: This acronym stands for wide-area information service, and it refers to a program that is used for searching the *Internet* for content that has been appropriately indexed.

Walkthrough: This is a subtype of the *surrogate travel* genre, wherein one is able to navigate the hallways and rooms of remote, or even nonexistent, buildings. Walkthroughs rely heavily on *CAD*-based (computer aided design-based) libraries of algorithms, wherewith architectural building designs are used to create rooms and hallways on the fly as users exercise their software-encoded, navigational freedom to move about within the simulated building. Common applications include *human-factors engineering* and real estate marketing.

WAN: Stands for wide area network, a term which refers to computer networks that are **not** limited to a geographic area within a range of 10 km, as are *LAN*s (local area networks). WANs often use common carrier facilities.

Water cooler syndrome: For the sociologist of media, this term refers to the tendency for people to talk the next day about what they watched on TV the night before. In the age multimedia, what will people talk about the morning after?

WAV: This is the file extension for the standard adopted by Microsoft and IBM for multimedia sound applications. WAV files contain *pulse code modulation* (PCM) waveform audio data.

Wavelet image compression: A sophisticated variant of *DCT* (discrete cosine transform) this is one of the frontier *compression* technologies; it is now receiving a considerable research and development effort.

Wave table synthesis: One of two primary forms of *MIDI* (musical instrument digital interface) synthesis (the other being *FM synthesis*), wave table is generally considered to be the superior of the two. It uses a store (or table) of digitally recorded instrument samples, and then blends those sampled sounds together on the basis of the sequence of MIDI commands it receives to create the programmed music or sound effects. The table of sounds, or *patches*, as they are sometimes called, are usually stored in ROM. Wave table players have ROM sizes that range in size from 1 to 6 megabytes, with the obvious quality advantage going to the larger tables, which hold correspondingly more, longer, or more intricate instrument samples. For playback, wave table players are measured in terms of two quality factors: 1) how many instruments they can play simultaneously, a feature called *timbrality*; and, 2) how many different notes they can play at the same time, a feature called *polyphony*.

Whiteboard: Also referred to as "electronic whiteboard," this device is one of the key *enabling technologies* of *document conferencing*. After two remote users establish a desktop-to-desktop connection, the session software presents a whiteboard window that both participants are permitted to view and manipulate. With the typical implementation of this concept, *bit maps* of the whiteboard are being transmitted back and forth over the network as each participant makes changes to the contents. Most implementations also enable either participant to save snapshots of the whiteboard for future reference.

White Book: Developed by Philips and JVC in 1993, this standard enables the storage of *MPEG* (Motion Picture Experts Group) video on *CD-ROM*.

Wide shot: From the world of filmmaking, this term refers to a *shot* that provides a broad view of all or a large part of the action in a scene.

Windows: From the world of graphical user interfaces (*GUIs*), this widely used term refers to independent regions created on the computer screen to segregate different functions and/or forms of information. Windows are made possible by the growth in *bit-mapped* displays, and, in turn, make it possible for several applications to display results on the same screen simultaneously. Thus, windows represent two basic graphical user interface design and *human interface design* principles: 1) people desire to, and are capable of working on more than one task at a time; and, 2) to maintain cognitive order during such multitasking activities, it is advisable to create a visible way of segregating, or compartmentalizing one task from another. The most ubiquitous windows graphical user interface application is the operating system by Microsoft, otherwise known as Microsoft *Windows*.

Windows™: Microsoft's graphical user interface (*GUI*) extension to their MS-DOS operating system, now an industry standard, it represents their implementation of the *desktop metaphor* interface that flowed from the early-eighties, pioneering work of the *Xerox PARC* research group on graphical user interfaces.

Wipe: From the world of *DVE* (digital video effects), this is a transitional effect wherein one scene supersedes another by wiping it off the screen. As with the other transitional effects, the more sophisticated *paint programs* and *authoring systems* now supply entire libraries of wipes, e.g., from side-to-side, top-to-bottom, etc.

Wireframe: In graphics, this is a 3-D outline image displayed as a series of connected *line segments*, including all of the *hidden lines*.

Wireless: This term refers to the emerging return to the radio airwaves for transmission *bandwidth*. Technologies such as *TDMA* (time division multiple access) and *CDMA* (code division multiple access) are being heralded as providing a substantial portion of the bandwidth required to feed the voracious appetite of *interactive multimedia* services. If wireless does prove to be as rich a source of bandwidth as experts are predicting, our TV set-tops will be visited once again by devices that are the futuristic equivalent of the rabbit ears that the baby boomers grew up with. Of course, these modern technologies are distinguished from their forebears by being based on digital, rather than analog encoding of the transmitted information. Wireless technologies will also enable the widespread use of *PDAs* (personal digital assistants), the handheld communications/computing devices that are now in their earliest forms.

Working plane: With respect to high-end visual modeling systems, this term refers to a visual reference system, a grid laid down on the screen at the outset of a given development project. This grid, or working plane, offers a spatial reference model to which items can be positioned, a feature also referred to as a *snap-to grid*. It is also very useful for scaling, wherein the feature is employed for sizing visual objects to fit a given context.

World-building software: This emergent term is used by practitioners of *virtual reality* to describe the authoring tools that they use to create simulated portions of the world.

WORM: Stands for write once, read many and refers to a standard form of compact disc technology that permits users to write their own data to CD, albeit only once. In effect, WORM technology turns the

CD mastering process over to the users, which is in contrast to the standard way of doing things with respect to *CD-ROM*, where, historically, the mastering has been done at specialized facilities that employ expensive equipment. Though far less expensive than these capital intensive facilities, WORM drives have remained beyond the financial reach of most desktops, and have typically been bought only by those organizations who have a high volume of CD mastering they must perform. As with almost every other form of *digital* technology, though, this expense factor is subject to change, as WORM drives are becoming increasingly affordable. Most contemporary WORMs permit *multisession* recording, which means that you cannot reuse the same disc geography, **but** you can take more than one session to make use of the entire geography of the disc. The Kodak Photo CD consumer technology is multisession, which makes it possible, for example, for families to make use of small chunks of a single CD as they grow their photo libraries over time, thus keeping the overall expense of the technology under check.

WYSIWYG: Stands for "what you see is what you get" and is pronounced "wizeewig." This term dates back to the earliest attempts to upgrade the graphical capabilities of personal computers so that users could get a realistic view of what their output would look like once it was committed to hard copy. For example, owing to the limited graphical capabilities of computer monitors, early word processing programs were unable to display any of the special formatting characteristics that the word processing software permitted, such as bold facing and underlining. To see these effects, early PC users had to wait until they printed the document. Obviously, they were often surprised (with "surprise" being a pejorative term in this context) with what they wound up getting. As the graphical capabilities of computers began to improve, the word processing programs were able to display these effects on the screen, thereby initiating the phrase "what you see is what you get," and, with it, this endearing acronym.

At PARC we coined the phrase "user illusion" to describe what we were about when designing user interface.
—Alan Kay, Apple Fellow, Apple Computer

Xanadu Project: Launched in the mid-sixties by Ted Nelson—the man also credited with coining the term *hypertext*—this project has been responsible for conducting breakthrough research on the impact of the computer on the textual creation enterprise. The obvious allusion that gave birth to this project's name is the magical place of creative imagination described in the nineteenth century poem, *Kubla Khan*, by Samuel Taylor Coleridge, in which seemingly discordant images are intermixed to create an other-worldly realm of "A Sunny Pleasure Dome with Caves of Ice!" One of the key concepts to emerge from this project is that of intermixing and matching portions of text from various sources to form composite works. Of obvious applicability to hypertext systems, Nelson has used the term "xanalogical storage" to refer to the shared document space that results from such intermixing of textual works. In 1988 the Xanadu Project was taken over by Autodesk, the California software maker most famous for its AutoCad and other visual processing tools.

Xerox PARC: The acronym stands for Palo Alto Research Center. Established in 1971, this now-famous R&D facility was responsible for developing some of the earliest prototypes for the personal computer. However, what has earned this center a rightful place in the creation myth of multimedia was its central role in devising some of the earliest concepts and standards for the design of graphical user interfaces (*GUI*), the fruits of which were brought to market in the form of the Apple Macintosh and Microsoft *Windows* desktop user interfaces. PARC was also largely responsible for developing the Smalltalk programming language, the *high level language* commonly given the credit for launching the *object-oriented* paradigm in software design. Of its more recent research projects, the most noteworthy to the continued progress of multimedia technology appears to be the Information Theater. This project is aimed at enhancing *text retrieval* technologies and at breeding a new form of presentation technology referred to as *information visualizers*.

Y/C: More commonly referred to as *S-video*, this video type provides a quality of signal that lies between *composite* and *component video*. The Y stands for *luminance*, the C for *chrominance*, which represent the two channels into which the form of video signal is broken.

Yellow Book: Is the Philips/Sony technical specifications reference for the physical structure and data layout of *CD-ROM* discs. These specifications are based on the *Red Book*'s description for audio CDs, also known as CD-DA. The Yellow Book standard has two modes: mode 1 is the basic specification based on CD-DA; and mode 2, also known as *CD ROM-XA*—the XA standing for extended architecture—which involves the interleaving of audio and graphic data, critical to enabling the synchronization of audio and visual components.

YUV: This is the industry standard way of transmitting and storing video information. Under this method, the *RGB* (red, green, blue) data for each *pixel* is converted to a format that uses one channel (Y) to represent the *luminance,* or overall intensity of that pixel, and two channels (UV) to represent the *chrominance,* or color. The advantage of this technique is that it makes it possible to reduce the overall data volume required for a video image by lowering the UV *resolution* relative to that of Y, which, in turn, takes advantage of the universally accepted principle that the human eye is less sensitive to color than it is to brightness.

Discovery favors the well-prepared mind.
—Jerome Bruner, Educational Philosopher

Zoom: In video and photography, this term refers to the facility to enlarge (zoom in on) or reduce (zoom out from) an area of an image. As a piece of the accepted cinematic nomenclature, the term *zoom* more precisely describes the enlargement of the film subject relative to its context or setting, in contrast to the term *pan*, which means to pull away from the subject.

Postscript

Failing to fetch me at first keep encouraged,
Missing me one place search another,
I stop somewhere waiting for you.
—Walt Whitman, poet of Leaves of Grass

ANNOTATED BIBLIOGRAPHY

In concert with the overall increase in interest regarding multimedia, we have witnessed a spate of written material over the past half-decade that hits in and around the subject. Books on multimedia, interactive multimedia, virtual reality, and cyberspace are beginning to appear at an accelerated rate and now threaten to take up entire stacks in libraries and bookstores across the country. New magazines and trade journals entirely devoted to the subject have appeared in the last few years, and many longstanding publications in related areas have begun to re-orient their content so that they are now invading the same conceptual turf. As if in a magnanimous gesture to its own cannibalizing forces—to its own executioner, if you will—the print and publishing industry is certainly doing its part to inform the public about the coming of multimedia.

Additionally, while it might be gratuitously facile to say that the intellectual foundations for multimedia start with Plato, or thereabouts, it would be accurate to say the serious people have been giving serious thought to the various forms that new media might take for at least the majority of this century. This vein of genetic thought leads, in particular, to the likes of Vannevar Bush, Marshall McLuhan, and Ted Nelson.

The entries in this book owe something to all of these sources, recent and otherwise. In this annotated bibliography, we attempt to give the reader some form of shoehorn into this now burgeoning bundle of source materials. We have broken the bibliography into two sections, one devoted to books and articles drawn from scholarly periodicals, the other to trade journals and magazines. In dealing with the latter, we have decided to treat the magazines as a whole, even though it should not be concluded from this that their individual feature articles are not as valuable as they might be. In fact, one of the happier trends in the industry right now is the appearance of some very high quality trades, to which—it should be pointed out—the authors have culled from and synthesized information to build the content for many of the entries of this book.

We make no claim of being comprehensive, or even of being close to comprehensive. Rather, we merely hope that this bibliography is somehow representative, and that it can lead the reader through a systematic swath of the mounting literature on multimedia.

Books and Scholarly Articles

Allen, Thomas B. *War Games*. New York: Berkley Books, 1987.

> Though this book does not make a single mention of multimedia, it is of note to the interactive community because it covers a subject that is of mounting importance to the future of media. The author points out that at, or near, the pinnacle of all of the branches of America's armed forces there is a penultimate form of training that is called "war games." These games, of course, strive to create as much of the complexity of the real world as possible, and so are perhaps more accurately referred to as simulations. But, then again, the difficulty we have in naming this highest form of military training may be a further reflection of the underlying instability and change that is part-in-parcel of the emerging age of multimedia. For the sake of fostering worthwhile reflection, this book is worth a read.

Ambron, Sueann, and Kristina Hooper. Editors. *Interactive Multimedia: Visions of Multimedia for Developers, Educators, & Information Providers*. Redmond, WA: Microsoft Press, 1988.

> This work is the third in a trilogy of readers published by Microsoft Press in conjunction with Apple Computer to pronounce the coming of multimedia. Of the three, this book does the best job of dealing with issues of interactive design and content development. The Foreword by John Sculley and articles by Stephen Weyer and Sueann Ambron are particularly noteworthy.

Aukstakalnis, Steve, and David Blatner. *Silicon Mirage: The Art and Science of Virtual Reality*. Berkeley, CA: Peachpit Press, 1992.

> This is a very competent survey of the enabling technologies and applications that are making virtual reality the cutting edge of multimedia. It does a fine job of explaining the scientific principles that are making the creation of such new and immersive technologies as force feedback possible. It also lays out an industry-by-industry survey of the current applications of virtual reality. Put simply, the book does its part to establish the legitamacy of VR.

Benedikt, Michael. Editor. *Cyberspace: First Steps*. Cambridge, MA: MIT Press, 1992.

> An excellent reader on the emerging subdiscipline of virtual reality known as "cyberspace," this book does more than any other in the industry thus far to explore the philosophical implications of new media. In particular, articles by the editor and by Michael Heim lay

out some of the dimensions of the deep structure of cyberspace. For those with an academic orientation, this book represents a good vehicle for placing the cutting edge of multimedia technologies in perspective.

Brand, Stewart. *The Media Lab: Inventing the Future at MIT.* New York: Viking, 1987.

When neophytes ask what book they should read to get their bearings with respect to multimedia, this is the one that we almost always recommend. It is a pleasureable, anecdotal read. But it also examines with considerable clarity the roots of new media thinking, if for no other reason but that it explores the background of Nicholas Negroponte, the founder of the Media Lab, and one of the industry's true visionaries. What is most heartening about this book is that, while all of the projects it describes were intended by virtue of the Lab's mission statement to conjure communications technologies 30 years out, several of them are actually starting to be implemented today. In particular, Negroponte's concept of "personal television" would appear to be just around the corner and will likely arrive—full blown, virtually as conceived—about a decade ahead of schedule. Written by the author of *The Whole Earth Catalog*, this book is both fun and informative.

Bush, Vannevar. "As We May Think." *Atlantic Monthly.* (July, 1945), pp. 101–08.

Any bibliography that purports to cover the multimedia industry is obliged to include this entry. This article is typically credited with being the first to articulate "hypertext." It would probably be a bit more accurate to say that it is the first description of the implications of hypertext, even though it predates the first use of that term by roughly two decades. Bush bemoaned the antiquated state of our library information systems (if you could have called them that in the 1940s), and foresaw a day when all of the contents of all of the world's print-based information would be inter-connected by associational links. Researchers and browsers, alike, would be able to traverse this structured labyrinth of information by simply following these links, either on the bases of their immediate research needs, or their current intellectual whims. Bush called this future haven of interlinked literature the Memex. As concepts go, . . . long live the Memex.

Gardner, Howard. *Frames of Mind: A Theory of Multiple Intelligences.* New York: Basic Books, 1983.

> Like a number of other entries in this bibliography, this one may seem a bit tangential. However, learning theory is one of the core competencies of one of the core applications of multimedia. Howard Gardner's contribution to learning theory has been considerable, and we could have included almost any of his works here. This one, though, ranks among his most memorable and should be required reading for anyone who wishes to practice the emerging profession of instructional design.

Greenfield, Patricia Marks. *Mind and Media: The Effects of Television, Video Games and Computers.* Cambridge, MA: Harvard University Press, 1984.

> Though this book predates most of the speculation over the coming of multimedia, it does a great deal to both anticipate it and light its way. Greenfield offers an excellent survey of the literature and research that occurred during the sixties and seventies pertaining to the comparative value of different learning media. She is absolutely prescient in her assessment of potential instructional benefits of the video game genre, and, as a case in point, lights the way in 1984 to the recent emergence of edutainment titles.

Holsinger, Erik. *How Multimedia Works.* Illustrated by Nevin Burger. Emeryville, CA: Ziff-Davis Press, 1994.

> This is the best exemplar of books that most successfully employ graphics and text to explain computer hardware and software technology. It succinctly and clearly defines and illustrates "how multimedia works" and is part of the Ziff-Davis "How It Works" series. Hats off to author, illustrator, and editorial staff for bringing an understandable view of multimedia to the masses.

Jacobson, Linda. Editor. *Cyberarts: Exploring Art and Technology.* San Francisco: Miller Freeman, 1992.

> This interesting reader ranges across a broad range of topics that are currently impacting the multimedia industry. The book is particularly useful in its coverage of the many categories of software that impinge on the interactive multimedia authoring process. Of particular note are entries that cover MIDI/MSC and the low cost, all-digital alternatives to high-end professional video that are now entering the market at a rapid pace. This book also contains a gem from Ted Nelson, who takes about ten rich pages to describe the current status of his life-quest Xanadu Project.

Kearsley, Greg P., Editor. *Artificial Intelligence & Instruction: Applications and Methods*. Reading, MA: Addison-Wesley, 1987.

> Heavy sledding, as they say, this is a worthwhile read for those who have an interest in the many academic projects launched during the seventies and eighties to explore the pedagogical potential of machine intelligence.

Khoshafian, Setrag, A. Brad Baker, Razmik Abnous, and Kevin Shepherd. *Intelligent Offices: Object-Oriented, Multi-Media Information Management in Client/Server Architectures*. New York: John Wiley & Sons, 1992.

> This is one in a series of very sound books published by John Wiley to explore the promising new conceptual areas in computer science. This book provides a synthesis of object-oriented software design, the integration of media into traditional applications, the design of graphical user interfaces, and the deployment of operational/computing resources over distributed, client-server architectures. For those interested in the technological foundations of multimedia—the enabling technologies—this is an excellent survey.

Lambert, Steve, and Suzanne Ropiequet. Editors. *CD ROM: The New Papyrus*. Redmond, WA: Microsoft Press, 1986.

> This is the first in a trilogy of readers published by Microsoft Press in conjunction with Apple Computer to pronounce the coming of multimedia; as you would expect, this title does the best of the three to frame the overall context of the emerging multimedia industry. The Foreword by Bill Gates does much to illustrate how much he was in tune with the graphical/media orientation of computing, even before he was able to successfully implement his *Windows* graphical user interface in the Intel-dominated PC world.

Laurel, Brenda. Editor. *The Art of Human-Computer Interface Design*. Reading, MA: Addison-Wesley, 1990.

> Of all the multimedia readers that have appeared over the past five years or so, this is probably the most representative of the industry's true range of interests. It is also distinguished by the general quality of its contributors—just about every industry thought leader has an entry in this volume. Perhaps the most noteworthy article is the editor's treatment of the exciting and complex concept of "interface agents."

Leebaert, Derek. Editor. *Technology 2001: The Future of Computing and Communications*. Cambridge, MA: The MIT Press, 1991.

Though this reader gives only scant treatment of multimedia, per se, it does an excellent job of speculating on the technical agenda of the industry's major enabling technologies: computer architectures, office automation, tele- and data communications, etc.

Lieberman, Debra A. "Learning to Learn Revisited: Computers and the Development of Self-Directed Learning Skills." *Journal of Research on Computing in Education.* Vol. 23 (Spring, 1991), pp. 391–95.

This scholarly article does a good job of relating the leading trends in learning theory to the use of instructional technology in school programs. Though there is a tendency in our country to be highly critical of our primary and secondary schools, this article is indicative of some of the cutting edge thinking that is going on with regard to the application of educational software.

McLuhan, Marshall. *Understanding Media: The Extensions of Man.* New York: Mentor, 1964.

McLuhan had a unique ability to identify the large historical arcs associated with media. And now that the forces of change have accelerated the forward evolution of media, McLuhan is being quoted with increasing frequency, particularly from the point of view represented in this book.

Mast, Gerald. *Film, Cinema, Movie: A Theory of Experience.* Chicago: University of Chicago Press, 1983.

As we labor to contemplate the future of media, it will no doubt be prudent for us to understand where we have been. Gerald Mast is one of the best film theorists going, and this is probably his most insightful discussion of the film medium—the medium, I think we all agree, to which the interactive arts will owe the most.

Nelson, Theodore Holm. "The Hypertext." *Proceedings of the World Documentation Federation.* (1965).

The first use of the term "hypertext" appears in this article, and, in effect, stands as the virtual starting gate for one of the most fecund intellectual careers in what is now being called multimedia.

Papert, Seymour. *Mindstorms: Children, Computers, and Powerful Ideas.* New York: Basic Books, 1980.

One of the earliest works to examine the use of computers in education, this book is notable for a number of reasons. It details the LOGO language, a high-level language developed explicitly for use by children for the sake of exploring math and science concepts. It covers a number of issues in instructional design which, if anything, are even more pertinent today than they were when they were written. Most notably, though, it captures the essence of Seymour Papert, a man who has been at the forefront of the entire computer revolution by virtue of his association with the MIT Artificial Intelligence Lab and of his ability to contribute to and articulate the thinking that has taken place therein.

Parsaye, Kamran, Mark Chignell, Setrag Khoshafian, and Harry Wong. *Intelligent Databases: Object-Oriented, Deductive, Hypermedia Technologies*. New York: John Wiley & Sons, 1989.

One in a series of books published by John Wiley, it explores some of the emerging concepts in computer science. This book does an excellent job of exploring the key issues in software engineering, particularly those having to do with object-oriented programming and hypermedia design, both of which impact very heavily on the enterprise of multimedia. It possesses one of the industry's most intelligent discussions of Ted Nelson's Xanadu Project and does an excellent job of analyzing the issues associated with designing and building knowledgebases.

Resnick, Lauren B., and L.E. Klopfer. "Toward Rethinking the Curriculum." In *Toward Rethinking the Curriculum*. L.B. Resnick and L.E. Klopfer, editors. Arlington, VA: Association for Supervision and Curriculum Development, 1987.

This article is one of many possible entries for Ms. Resnick, perhaps the leading American thinker in the field of educational reform. Throughout her canon of work, one finds a steady theme: curriculum needs to move away from the industrial-age traditions of drill-and-practice, emphasis on specific content, and other forms of regimentation, and in the direction of pedagogies that stimulate higher-order thinking, problem solving, and the acquisition of process knowledge. These pedagogies are much more difficult than their traditional forbears to encoded interactive multimedia programs . . . but so be it.

Robbe-Grillet, Alain. *For a New Novel: Essays on Fiction*. New York: Grove Press, 1965.

For anyone who sees the production of interactive forms of art as a mission against which are stacked incalculable odds, these essays from Robbe-Grillet will prove comforting, if not insightful. Though his fictional works were never widely accepted in his own time, Robbe-Grillet stands as probably the most inventive practitioner of the narrative arts in our century. These essays articulate the rebellious, iconoclastic vision that is so abundantly present in his novels. Had he "bloomed" during the 1990s, we have no doubt that Robbe-Grillet would be devoted to interactivity and the cyberarts.

Ropiequet, Suzanne. Editor. *CD ROM: Optical Publishing*. Redmond, WA: Microsoft Press, 1987.

The second in a trilogy of readers published by Microsoft Press in conjunction with Apple Computer to pronounce the coming of multimedia, this one has the stongest orientation of the three toward the engineering issues associated with CD-ROM technology.

Schneiderman, Ben. *Designing the User Interface: Strategies for Effective Human-Computer Interaction*. Reading, MA: Addison-Wesley, 1986.

This work serves as a de facto standard in the area of interface design, a discipline which possesses near-complete overlap with the field of interactive multimedia design. Schneiderman's text is particularly insightful in its treatment of the concept of "direct manipulation."

White, Mary Alice. *What Curriculum for the Information Age?* Hillsdale, NJ: Lawrence Erlbaum Associates, 1987.

This is an excellent treatment of educational concepts that should deeply concern everyone in the multimedia industry.

Magazines and Trade Journals

Byte. Published by McGraw-Hill. One Phoenix Mill Lane, Peterborough, NH 03458.

From its inception, *Byte* established itself as the most credible technical read in the small systems (desktop) world. For those in the multimedia industry responsible for following technical trends, this is the key journal. In recent years, with the rise of multimedia, *Byte* has become exceptional at following relevant technical trends in computer architectures and software engineering.

CD-ROM Professional. Published by Pemberton Press, Inc. 407 Kingston Avenue, St. Paul, MN 55117–2424.

This magazine has gained a high level of credibility with multimedia content developers. Appropriate to its name, the magazine focuses on technical and marketing issues having to do with CD-ROM as a delivery medium for multimedia content.

CD-ROM World. Published by Mecklermedia, 11 Ferry Lane West, Westport, CT 06880.

> Though this magazine covers much of the same ground as the other multimedia trades, it does seem to be developing a specialization in one area: the review of CD-ROM titles. In an industry that is crying for standards of criticism, this orientation is a welcome one.

Computer Graphics World. Published by PennWell Publishing Company, 10 Tara Boulevard, Suite 500, Nashua, NH 03062–2801.

> Increasingly, this magazine is becoming a must-read for those involved in the authoring of multimedia content. From a tradition heavily focused on specialized computer graphics programs, *CGW* has transitioned into the center of the multimedia industry by re-orienting its feature articles that deal with the cutting edge of authoring technologies. The magazine is particularly strong in the field of nonlinear, all digital software tools; a hotbed of activity that is leading Hollywood in the direction of a collision with Silicon Valley perhaps a year or two ahead of the schedule set by the San Andreas fault.

Desktop Video World. Published by TechMedia Publishing, Inc. 80 Elm Street, Peterborough, NH 03458.

> A relative newcomer, this trade journal focuses on issues surrounding the use of digital media on desktop machines, primarily the PC, Mac, and Amiga platforms.

Morph's Outpost (on the Digital Frontier). Published by Morph's Outpost, Inc. P.O. Box 578, Orinda, CA 94563.

> Appropriately, this tabloid-style publication is one of the most unusual trade journals in the industry. Its content profiles *NewMedia* fairly closely, though it possesses a somewhat stronger orientation to content creation and interviews. This publication may validate the long-held suspicion about the screws and bolts rattling free in California.

Macworld. Published by Macworld Communications, Inc. 501 Second Street, San Francisco, CA 94107.

> Inasmuch as the Macintosh has continued its two to three year lead over the PC platform with respect to media capabilities, this magazine finds itself in the center of the multimedia industry almost by default. Though its product range is narrow, this is an excellent magazine for following developments in multimedia, particularly with respect to the many authoring tools that have become

frontrunners through their historical tie to the Macintosh platform. *Macworld* also does an excellent job of illustrating basic computer concepts for the neophytes, possessing perhaps the best art department in the trade magazine industry.

Multimedia Today. Published by IBM Multimedia Solutions, 4111 Northside Parkway, HO4L1, Atlanta, GA 30327.

This publication raises the concept of consultative selling to an art, using a trade journal to showcase and explore IBM's multimedia product offerings. The magazine is particularly strong on case studies, and each issue provides an extensive, detailed catalog of IBM business partner multimedia products, including sections on courseware and production tools.

Multimedia World. Published by PC World Communications, Inc., 501 Second Street, #600, San Francisco, CA 94107.

Brought to us by the same people who publish *PC World*, this magazine is positioned in the same approximate niche as *NewMedia*. Its content—to use the term *du jour*—is not of the same consistency or quality.

NewMedia Magazine. Published by Hypermedia Communications, Inc. 901 Mariner's Island Boulevard, Suite 365, San Mateo, CA 94404.

In many respects, this magazine has become the *Byte* of multimedia. Its lead features are uniformly strong and strike at the key issues facing the industry. Their annual *Multimedia Buyer's Guide* represents a substantial contribution to the industry, not just because it helps organize the information about who is selling what, but also because the editors have taken the effort to have it also help categorize the exploding media phenomena that are multimedia.

PC Magazine. Published by Ziff-Davis Publishing Company, One Park Avenue, New York, NY 10016.

A stalwart of the PC industry, this magazine has its fair share of multimedia articles, in parallel with the overall industry trends in that direction.

Upside. Published by the Upside Publishing Company, 1159–B Triton Drive, Foster City, CA 94404.

This magazine has a well-executed focus on technology issues as they relate specifically to investment. Though the topics range primarily in the direction of general computing and telecommunications, it is an excellent source for those in the investment banking business, or for those who are investors in the stock market.

Videomaker. Published by Videomaker, Inc. P. O. Box 4591, Chico, CA 95927.

As media production equipment becomes increasingly digital, magazines such as these become as excellent source for those members of the multimedia development team who are responsible for producing the clay.

Virtual Reality World. Published by Mecklermedia, 11 Ferry Lane West, Westport, CT 06880.

A sign of the times, this publication brings a sober approach to virtual reality. Though some of its entries tend to evangelize a bit, most attack their futuristic subject matter from an appropriate, even scholarly perspective. Refreshingly, many of the articles come with detailed footnotes and bibliographies.